2020
SUN SIGN
BOOK

Forecasts by
Lesley Francis

Cover design by Kevin R. Brown
Editing by Andrea Neff
Interior illustration on page 19 by the Llewellyn Art Department
iStockphoto.com/165969046/©PaCondryx
iStockphoto.com/168312684/©RomanOkopny
iStockphoto.com/952773584/©Cobalt88

© 2019 by Llewellyn Publications
ISBN: 978-0-7387-4950-1
Llewellyn is a registered trademark of Llewellyn Worldwide Ltd.
2143 Wooddale Drive, Woodbury, MN 55125-2989
www.llewellyn.com
Printed in the United States of America

Contents

2019

SEPTEMBER
S	M	T	W	T	F	S
1	2	3	4	5	6	7
8	9	10	11	12	13	14
15	16	17	18	19	20	21
22	23	24	25	26	27	28
29	30					

OCTOBER
S	M	T	W	T	F	S
		1	2	3	4	5
6	7	8	9	10	11	12
13	14	15	16	17	18	19
20	21	22	23	24	25	26
27	28	29	30	31		

NOVEMBER
S	M	T	W	T	F	S
					1	2
3	4	5	6	7	8	9
10	11	12	13	14	15	16
17	18	19	20	21	22	23
24	25	26	27	28	29	30

DECEMBER
S	M	T	W	T	F	S
1	2	3	4	5	6	7
8	9	10	11	12	13	14
15	16	17	18	19	20	21
22	23	24	25	26	27	28
29	30	31				

2020

JANUARY
S	M	T	W	T	F	S
			1	2	3	4
5	6	7	8	9	10	11
12	13	14	15	16	17	18
19	20	21	22	23	24	25
26	27	28	29	30	31	

FEBRUARY
S	M	T	W	T	F	S
						1
2	3	4	5	6	7	8
9	10	11	12	13	14	15
16	17	18	19	20	21	22
23	24	25	26	27	28	29

MARCH
S	M	T	W	T	F	S
1	2	3	4	5	6	7
8	9	10	11	12	13	14
15	16	17	18	19	20	21
22	23	24	25	26	27	28
29	30	31				

APRIL
S	M	T	W	T	F	S
			1	2	3	4
5	6	7	8	9	10	11
12	13	14	15	16	17	18
19	20	21	22	23	24	25
26	27	28	29	30		

MAY
S	M	T	W	T	F	S
					1	2
3	4	5	6	7	8	9
10	11	12	13	14	15	16
17	18	19	20	21	22	23
24	25	26	27	28	29	30
31						

JUNE
S	M	T	W	T	F	S
	1	2	3	4	5	6
7	8	9	10	11	12	13
14	15	16	17	18	19	20
21	22	23	24	25	26	27
28	29	30				

JULY
S	M	T	W	T	F	S
			1	2	3	4
5	6	7	8	9	10	11
12	13	14	15	16	17	18
19	20	21	22	23	24	25
26	27	28	29	30	31	

AUGUST
S	M	T	W	T	F	S
						1
2	3	4	5	6	7	8
9	10	11	12	13	14	15
16	17	18	19	20	21	22
23	24	25	26	27	28	29
30	31					

SEPTEMBER
S	M	T	W	T	F	S
		1	2	3	4	5
6	7	8	9	10	11	12
13	14	15	16	17	18	19
20	21	22	23	24	25	26
27	28	29	30			

OCTOBER
S	M	T	W	T	F	S
				1	2	3
4	5	6	7	8	9	10
11	12	13	14	15	16	17
18	19	20	21	22	23	24
25	26	27	28	29	30	31

NOVEMBER
S	M	T	W	T	F	S
1	2	3	4	5	6	7
8	9	10	11	12	13	14
15	16	17	18	19	20	21
22	23	24	25	26	27	28
29	30					

DECEMBER
S	M	T	W	T	F	S
		1	2	3	4	5
6	7	8	9	10	11	12
13	14	15	16	17	18	19
20	21	22	23	24	25	26
27	28	29	30	31		

2021

JANUARY
S	M	T	W	T	F	S
					1	2
3	4	5	6	7	8	9
10	11	12	13	14	15	16
17	18	19	20	21	22	23
24	25	26	27	28	29	30
31						

FEBRUARY
S	M	T	W	T	F	S
	1	2	3	4	5	6
7	8	9	10	11	12	13
14	15	16	17	18	19	20
21	22	23	24	25	26	27
28						

MARCH
S	M	T	W	T	F	S
	1	2	3	4	5	6
7	8	9	10	11	12	13
14	15	16	17	18	19	20
21	22	23	24	25	26	27
28	29	30	31			

APRIL
S	M	T	W	T	F	S
				1	2	3
4	5	6	7	8	9	10
11	12	13	14	15	16	17
18	19	20	21	22	23	24
25	26	27	28	29	30	

MAY
S	M	T	W	T	F	S
						1
2	3	4	5	6	7	8
9	10	11	12	13	14	15
16	17	18	19	20	21	22
23	24	25	26	27	28	29
30	31					

JUNE
S	M	T	W	T	F	S
		1	2	3	4	5
6	7	8	9	10	11	12
13	14	15	16	17	18	19
20	21	22	23	24	25	26
27	28	29	30			

JULY
S	M	T	W	T	F	S
				1	2	3
4	5	6	7	8	9	10
11	12	13	14	15	16	17
18	19	20	21	22	23	24
25	26	27	28	29	30	31

AUGUST
S	M	T	W	T	F	S
1	2	3	4	5	6	7
8	9	10	11	12	13	14
15	16	17	18	19	20	21
22	23	24	25	26	27	28
29	30	31				

Meet Lesley Francis

Lesley is a full-time practicing astrologer, intuitive, professional writer, teacher/facilitator, and speaker. She began her study of astrology in early 1974 while working as a journalist for Canada's fourth-largest newspaper and quickly found a lifelong passion, one that ultimately took her down a completely different path in the late 1990s after she left behind her 25-year career in journalism. This shift led to still more changes as Lesley developed both her psychic gifts and her very own intuitive tool, a deck of cards based in astrology.

Her monthly predictions graced *Llewellyn's Astrological Calendar*, the largest-selling calendar of its kind worldwide, for seven years, from 2012 to 2018, and she is a past contributor to other Llewellyn publications. Lesley has spoken at numerous astrological conferences, including NORWAC, SOTA, and the inaugural Canadian Astrology Conference in 2015.

Lesley can be reached through her website at www.lesleyfrancis.com.

How to Use This Book

by Kim Rogers-Gallagher

Hi there! Welcome to the 2020 edition of *Llewellyn's Sun Sign Book*. This book centers on Sun sign astrology—that is, the set of general attributes and characteristics that those of us born under each of the twelve particular Sun signs share. You'll find descriptions of your sign's qualities tucked into your sign's chapter, along with the type of behavior you tend to exhibit in different life situations—with regard to relationships, work situations, and the handling of money and possessions, for example. Oh, and there's a section that's dedicated to good old-fashioned fun, too, including what will bring you joy and how to make it happen.

There's a lot to be said for Sun sign astrology. First off, the Sun's sign at the time of your birth describes the qualities, talents, and traits you're here to study this time around. If you believe in reincarnation, think of it as declaring a celestial major for this lifetime. Sure, you'll learn other things along the way, but you've announced to one and all that you're primarily interested in mastering this one particular sign. Then, too, on a day when fiery, impulsive energies are making astrological headlines, if you're a fiery and/or impulsive sign yourself—like Aries or Aquarius, for example—it's easy to imagine how you'll take to the astrological weather a lot more easily than a practical, steady-handed sign like Taurus or Virgo.

Obviously, astrology comes in handy, for a variety of reasons. Getting to know your "natal" Sun sign (the sign the Sun was in when you were born) can most certainly give you the edge you need to ace the final and move on to the next celestial course level—or basically to succeed in life, and maybe even earn a few bonus points toward next semester. Using astrology on a daily basis nicely accelerates the process.

Now, there are eight other planets and one lovely Moon in our neck of the celestial woods, all of which also play into our personalities. The sign that was on the eastern horizon at the moment of your birth—otherwise known as your *Ascendant*, or *rising sign*—is another indicator of your personality traits. Honestly, there are all kinds of cosmic factors, so if it's an in-depth, personal analysis you're after, a professional astrologer is the only way to go—especially if you're curious about relationships, past lives, future trends, or even the right time to schedule an important life event. Professional astrologers calculate your birth chart—again, the "natal" chart—based on the date, place, and exact time of your birth—which allows for a far more personal and specific reading. In the meantime, however, in addition to reading up on your Sun sign, you can use the tables on pages 8 and 9 to find the sign of your Ascendant. (These tables, however, are approximate and tailored to those of us born in North America, so if the traits of your Ascendant don't sound familiar, check out the sign directly before or after.)

There are three sections to each sign chapter in this book. As I already mentioned, the first section describes personality traits, and while it's fun to read your own, don't forget to check out the other Sun signs. (Oh, and do feel free to mention any rather striking behavioral similarities to skeptics. It's great fun to watch a Scorpio's reaction when you tell them they're astrologically known as "the sexy sign," or a Gemini when you thank them for creating the concept of multitasking.)

The second section is entitled "The Year Ahead" for each sign. Through considering the movements of the outer planets (Uranus, Neptune, and Pluto), the eclipses, and any other outstanding celestial movements, this segment will provide you with the big picture of the year—or basically the broad strokes of what to expect, no matter who you are or where you are, collectively speaking.

The third section includes monthly forecasts, along with rewarding days and challenging days, basically a heads-up designed to alert you to potentially easy times as well as potentially tricky times.

At the end of every chapter you'll find an Action Table, providing general information about the best time to indulge in certain activities. Please note that these are only suggestions. Don't hold yourself back or rush into anything your intuition doesn't wholeheartedly agree with—and again, when in doubt, find yourself a professional.

Well, that's it. I hope that you enjoy this book, and that being aware of the astrological energies of 2020 helps you create a year full of fabulous memories!

Kim Rogers-Gallagher has written hundreds of articles and columns for magazines and online publications and has two books of her own, *Astrology for the Light Side of the Brain* and *Astrology for the Light Side of the Future*. She's a well-known speaker who's been part of the UAC faculty since 1996. Kim can be contacted at KRGPhoenix313@yahoo.com for fees regarding readings, classes, and lectures.

Ascendant Table

Your Sun Sign	6–8 am	8–10 am	10 am–Noon	Noon–2 pm	2–4 pm	4–6 pm
Aries	Taurus	Gemini	Cancer	Leo	Virgo	Libra
Taurus	Gemini	Cancer	Leo	Virgo	Libra	Scorpio
Gemini	Cancer	Leo	Virgo	Libra	Scorpio	Sagittarius
Cancer	Leo	Virgo	Libra	Scorpio	Sagittarius	Capricorn
Leo	Virgo	Libra	Scorpio	Sagittarius	Capricorn	Aquarius
Virgo	Libra	Scorpio	Sagittarius	Capricorn	Aquarius	Pisces
Libra	Scorpio	Sagittarius	Capricorn	Aquarius	Pisces	Aries
Scorpio	Sagittarius	Capricorn	Aquarius	Pisces	Aries	Taurus
Sagittarius	Capricorn	Aquarius	Pisces	Aries	Taurus	Gemini
Capricorn	Aquarius	Pisces	Aries	Taurus	Gemini	Cancer
Aquarius	Pisces	Aries	Taurus	Gemini	Cancer	Leo
Pisces	Aries	Taurus	Gemini	Cancer	Leo	Virgo

Your Time of Birth

	Your Time of Birth					
Your Sun Sign	6–8 pm	8–10 pm	10 pm–Midnight	Midnight–2 am	2–4 am	4–6 am
Aries	Scorpio	Sagittarius	Capricorn	Aquarius	Pisces	Aries
Taurus	Sagittarius	Capricorn	Aquarius	Pisces	Aries	Taurus
Gemini	Capricorn	Aquarius	Pisces	Aries	Taurus	Gemini
Cancer	Aquarius	Pisces	Aries	Taurus	Gemini	Cancer
Leo	Pisces	Aries	Taurus	Gemini	Cancer	Leo
Virgo	Aries	Taurus	Gemini	Cancer	Leo	Virgo
Libra	Taurus	Gemini	Cancer	Leo	Virgo	Libra
Scorpio	Gemini	Cancer	Leo	Virgo	Libra	Scorpio
Sagittarius	Cancer	Leo	Virgo	Libra	Scorpio	Sagittarius
Capricorn	Leo	Virgo	Libra	Scorpio	Sagittarius	Capricorn
Aquarius	Virgo	Libra	Scorpio	Sagittarius	Capricorn	Aquarius
Pisces	Libra	Scorpio	Sagittarius	Capricorn	Aquarius	Pisces

How to use this table:
1. Find your Sun sign in the left column.
2. Find your approximate birth time in a vertical column.
3. Line up your Sun sign and birth time to find your Ascendant.

This table will give you an approximation of your Ascendant. If you feel that the sign listed as your Ascendant is incorrect, try the one either before or after the listed sign. It is difficult to determine your exact Ascendant without a complete natal chart.

Astrology Basics

Natal astrology is done by freeze-framing the solar system at the moment of your birth, from the perspective of your birth place. This creates a circular map that looks like a pie sliced into twelve pieces. It shows where every heavenly body we're capable of seeing was located when you arrived. Basically, it's your astrological tool kit, and it can't be replicated more than once in thousands of years. This is why we astrologers are so darn insistent about the need for you to either dig your birth certificate out of that box of ancient paperwork in the back of your closet or get a copy of it from the county clerk's office where you were born. Natal astrology, as interpreted by a professional astrologer, is done exactly and precisely for you and no one else. It shows your inherent traits, talents, and challenges. Comparing the planets' current positions to their positions in your birth chart allows astrologers to help you understand the celestial trends at work in your life—and most importantly, how you can put each astrological energy to a positive, productive use.

Let's take a look at the four main components of every astrology chart.

Planets

The planets represent the needs or urges we all experience once we hop off the Evolutionary Express and take up residence inside a human body. For example, the Sun is your urge to shine and be creative, the Moon is your need to express emotions, Mercury is in charge of how you communicate and navigate, and Venus is all about who and what you love—and more importantly, how you love.

Signs

The sign a planet occupies is like a costume or uniform. It describes how you'll go about acting on your needs and urges. If you have Venus in fiery, impulsive Aries, for example, and you're attracted to a complete stranger across the room, you won't wait for them to come to you. You'll walk over and introduce yourself the second the urge strikes you. Venus in intense, sexy Scorpio, however? Well, that's a different story. In this case, you'll keep looking at a prospective beloved until they finally give in, cross the room, and beg you to explain why you've been staring at them for the past couple of hours.

Houses

The houses represent the different sides of our personalities that emerge in different life situations. For example, think of how very different you act when you're with an authority figure as opposed to how you act with a lover or when you're with your BFF.

Aspects

The aspects describe the distance from one planet to another in a geometric angle. If you were born when Mercury was 90 degrees from Jupiter, for example, this aspect is called a square. Each unique angular relationship causes the planets involved to interact differently.

Meet the Planets

The planets represent energy sources. The Sun is our source of creativity, the Moon is our emotional warehouse, and Venus describes who and what we love and are attracted to—not to mention why and how we go about getting it and keeping it.

Sun

The Sun is the head honcho in your chart. It represents your life's mission—what will give you joy, keep you young, and never fail to arouse your curiosity. Oddly enough, you weren't born knowing the qualities of the sign the Sun was in when you were born. You're here to learn the traits, talents, and characteristics of the sign you chose—and rest assured, each of the twelve is its own marvelous adventure! Since the Sun is the Big Boss, all of the other planets, including the Moon, are the Sun's staff, all there to help the boss by helping you master your particular area of expertise. Back in the day, the words from a song in a recruitment commercial struck me as a perfect way to describe our Sun's quest: "Be all that you can be. Keep on reaching. Keep on growing. Find your future." The accompanying music was energizing, robust, and exciting, full of anticipation and eagerness. When you feel enthused, motivated, and stimulated, that's your Sun letting you know you're on the right path.

Moon

If you want to understand this lovely silver orb, go outside when the Moon is nice and full, find yourself a comfy perch, sit still, and have a nice, long look at her. The Moon inspires us to dream, wish, and sigh, to reminisce, ruminate, and remember. She's the Queen of Emotions, the astrological purveyor of feelings and reactions. In your natal chart, the condition of the Moon—that is, the sign and house she's in and the connections she makes with your other planets—shows how you'll deal with whatever life tosses your way—how you'll respond, how you'll cope, and how you'll pull it all together to move on after a crisis. She's where your instincts and hunches come from, and the source of every gut feeling and premonition. The Moon describes your childhood home, your relationship with your mother, your attitude toward childbearing and children in general, and what you're looking for in a home. She shows what makes you feel safe, warm, comfy, and loved. On a daily basis, the Moon describes the collective mood.

Mercury

Next time you pass by a flower shop, take a look at the FTD logo by the door. That fellow with the wings on his head and his feet is Mercury, the ancient Messenger of the Gods. He's always been a very busy guy. Back in the day, his job was to shuttle messages back and forth between the gods and goddesses and we mere mortals—obviously, no easy feat. Nowadays, however, Mercury is even busier. With computers, cell phones, social media, and perhaps even the occasional human-to-human interaction to keep track of—well, he must be just exhausted. In a nutshell, he's the astrological energy in charge of communication, navigation, and travel, so he's still nicely represented by that winged image. He's also the guy in charge of the five senses, so no matter what you're aware of right now, be it taste, touch, sound, smell, or sight—well, that's because Mercury is bringing it to you, live. At any rate, you'll hear about him most when someone mentions that Mercury is retrograde, but even though these periods have come to be blamed for all sorts of problems, there's really no cause for alarm. Mercury turns retrograde (or, basically, appears to move backwards from our perspective here on Earth) every three months for three weeks, giving us all a chance for a do-over—and who among us has never needed one of those?

Venus

So, if it's Mercury that makes you aware of your environment, who allows you to experience all kinds of sensory sensations via the five senses? Who's in charge of your preferences in each department? That delightful task falls under the jurisdiction of the lovely lady Venus, who describes the physical experiences that are the absolute best—in your book, anyway. That goes for the music and art you find most pleasing, the food and beverages you can't get enough of, and the scents you consider the sweetest of all—including the collar of the shirt your loved one recently wore. Touch, of course, is also a sense that can be quite delightful to experience. Think of how happy your fingers are when you're stroking your pet's fur, or the delicious feel of cool bed sheets when you slip between them after an especially tough day. Venus brings all those sensations together in one wonderful package, working her magic through love of the romantic kind, most memorably experienced through intimate physical interaction with an "other." Still, your preferences in any relationship also fall under Venus's job description.

Mars

Mars turns up the heat, amps up the energy, and gets your show on the road. Whenever you hear yourself grunt, growl, or grumble—or just make any old "rrrrr" sound in general—your natal Mars has just made an appearance. Adrenaline is his business and passion is his specialty. He's the ancient God of War—a hot-headed guy who's famous for having at it with his sword first and asking questions later. In the extreme, Mars is often in the neighborhood when violent events occur, and accidents, too. He's in charge of self-assertion, aggression, and pursuit, and one glance at his heavenly appearance explains why. He's The Red Planet, after all—and just think of all the expressions about anger and passion that include references to the color red or the element of fire: "Grrr!" "Seeing red." "Hot under the collar." "All fired up." "Hot and heavy." You get the idea. Mars is your own personal warrior. He describes how you'll react when you're threatened, excited, or angry.

Jupiter

Santa Claus. Luciano Pavarotti with a great big smile on his face as he belts out an amazing aria. Your favorite uncle who drinks too much, eats too much, and laughs far too loud—yet never fails to go well above and beyond the call of duty for you when you need him. They're all perfect examples of Jupiter, the King of the Gods, the giver of all things good, and the source of extravagance, generosity, excess, and benevolence in our little corner of the Universe. He and Venus are the heavens' two most popular planets—for obvious reasons. Venus makes us feel good. Jupiter makes us feel absolutely over-the-top excellent. In Jupiter's book, if one is good, it only stands to reason that two would be better, and following that logic, ten would be just outstanding. His favorite words are "too," "many," and "much." Expansions, increases, and enlargements—or basically, just the whole concept of growth—are all his doing. Now, unbeknownst to this merry old fellow, there really is such a thing as too much of a good thing—but let's not pop his goodhearted bubble. Wherever Jupiter is in your chart, you'll be prone to go overboard, take it to the limit, and push the envelope as far as you possibly can. Sure, you might get a bit out of control every now and then, but if envelopes weren't ever pushed, we'd never know the joys of optimism, generosity, or sudden, contagious bursts of laughter.

Saturn

Jupiter expands. Saturn contracts. Jupiter encourages growth. Saturn, on the other hand, uses those rings he's so famous for to restrict growth. His favorite word is "no," but he's also very fond of "wait," "stop," and "don't even think about it." He's ultra-realistic and quite pessimistic, a cautious, careful curmudgeon who guards and protects you by not allowing you to move too quickly or act too recklessly. He insists on preparation and doesn't take kindly when we blow off responsibilities and duties. As you can imagine, Saturn is not nearly as popular as Venus and Jupiter, mainly because none of us like to be told we can't do what we want to do when we want to do it. Still, without someone who acted out his part when you were too young to know better, you might have dashed across the street without stopping to check for traffic first, and—well, you get the point. Saturn encourages frugality, moderation, thoughtfulness, and self-restraint, all necessary habits to learn if you want to play nice with the other grown-ups. He's also quite fond of building things, which necessarily starts with solid foundations and structures that are built to last.

Uranus

Say hello to Mr. Unpredictable himself, the heavens' wild card—to say the very least. He's the kind of guy who claims responsibility for lightning strikes, be they literal or symbolic. Winning the lottery, love at first sight, accidents, and anything seemingly coincidental that strikes you as oddly well-timed are all examples of Uranus's handiwork. He's a rebellious, headstrong energy, so wherever he is in your chart, you'll be defiant, headstrong, and quite unwilling to play by the rules, which he thinks of as merely annoying suggestions that far too many humans adhere to. Uranus is here to inspire you to be yourself—exactly as you are, with no explanations and no apologies whatsoever. He motivates you to develop qualities such as independence, ingenuity, and individuality—and with this guy in the neighborhood, if anyone or anything gets in the way, you'll 86 them. Period. Buh-bye now. The good news is that when you allow this freedom-loving energy to guide you, you discover something new and exciting about yourself on a daily basis—at least. The tough but entirely doable part is keeping him reined in tightly enough to earn your daily bread and form lasting relationships with like-minded others.

Neptune

Neptune is the uncontested Mistress of Disguise and Illusion in the solar system, beautifully evidenced by the fact that this ultra-feminine energy has been masquerading as a male god for as long as gods and goddesses have been around. Just take a look at the qualities she bestows: compassion, spirituality, intuition, wistfulness, and nostalgia. Basically, whenever your subconscious whispers, it's in Neptune's voice. She activates your antennae and sends you subtle, invisible, and yet highly powerful messages about everyone you cross paths with, no matter how fleeting the encounter. I often picture her as Glinda the Good Witch from *The Wizard of Oz*, who rode around in a pink bubble, singing happy little songs and casting wonderful, helpful spells. Think "enchantment"—oh, and "glamour," too, which, by the way, was the old-time term for a magical spell cast upon someone to change their appearance. Nowadays, glamour is often thought of as a rather idealized and often artificial type of beauty brought about by cosmetics and airbrushing, but Neptune is still in charge, and her magic still works. When this energy is wrongfully used, deceptions, delusions and fraud can result—and since she's so fond of ditching reality, it's easy to become a bit too fond of escape hatches like drugs and alcohol. Still, Neptune inspires romance, nostalgia, and sentimentality, and she's quite fond of dreams and fantasies, too—and what would life be like without all of that?

Pluto

Picture all the gods and goddesses in the heavens above us living happily in a huge mansion in the clouds. Then imagine that Pluto's place is at the bottom of the cellar stairs, and on the cellar door (which is in the kitchen, of course) a sign reads "Keep out. Working on Darwin Awards." That's where Pluto would live—and that's the attitude he'd have. He's in charge of unseen cycles—life, death, and rebirth. Obviously, he's not an emotional kind of guy. Whatever Pluto initiates really has to happen. He's dark, deep, and mysterious—and inevitable. So yes, Darth Vader does come to mind, if for no other reason than because of James Earl Jones's amazing, compelling voice. Still, this intense, penetrating, and oh-so-thorough energy has a lot more to offer. Pluto's in charge of all those categories we humans aren't fond of—like death and decay, for example—but on the less drastic side, he also inspires recycling, repurposing, and reusing. In your chart, Pluto represents a place where you'll be ready to go big or go home, where investing all or nothing is a given. When a crisis comes up—when you need to be totally committed and totally authentic to who you really are to get through it—that's when you'll meet your Pluto. Power struggles and mind games, however—well, you can also expect those pesky types of things wherever Pluto is located.

A Word about Retrogrades

"Retrograde" sounds like a bad thing, but I'm here to tell you that it isn't. In a nutshell, retrograde means that from our perspective here on Earth, a planet appears to be moving in reverse. Of course, planets don't ever actually back up, but the energy of retrograde planets is often held back, delayed, or hindered in some way. For example, when Mercury—the ruler of communication and navigation—appears to be retrograde, it's tough to get from point A to point B without a snafu, and it's equally hard to get a straight answer. Things just don't seem to go as planned. But it only makes sense. Since Mercury is the planet in charge of conversation and movement, when he's moving backward—well, imagine driving a car that only had reverse. Yep. It wouldn't be easy. Still, if that's all you had to work with, you'd eventually find a way to get where you wanted to go. That's how all retrograde energies work. If you have retrograde planets in your natal chart, don't rush them. These energies may need a bit more time to function well for you than other natal planets, but if you're patient, talk about having an edge! You'll know these planets inside and out. On a collective basis, think of the time when a planet moves retrograde as a chance for a celestial do-over.

Signs of the Zodiac

The sign a planet is "wearing" really says it all. It's the costume an actor wears that helps them act out the role they're playing. It's the style, manner, or approach you'll use in each life department—whether you're being creative on a canvas, gushing over a new lover, or applying for a management position. Each of the signs belongs to an element, a quality, and a gender, as follows.

Elements

The four elements—fire, earth, air, and water—describe a sign's aims. Fire signs are spiritual, impulsive energies. Earth signs are tightly connected to the material plane. Air signs are cerebral, intellectual creatures, and water signs rule the emotional side of life.

Qualities

The three qualities—cardinal, fixed, and mutable—describe a sign's energy. Cardinal signs are tailor-made for beginnings. Fixed energies are solid, just as they sound, and are quite determined to finish what they start. Mutable energies are flexible and accommodating but can also be scattered or unstable.

Genders

The genders—masculine and feminine—describe whether the energy attracts (feminine) or pursues (masculine) what it wants.

The Twelve Signs

Here's a quick rundown of the twelve zodiac signs.

Aries

Aries planets are hotheads. They're built from go-getter cardinal energy and fast-acting fire. Needless to say, Aries energy is impatient, energetic, and oh-so-willing to try anything once.

Taurus

Taurus planets are aptly represented by the symbol of the bull. They're earth creatures, very tightly connected to the material plane, and fixed—which means they're pretty much immovable when they don't want to act.

Sequence	Sign	Glyph	Ruling Planet	Symbol
1	Aries	♈	Mars	Ram
2	Taurus	♉	Venus	Bull
3	Gemini	♊	Mercury	Twins
4	Cancer	♋	Moon	Crab
5	Leo	♌	Sun	Lion
6	Virgo	♍	Mercury	Virgin
7	Libra	♎	Venus	Scales
8	Scorpio	♏	Pluto	Scorpion
9	Sagittarius	♐	Jupiter	Archer
10	Capricorn	♑	Saturn	Goat
11	Aquarius	♒	Uranus	Water Bearer
12	Pisces	♓	Neptune	Fish

Gemini

As an intellectual air sign that's mutable and interested in anything new, Gemini energy is eternally curious—and quite easily distracted. Gemini planets live in the moment and are expert multitaskers.

Cancer

Cancer is a water sign that runs on its emotions, and since it's also part of the cardinal family, it's packed with the kind of start-up energy that's perfect for raising a family and building a home.

Leo

This determined, fixed sign is part of the fire family. As fires go, think of Leo planets as bonfires of energy—and just try to tear your eyes away. Leo's symbol is the lion, and it's no accident. Leo planets care very much about their familial pride—and about their personal pride.

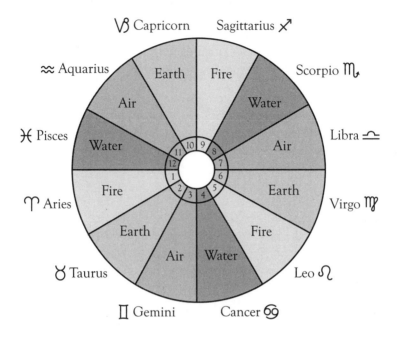

Virgo

Virgo is mutable and therefore easily able to switch channels when necessary. It's part of the earth family and connected to the material world (like Taurus). Virgo energy loves to work, organize, and sort, but most of all, to fix what's broken.

Libra

This communicative air sign runs on high. It's cardinal, so when it comes to making connections, Libra is second to none. Libra planets are people pleasers and the honorary cruise directors of the zodiac, and are as charming and accommodating as the day is long.

Scorpio

Scorpio is of the water element and a highly emotional creature. Scorpio energy is fixed, too, so feelings are tough to shake and obsessions are easy to come by. Planets in this sign are devoted and determined and can be absolutely relentless.

Sagittarius

Sagittarius has all the fire of Aries and Leo but, due to its mutable nature, tends to be distracted, spreading its energy among projects and interests. Think of Sagittarius energy as a series of red-hot brushfires, firing up and dying down and firing up again in a new location.

Capricorn

As the third earth sign, Capricorn is concerned with reality and practicality, complete with all the rules and regulations it takes to build and maintain a life here on Planet Number Three. Capricorn energy takes charge and assumes responsibility quite easily.

Aquarius

The last of the three communicative air signs, Aquarius prefers mingling and interacting with a group via friendships. Freedom-loving Aquarius energy won't be restricted—not for long, anyway—and is willing to return the favor, in any and all relationships.

Pisces

Watery Pisces runs on its emotions—and even more so on its intuition, which is second to none. This mutable, flexible sign is aptly represented by the constant fluctuating movements of its symbol, the two fish.

Aspects

Astrological aspects describe the relationships between planets and important points in a horoscope chart. Basically, they're the mathematical angles that measure the distance between two or more planets. Planets in square aspect are 90 degrees apart, planets in opposition are 180 degrees apart, and so forth. Each of these aspect relationships seems to link energies in a very different way. For example, if two planets are in square aspect, think of what you know about "squaring off," and you'll understand exactly how they're interacting. Think of aspects as a way of describing the type of conversation going on between celestial bodies.

Here's a brief description of the five major aspects.

Conjunction

When two planets are within a few degrees of each other, they're joined at the hip. The conjunction is often called the aspect of "fusion," since the energies involved always act together.

Sextile

Planets in sextile are linked by a 60-degree angle, creating an exciting, stimulating astrological "conversation." These planets encourage, arouse, and excite each other.

Square

The square aspect is created by linking energies in a 90-degree angle—which tends to be testy and sometimes irritating but always action-oriented.

Trine

The trine is the "lazy" aspect. When planets are in this 120-degree angle, they get along so well that they often aren't motivated to do much. Trines make things easy—too easy, at times—but they're also known for being quite lucky.

Opposition

Oppositions exist between planets that are literally opposite one another. Think about seesaws and playing tug-of-war, and you'll understand how these energies get along. Sure, it can be a power struggle at times, but balance is the key.

2020 at a Glance

What stands out about 2020 is that it begins and ends with two separate and distinct calls to action, one on January 12 and the other on December 21. The year is barely days old when we find ourselves knee-deep in the most intense event of 2020: full-on contact between Saturn and Pluto. Of course, the tension between these two heavyweights has been building for the last year, but now it reaches its climax. But the questions remains: What kind of culmination will it be? One thing is certain. It will pack a profound and potentially life-altering punch. This experience will be visceral. You *will* feel it, most likely in every cell of your body and in every corner of your consciousness. It will be intense and overwhelming. It may even make you feel like you want to crawl out of your skin.

The first thing you need to know is that if you decide that you must choose between maintaining control at all costs over any aspect of your life that this event touches or essentially taking out the garbage you accumulated and using that newfound space to ignite new passion and new vitality, then you are creating an unnecessary dilemma. Because there is enough to master in this challenging process without giving in to the inherent push-pull symbolized by the interaction between Saturn and Pluto. It may be difficult to refrain from dragging yourself back and forth between what, on the surface, appears to be two opposites. On the one hand, Saturn conjures up fear at even the thought that control is unattainable, while on the other hand, Pluto asks for complete vulnerability, a complete letting go.

It's not easy to find common ground between these two very different drives. The key is to recognize that you cannot change the basic nature of Saturn or Pluto. What you can do is find a common goal that each can pursue authentically. And that common goal is purifying your life so you can build a new foundation. Would you build a house on a foundation that was crumbling and no longer safe or supportive? No. In this case, you are the house whose foundation is falling apart. Pluto wants to help you clear out the rubble so that Saturn can then build a new base, one that gives you the best chance of succeeding far into the future without being destroyed by anything that limits you. No matter how this manifests in your life—and it will be different for each individual Sun sign and for each individual born under that Sun sign—Saturn offers the fortitude and Pluto the passion to commit yourself completely to this process throughout almost all of 2020 and to emerge rebuilt and reborn.

Ready to use your wisdom and newly developed skills to respond to the invitation issued by Saturn and Jupiter as 2020 comes to a close and they meet up in the very first degree of Aquarius? How will you choose to take yourself into the future? Because it's not enough to do the work of stripping yourself down, transforming, and creating that new beginning. Now you must not just do something with it but also grow some more. You must be willing to step confidently and optimistically into the future, even if you have no idea what it looks like and even if you are stepping outside the known qualities and quantities of your life. After all, you just finished proving to yourself beyond a shadow of a doubt that you can take charge of your life and master any set of circumstances you encounter. You are your strength, your security, your inspiration, your own source of power. And that is more valuable to who you are and who you are becoming than anything on the outside.

2020 SUN SIGN BOOK

Forecasts by

Lesley Francis

Aries

The Ram
March 21 to April 20

♈

Element: Fire	Glyph: Ram's head
Quality: Cardinal	Anatomy: Head, face, throat
Polarity: Yang/masculine	Colors: Red, white
Planetary Ruler: Mars	Animal: Ram
Meditation: I build on my strengths	Myths/Legends: Artemis, Jason and the Golden Fleece
Gemstone: Diamond	House: First
Power Stones: Bloodstone, carnelian, ruby	Opposite Sign: Libra
	Flower: Geranium
Key Phrase: I am	Keyword: Initiative

The Aries Personality

Strengths, Talents, and the Creative Spark

You are always itching to initiate something, anything. After all, you love the rush of adrenaline that comes with those first steps down the path of possibility. You love the anticipation of finding yourself in circumstances that test you, push you, challenge you. You love knowing you have the capacity to step up to the plate and knock it out of the park. For you, life is not life without the promise of new beginnings. If you thought everything could be predicted day in and day out, you'd find yourself on the road to instant depression because such a life is incomprehensible to you. This is a strength, a talent, and the spark to your creativity all rolled into one—that indefinable urge that comes from deep within you to begin anew over and over again, with no end in sight.

This is what sustains you: that call to take a risk, to leap into the unknown with a confidence and a knowing that quite often astounds you and everyone around you. That surety allows you to fall down and immediately pick yourself up again, without hesitation, without fear, without second-guessing yourself. In your world, you know what you know. Label it what you will: instinct, intuition, or hunch. It's what drives you and what it's labeled doesn't interest you as much as where it takes you, and what it shows you about who you are and what you can accomplish.

Blind Spots and Blockages

Did you consider, as you were rushing headlong down the trail, that everything in life is not a battle? You can butt those horns as much as you want, but not everyone is interested in being the target you use to prove how strong and courageous you are. Life requires more than just pure adrenaline. Sometimes it demands a more measured response— one that is assertive rather than aggressive, one that is considerate and not pushy, one that acknowledges you are not alone on the planet. Looking for obstacles to overcome or trying to prove yourself all the time can get a bit tiring. True, you are hard-wired to continually look for something new to engage you and give you the chance to conquer one more little corner of life. However, your fear of failure and of lacking what it takes to triumph often impels you past the point where common sense should kick in.

Your blind spot is not recognizing that always testing yourself, always wanting to go beyond what you did yesterday, leaves little room to be in the moment and appreciate what you've done, because you are already looking for the next challenge. Plus it's not particularly kind or effective to expect the utmost and the extraordinary from yourself every minute of every day. Not only is it unrealistic but it undermines you at your core and triggers deep feelings of inadequacy. Time to recognize that inherent in risk is the possibility that things will go sideways, and that you have the resiliency to turn what looks like failure into a testament to the sheer force of your will to make it through adversity and come out the other side stronger.

Intimacy and Connection

This aspect of life can be a challenge for you, not because you don't like people but because you are often mystified by what motivates others. This leads you to talk about yourself—not for self-glorification, because you really don't seek or need other people's approval, but because you are looking for something in others that reminds you of yourself. You want to see that flicker of recognition on the other person's face that demonstrates you have something in common. Otherwise you aren't sure exactly where or how you can make a connection, never mind build intimacy. The key here is to realize that if everyone was exactly like you, you'd be bored out of your mind. You don't really need to see yourself in others because you already have a strong sense of who you are. What will actually nurture you is embracing the differences in others, because that leads to new experiences and new perspectives that enrich your life, and introduces you to even more of what life has to offer. It can be limiting and stultifying to spend your life locked in your own view of the world. So let go of the need to know everything and be right. Open your heart and your ears, and use your infinite capacity to take risks to connect with all those marvelous humans just waiting to be your friend, your lover, etc.

Values and Resources

The cornerstone of everything you value is based completely on being self-reliant and self-sufficient. Your heart beats a little faster and your happiness rises ever higher when you can look at your world and know you created it, whether it's your physical, emotional, intellectual or spiritual world you are contemplating. And, because you love to test yourself, you are extremely resourceful in finding ways to meet any challenge you deem worthy. The truth is you feel that you alone are the only resource you really need or can truly rely on. Which is why you are almost allergic to asking for *help*. That automatically implies some failure on your part. You will, however, accept support from others, because that still puts you in the driver's seat. As long as you are leading the way, all is right with the world. As for the external measuring sticks used to determine self-worth—money and possessions—they hold little value to you on their own. They only matter as a symbol of what you did and what you accomplished. You don't need them to validate any aspect of this adventure you call life.

Goals and Success

You definitely enjoy making things happen, big or small, short term or long term, practical or spiritual. The satisfaction is always in the doing, in forging a new path for yourself, and in expanding your awareness and your skill set—definitely worthy goals you seek to exemplify over and over again throughout the course of your life. For you, success is simple and straightforward. Act on your ability to initiate, feel that fire within that lights you up, push yourself to go further, and, finally, enjoy the moment when you prove to yourself yet again that you can meet the challenge of life.

Aries Keywords for 2020
Perseverance, preparation, passion

The Year Ahead for Aries

The year 2020 promises to be one of deep sensitivity coupled with a powerful urge to express your personal power by overcoming obstacles both internal and external. The need to be seen as more than a flash in the pan or that individual who will do anything for a shot of adrenaline requires a deep transformation of how you show up in the world. Recognize that the dissatisfaction you identify as coming from others actually has its genesis within. You are strong and capable. You always have been. It's just that now you want your life to reflect a gravitas, *your* gravitas. No longer are you satisfied with being the person who initiates things or the person who takes risks when no one else will, whether those risks are physical, emotional, intellectual, or spiritual. You definitely find yourself wanting to be taken more seriously, which translates to deepening your commitment to life in all its shades and nuances, not just those that make your heart beat a little faster in the moment but fade because they contain no real substance or sustenance. So make use of your greatest asset: your ability to take action. Just remember to create a plan before you take action. Begin by channeling that powerful instinct you have into redefining what you value in yourself and what is meaningful to you in your life. Allow it to guide you to a deeper understanding of what you truly seek. Then build a foundation for that risk you want to take.

This process is bound to surprise you to the very core of your being as you open inner doors you didn't know you had. And, it will create a challenge to integrate two very powerful impulses: one that asks you to change from the inside out, creating a new way of taking risks and setting you up for long-term growth, and another that whispers in your ear that everything is fine just the way it is and that you need to protect yourself at all costs by shutting down any urge to grow. Why? Because you are afraid that kind of change equates to admitting that somehow you've been wrong all your life. Well, that's the furthest thing from the truth. You are on the verge of a major rebirth that will take everything you've been and done and use it as fuel to fashion the very best person you can be.

Jupiter

It would be lovely to think that Jupiter could ease some of the tension gripping you from the inside out, that he can ameliorate that hypersensitivity that seems to be there every time you take a breath. And he just might do both of those things, but it really depends on your mood, on your current perception of life. Because the reality is that Jupiter amplifies whatever he touches. So if you are convinced that the energies floating around in your consciousness are just there to torment you, Jupiter will keep reminding you of that. If, on the other hand, you greet all the internal shifting and pushing and discomfort with grace and acceptance, Jupiter will illuminate and accentuate that feeling of grace and acceptance. He will show you that the journey you are on is meaningful, and he will guide you to that space in your reality where you discover a deeper faith in yourself. It all depends on you—on you embracing your innate belief that no one is in charge of your reality but you. Granted, that is being tested in some very intense and twisty ways in 2020, and there will be days when you wonder if you have permanently lost your famous talent for meeting all challenges with a smile and a little bit of defiance on your face. But you will prevail. Just remember to avoid taking any path that looks like the easy way out. There isn't one. Not even Jupiter can produce that for you this year. He can, however, lead you to a profound joy in being able to live life anew.

Saturn

No sense in pretending that Saturn is not going to test your resiliency, your intentions, and your capacity to stand firm in the face of his unrelenting demand that you get it together right now and create something of lasting value. You are definitely ready to respond to this call to action. You just aren't sure how. After all, there are days when you aren't sure about anything: who you are, what you are doing here, and, most importantly, what the heck is really going on. This leaves you feeling like you are swimming in the middle of the ocean with nothing to grab on to. How can you possibly create anything when you are on the verge of drowning? And, yes, that is an accurate description of how life is affecting you. Of course, Saturn may urge you to ignore all those questions and feelings. They can't possibly be that useful. On the contrary, you need to answer those questions and honor those feelings if you want to respond to Saturn's challenge.

So what's the solution? Accept that all this confusion is a sign that you are leaving behind anything that interferes with that deep desire to completely overhaul your life in preparation for something indescribable (which it is) and magnificent. Turn inward and trust your instincts. How many times in life have you thrown caution to the wind and just jumped in? Countless times. True, this feels different, because it is different. The risk you take now ushers you into a space and a place beyond your usual mastering of life. Accept the challenge and it will lead to a purpose and a plan that you simply can't visualize right now. Just know it will be worth every ounce of the struggle it takes to get there.

Uranus

The need to take stock of the practical foundation of your life continues to push itself to the forefront of your life when you least expect it. Since you already feel your life is undergoing a major recalibration, it doesn't surprise you that it's time to think about what you really value and reassess your resources, both internal and external. What keeps knocking you off balance is that you don't seem to be making any headway in sorting and sifting through all the aspects of your life so you can strip away the unnecessary and create a new point of initiation. After all, the one thing that always stalls your forward movement is not knowing where to begin. And, if that wasn't disconcerting enough, you feel, at least once every day, that anything and everything could explode or implode at any moment. The combination of these two competing perceptions feels a lot like riding a bucking bronco. You know you need to be strong and centered at the same time you are sure you are going to go crashing to the ground. This is definitely Uranus at work, stirring the pot of the things you take for granted as solid and dependable (because even you need enough certainty in your life to be able to take risks) while at the same time disrupting the very parts of you that you rely on, leaving you wondering if you can make a decision, take a direction, or simply be confident in your ability to navigate life. The key here is to do something you do really well. Be in the moment. Try not to project too far into the future, even though it feels like that's what you should be doing. That way, the appropriate steps, plans, opportunities, and/ or perceptions have the space to rise up organically, giving you the best chance to use all this upheaval to your advantage.

Neptune

The misty—or is that the murky?—messages emerging from the ethers, aka your unconscious, don't appear to have any connection to your life. And that's the point. How can you step outside what you know and have known if you are not able to entertain the unfettered and limitless things swishing around in a part of your brain that has nothing to do with cognitive thought? Now, before you resist, recognize that the purpose of all these imaginings is to keep you open to the wildly improbable, to keep your consciousness fluid, and to keep inspiration always just a heartbeat away. This is the stuff of life, all that weird and wonderful flotsam and jetsam floating around, shifting and changing your perceptions and your sense of where you might be going. Because somewhere in all of this is something that will stick, something that will provide you with the kind of sustenance that makes life that much deeper, and something that will make life feel much more magical. And you definitely need that right now: the buoyancy that releases you from the bonds and bounds of all that intense work you are putting in to transform you and your life. Of course, part of you will want to dismiss what looks like nonsense, but remember that not all experiences need to fit into a third-dimensional box. They just need to lift you up and create delight, wonder, and hope. So invite more of this into your life by meditating, keeping track of your dreams, paying attention to the unscheduled insights that show up, and laughing at the silliness that your consciousness has such a powerful capacity to conjure up.

Pluto

Mark January 12 on your calendar. It's the day when Saturn finally catches up to Pluto and the on-and-off dialogue they've been having since December 19, 2017, comes to a head, putting tremendous pressure on you, inside and out. In fact, you may feel that your life is about to come apart at the seams. And that may not be very far from the truth. Now, before you panic, take stock of how much you have prepared yourself for this particular moment. If, in the last eight to ten years, you've welcomed every opportunity to rid yourself of what no longer works for you, gone deeper into your feeling world than you ever thought possible, processed unhealthy patterns that robbed you of energy, and committed yourself to finding a purpose in life that fuels your inner passion, then this day has the potential to create a powerful turning point—one that opens an overwhelming yet exciting vision of where your life is going and, in doing so, asks you to let go of anything else that inhibits you. And that's scary. Embrace that fear and recognize it for what it is: a final attempt by the part of you that wants to hold on to what is familiar, even if it's toxic or counterproductive. Know that this day *is* a turning point, not the final test. It's a beginning, an initiation that gives the rest of this year a joyful and positive focus.

How Will This Year's Eclipses Affect You?

Eclipses signal intense periods that highlight major growth opportunities for us in the process of creating our lives. They are linked to the lunar phases—specifically the New and the Full Moon—and involve the relationship between the Sun, the Moon, and the Earth. A Solar Eclipse is a magnified New Moon, while a Lunar Eclipse is a magnified Full Moon. Eclipses unfold in cycles involving all twelve signs of the zodiac, and they occur in pairs, usually about two weeks apart.

This year there are six eclipses: two Solar Eclipses (one in Cancer and one in Sagittarius) and four Lunar Eclipses (one in Cancer, one in Sagittarius, one in Capricorn, and one in Gemini). This mixed bag of energies signals a shift from last year's focus on redefining nurturing versus babysitting, obligation versus accountability, family versus career, time for self versus taking care of business, and feelings versus rational thought. Three of this year's eclipses (the Lunar Eclipse on January 10 and the Solar Eclipse on June 21, both in Cancer, as well as the Lunar Eclipse on July 5 in Capricorn) complete this cycle, while the new eclipse cycle calls on us to understand that there is no wisdom in living in an ivory tower, stuck in our belief that there is only one way to live life while cut off from that very life. Instead, we need to get down to the streets and actually experience our environment, talk to people, create a dialogue, and embrace diversity. Only then can we create a world that truly embodies freedom and opportunity. Three eclipses (the Lunar Eclipse on June 5 in Sagittarius, the Lunar Eclipse on November 30 in Gemini, and the Solar Eclipse on December 14 in Sagittarius) begin this process.

The first eclipse of 2020 takes place on January 10, and it's a Lunar Eclipse in Cancer, highlighting your ongoing need to find new ways to take care of yourself, if you want to fuel that big transformation burbling just below the surface of your consciousness. No amount of practical preparation or rational thought can support you through a time when you are birthing a new you and a new life. This requires a connection to that deep well of feeling that underlies everything you do. Remember that this eclipse truly sets the tone for you this year and, if you choose to ignore its invitation, you really will be playing catch-up with yourself all year, trying to find the footing that you need to move forward and put into practice all those new dreams and visions you have. The path and the potential are clear. Embrace the emergence of the new you rather than stifling it and the opportunities represented by the remaining eclipses in 2020. They point to the kind of success that satisfies you both internally and externally. Eclipses truly are signposts. But they are not the journey. That's totally up to you.

Aries | January

Overall Theme

So, there is a reckoning at hand. Sounds ominous. Well, there's no avoiding the fact that this month feels like the biggest upheaval you've ever experienced. However, it relieves a lot of the internal pressure you've been confronting, leaving space and breathing room. This, in itself, is cause for celebration. You feel free, so get ready to make your mark.

Relationships

Stripped down to your essence by a whole lot of converging energies, you really aren't sure exactly what you have to share with anyone, or even if you want to. Rather than building walls to avoid that tremendous feeling of vulnerability surging through your entire being, remain transparent and you will discover everyone else is in the same boat. This leads to the opportunity to build real intimacy.

Success and Money

You definitely feel the urge to push the limits in your work/career life because it is the one area of your life that seems not only tangible but safe, where you can actually *do* something. Be careful. What you accomplish may be the opposite of what you desire if it's based in a push for power rather than a drive for mastery.

Pitfalls and Potential Problems

Relinquish any idea that you are in charge of anything, not even yourself, this month and you find new gears you didn't know you had. Of course, this is likely to offend you to your very core until you realize that the challenge you are facing really comes from inside of you, and that you need to experience the process instead of trying to drive it in any particular direction. Now that's self-determination.

Rewarding Days

5, 6, 13, 14

Challenging Days

9, 10, 22, 23

Aries | February

Overall Theme

It's going to be hard to focus your attention on the reality of life as your creative mind goes into overdrive, taking you into uncharted territory that lights you up from the inside. It really feels like you've struck gold, and in many ways you have. But until you find a way to manifest all those magical musings, they remain seeds that still need to be planted.

Relationships

A lot of time gets spent on wondering what it is people expect from you, because everywhere you turn it feels like someone is waiting to push all your buttons or, worse, challenge you to a duel. There's a lot of push-pull going on mixed in with an unhealthy amount of passive-aggressive snarkiness. The best thing you can do is take a deep breath and step back. These are definitely lose-lose situations, so ignore the challenges.

Success and Money

It's going to be tough to stay grounded in this area of your life, because most days it feels like an albatross around your neck. Well, take some of that creative energy lighting up your circuits and apply it to some real-life challenges that suddenly crop up. You'll save the day and save yourself.

Pitfalls and Potential Problems

Stop trying to convince yourself that your life is in perfect alignment. You are still shiny and fresh and new *and* wobbly. After all, you are essentially a newborn. Which is a double-edged sword. Yes, the old crap is gone—at least, you feel like it is—and there is so much more space in your consciousness and your body. However, you don't know exactly what you are doing yet. And that's okay. Relax.

Rewarding Days

8, 9, 16, 17

Challenging Days

6, 7, 18, 19

Aries | March

Overall Theme

This is a month of mixed messages. It begins with a general feeling that you are not actually inhabiting your physical reality, making it difficult to actually navigate life. Everything is fuzzy and more than a little out of focus. And then, while you are struggling to make sense of that, suddenly everything shifts into overdrive and you are pushed from deep inside to get busy and take all that new, transformative energy you created in January and *do* something *now*. Refrain from acting hastily. Make a plan instead.

Relationships

Nothing is likely to irritate you more right now than any demand on you that contains a sense of obligation. You are trying to figure out just what is best for you while mulling over how to change the way relationships actually function in your world. These are huge questions for you, ones that demand a lot of your attention and don't leave much space for actually connecting. And that's just fine.

Success and Money

It really is best to maintain the status quo in this area of your life. No hasty moves and no sudden decisions, no matter what your impulses push you toward. First of all, you don't have enough information, and second, the need to do something just to do something is not a sufficient reason to take a risk at a time that doesn't support that kind of action.

Pitfalls and Potential Problems

Don't fight the floaty, wispy, ephemeral feeling that engulfs you and leaves you totally discombobulated. It won't do any good. And it serves a purpose. There are times when you need to move beyond your comfort zone—the physical world—so you can clean out your psyche and connect to something larger than yourself. It helps keep life in perspective.

Rewarding Days

17, 18, 24, 25

Challenging Days

4, 5, 29, 30

Aries | April

Overall Theme

It's going to feel like the shackles have finally come off and you can get back to normal. And then you discover that you need a new normal because you really have changed, both who you are and what galvanizes you to get up every morning. It's no longer enough to take action. You must take purposeful action that results in deep and meaningful results.

Relationships

Part of your new normal is finding ways to connect to others that actually enrich you on an emotional level. This leads to a level of curiosity that astounds you because it's solely about knowing the other person inside and out, rather than making sure they are interesting enough to deserve your attention. They blossom and you blossom.

Success and Money

You feel ready to take on a whole new life, based on a more integrated definition of success. It's not enough to climb to the top of the mountain anymore. You need to have a vision of what that means and how you want it to impact your life. Time to take the first steps.

Pitfalls and Potential Problems

All systems are unquestionably ready to go. Just don't blow your circuits by trying to do everything all at once. This new path you've embarked on needs a wiser use of that dynamo that lives inside you. The long-term results of taking a more measured approach will ultimately blow your mind and leave you with a deeper appreciation of who and what you are.

Rewarding Days

15, 16, 20, 21

Challenging Days

7, 8, 13, 14

Aries | May

Overall Theme

A number of subtle shifts open up new doors and perceptions, creating a bit of a logjam in your brain. You are not always the most adept at considering a number of powerful and intriguing ideas simultaneously, because you prefer to react to one thing at a time. So rather than trying to figure out how to act on all this, take one simple step. Write everything down and process it later.

Relationships

Before you open your mouth to say anything to anyone, take a deep breath. And then take another one. This is definitely a month when what you say carries the extra added responsibility of making sure you are not opening your mouth and inserting your foot. You often don't use much of a filter when you talk, and you expect others to know that you don't mean any harm. Be aware that no one is likely to afford you that courtesy this month.

Success and Money

It's definitely time to consider where you are in the arc of your life when it comes to your long-term future. This means it's time to reflect on what you value and what you care about, and whether you are currently in alignment with either of those things. This doesn't equal nailing yourself to the floor. It means finding new pathways.

Pitfalls and Potential Problems

It might feel a lot like the old is colliding with the new when the old is actually falling away so there is space for the new. And this applies to whatever area of your life is demanding your attention. You know you are ready to let go of anything that inhibits your forward movement. To do this, be honest with yourself about any long-cherished ideas about yourself or your life that just don't work.

Rewarding Days

5, 6, 22, 23

Challenging Days

10, 11, 27, 28

Aries | June

Overall Theme

Life is just so much easier when the only thing you need to respond to is that familiar call to just do it. Well, that seems to be in short supply, as the one thing consistently knocking on your door is an overwhelming sensitivity to anything and everything. Embrace it and you discover a vision for your future that is exhilarating, even if it seems impossible.

Relationships

You are suddenly overwhelmingly aware of the feelings and fears of those closest to you. And, as always, it leaves you breathless—but not with anticipation. Not only is this outside your comfort zone, but it takes you to places you are not sure you can navigate. Remember this: You are already doing what needs to be done, both for yourself and for others. You are present.

Success and Money

The challenge this month is to balance the need for security with the equally demanding call for freedom, adventure, and meaningful endeavor. That's quite a tall order, so take your time, examine all the possibilities (you will have a number to consider), and recognize you are searching for the next big thing in your life.

Pitfalls and Potential Problems

A push-pull feeling dominates your world, leaving you unable to decide whether you want to run away from home or hide out in your basement so no one can see just how overwhelmed you are by your emotions. You can release yourself from this self-imposed purgatory by acknowledging that your emotions are a signal that you need to listen more closely to all the knowing behind the discomfort.

Rewarding Days

2, 3, 27, 28

Challenging Days

4, 5, 21, 22

Aries | July

Overall Theme

No sooner are you feeling that all is right with your world than the sky turns dark again and you find yourself laboring once more to get out from under this fear that you are not only running out of gas but also running out of the will and the desire to push past life's challenges. This is not a setback as much as it is an opportunity to let go of emotional detritus.

Relationships

Who needs people? You aren't sure you do. Because, after all, you have enough on your plate trying to keep the fire inside you—the one that you believed could not be extinguished—from going out. You just don't have time for even the most basic requests from others. Rather than putting your famous impatience on display, stretch yourself and share what you are going through.

Success and Money

The only thing that truly matters to you right now is maintaining the status quo in this area of your life. In a stroke of insight, you realize that all those wonderful new plans you've been playing with and nursing along are not ready for the full light of day because you simply don't have the energy to push forward. And that's okay.

Pitfalls and Potential Problems

It's true that everything feels not just stuck, not just impossible, not just immovable, but also without life. Which is, no doubt, the worst thing in your world. Accept that you are suffering from tunnel vision and that there is a purpose to all this. What you are staring at so intently is all the fear and apprehension you have shoved aside before in order to do and be. The time has come to release it. And to do that, you need to see it.

Rewarding Days

11, 12, 29, 30

Challenging Days

4, 5, 18, 19

Aries | August

Overall Theme

Your boundless energy returns, accompanied by a newfound wisdom that allows you to see what brings you great joy, how you intend to create it, and how to remain true to your initial vision even when confronted with obstacles. You really aren't quite sure what to do with this new outlook. Instead of getting fidgety, embrace it.

Relationships

The highly reactionary phase of last month softens. First, because you realize that not everyone expects you to always be the person with all the answers. (The truth is that's really what you expect of yourself.) Second, because opening up to others actually strengthens you. This almost stops you in your tracks until you realize how good that makes you feel.

Success and Money

There's a deep desire to try to push, push, push your agenda this month as a way to remind you and those around you that you are still a force to be reckoned with. Take that energy and focus it on inviting people to play with you rather than running over them. This creates better long-term results and a deeper appreciation of what you are capable of.

Pitfalls and Potential Problems

Too often you have allowed frustration and irritation to get in the way of what you truly desire. Which, you now realize, is more than just being in motion, more than just getting something done. This is a new feeling, this need for your life to stand for something and to mean something that goes beyond your infinite capacity to take a risk. This is new territory, so sit with it and let it settle into your whole being.

Rewarding Days

7, 8, 17, 18

Challenging Days

15, 16, 21, 22

Aries | September

Overall Theme

You feel like you are in full flight when someone tries to clip your wings. Actually, it's just time to slow things down a bit and assess your forward progress. It's not a secret plot to get in the way of your objectives but a necessary recalibration. To do this, you need to conserve your energy so your body, mind, and heart can recharge.

Relationships

Before you have time to resent what you consider an unnecessary break from setting the world on fire (not literally, of course), this part of your world takes on new color and vibrancy. People you know and those you don't suddenly offer you new awareness and new vistas that lift your spirits and keep you playful and happy.

Success and Money

This is a good month to listen to others because there promises to be an insight, a gem of awareness, that illuminates just how and where you've created an ongoing glitch that threatens to derail your plans. The gift is finding that it's something you can actually change by simply shifting your perspective.

Pitfalls and Potential Problems

You are still learning that there is much to be enjoyed and experienced when you are not going a hundred miles an hour. Suddenly you recognize that your constant chafing at the bit is not only tiresome but unproductive. Of course, the part of you that insists on something, anything, in your life being in overdrive isn't about to agree to a complete change in approach. So satisfy it by finding a place in your life where that energy works so you can practice your new attitude everywhere else.

Rewarding Days

9, 10, 13, 14

Challenging Days

11, 12, 24, 25

Aries | October

Overall Theme
The slowdown continues and you are unquestionably losing your patience. Or is that faith? It definitely feels like one step forward and two steps back. Unfortunately that's the nature of the outward energies right now. The key here is to go inward. There's still a lot of internal shifting needed to implement the transformation that pushed its way onto your plate in January.

Relationships
Be careful not to let any frustration you feel about what's happening or not happening in your life dictate how you relate to others. This is a time when saying nothing at all is much better than turning your crankiness into a verbal weapon. Recognize that you are always compelled to get things up and out of your consciousness. Best to take your exasperation to the gym.

Success and Money
The most productive thing to do this month is probably nothing at all in this area of your life. You are not at your best when you are confronted with what you perceive to be obstacle after obstacle. It leads you to make hasty decisions just so you can take action. Which is highly probable right now. So resist that very strong impulse to take any risk. That way you can avoid some awkward consequences.

Pitfalls and Potential Problems
This is a time when you really need to develop a deeper connection to your inner self so you can truly know yourself better. It may come as a surprise to you, but knowing yourself is actually a lifelong journey. After all, you are more complex than you acknowledge, partly because you are convinced that what you consider navel gazing is a waste of time. Consider this. Exploring all your nooks and crannies is actually a fantastic journey.

Rewarding Days
1, 2, 19, 20

Challenging Days
8, 9, 15, 16

Aries | November

Overall Theme

Life is really hard to pin down now. Or is it you that's hard to pin down? And that's not because you are moving too fast. The mix of energies currently knocking on your door makes it hard for you to get a clear sense of what your next step should be. Accept that things are really fluid and that it's best to take one day and perhaps one hour at a time.

Relationships

You find yourself being awfully nice to everyone, in part because it's one thing you know you can do that brings positive results, and in part because you want to camouflage the deeply disturbing feeling that you don't have a clue what's going on. No matter the reason, this makes relationships the one part of your life that makes sense, whether they are rewarding or challenging.

Success and Money

A wealth of opportunities present themselves, from the consequential to the inconsequential. File each and every one of them away until you feel more grounded, because right now you can't really discern which is which. This may be disconcerting to those offering up what they believe is the opportunity of a lifetime. Don't worry about them. Take care of yourself.

Pitfalls and Potential Problems

Everything absolutely amps up exponentially, leading to a level of confusion that is mind-boggling. It's like looking at a soup that has so many ingredients that it's hard to determine what kind it is. All you can do is trust that you have the will and determination as well as the insight to navigate all this weird intensity and come out the other side feeling renewed and ready to take on the world.

Rewarding Days
15, 16, 21, 22

Challenging Days
5, 6, 29, 30

Aries | December

Overall Theme

You enter the last month of 2020 with a hint of trepidation that is immediately swept away by a wave of confidence and enthusiasm that leaves you a little breathless. Once you exhale, you are all systems go and you recognize you've been preparing for this all year long. Finally you get to do more than start and stop, start and stop, start and stop. You get to go!

Relationships

This is an area of your life where you've grown immeasurably in 2020. Gone are some of your tendencies to be reactive, defensive, combative, and impulsive. You now know how to take a deep breath and truly listen to what is being shared, aware that people are speaking from inside their own reality. This has led you to see how multidimensional relationships can be. And, oh yes, how rewarding it is to be more vulnerable.

Success and Money

It's been quite the year of reevaluating yourself, your values, your definition of success, and your relationship to abundance. You've emerged from this process feeling shinier and newer. Realize that this is truly all you need right now. Life is going to give you lots of opportunities to act using this new template.

Pitfalls and Potential Problems

The biggest challenge facing you is your innate tendency to measure your life based on the success/failure model. This is just a return to old habits, old thinking, old patterns. As 2020 comes to a close, there's a very powerful opportunity to begin 2021 with a profound appreciation for the gifts inherent in every situation that didn't go according to plan. You just need to look past the end result.

Rewarding Days

4, 5, 17, 18

Challenging Days

2, 3, 15, 16

Aries Action Table

These dates reflect the best—but not the only—times for success and ease in these activities, according to your Sun sign.

	JAN	FEB	MAR	APR	MAY	JUN	JUL	AUG	SEP	OCT	NOV	DEC
Move		1, 2										
New romance				14, 15			11, 12	2, 3				
Seek coaching/counseling			8, 9						1, 2			
Ask for a raise	5, 6									3, 4		
Vacation						11, 12						16, 17
Get a loan			12, 13								17, 18	

Taurus

The Bull
April 21 to May 21

♉

Element: Earth

Quality: Fixed

Polarity: Yin/feminine

Planetary Ruler: Venus

Meditation: I trust myself and others

Gemstone: Emerald

Power Stones: Diamond, blue lace agate, rose quartz

Key Phrase: I have

Glyph: Bull's head

Anatomy: Throat, neck

Color: Green

Animal: Cattle

Myths/Legends: Isis and Osiris, Ceridwen, Bull of Minos

House: Second

Opposite Sign: Scorpio

Flower: Violet

Keyword: Conservation

The Taurus Personality

Strengths, Talents, and the Creative Spark

At the very core of who you are is an inexhaustible supply of determination, perseverance, and tenacity. No one, but no one, can stick to a plan quite the way you do. Once you make a decision, you make a commitment. That's just the way it is. The only thing left to do is put in the hard work necessary to make good on that promise, whether you made it to yourself or to someone or something else. It's all the same. You gave your word and it would never occur to you to back out, no matter what challenges or difficulties you confront along the way.

After all, you would rather die than be considered a quitter. In fact, it's quite likely that the word *quit* is not even in your vocabulary. Because, for you, it's just another word for failure, and that is something you cannot and will not accept. Which, of course, leads you to work harder until you finally triumph. This capacity for dedication often overshadows the true source of your success: a deep, practical creativity that sparks your imagination, allowing you to see the fruits of your labor before you actually do anything. It is so innate that it often goes unrecognized by you and others. You instinctively understand how the physical world works, as well as what is needed in any situation to create the required outcome. Your greatest joy is using that knowledge to master life.

Blind Spots and Blockages

You really do believe that everything not only should but will last forever. This leads you to build a reality that, in the long run, becomes a rut. And no matter how you decorate it, a rut is still a rut. But oh, how you love that rut. It's safe and secure, and it keeps the bogeyman at bay. Or so you think. The reality is that nothing stays the same. Change truly is inevitable, so you've got a choice. You can climb out of the rut, welcome uncertainty, and trust your inner resolve to see you through whatever life dishes up. Or you can redecorate the rut—new paint, new art, and new furniture—convinced that's all the change you need to make. There's just one problem with that approach. It eventually leads to disaster, because it actually disconnects you from the very parts of yourself that are the cornerstones of who you are.

You can survive. You can create security out of nothing. You can thrive no matter what. You've already done it. Many times. In small ways and in big ways. Your blind spot is not recognizing that you can do it over and over again. This refusal leads to perhaps your biggest blockage: you really don't know when to let go. You hang on and hang on, unwilling to acknowledge that someone or something, once so important to you, no longer serves or supports you. That's life. You don't have to like it. But you do need to give yourself permission to stop nailing everything to the floor, to get rid of the tunnel vision, and to look around. Life is full of opportunity, not disaster.

Intimacy and Connection

Your motto is "Approach with caution." That's because your basic desire is to build long-lasting, deeply felt relationships, not just fleeting, insubstantial connections that don't stand the test of time. And in order to do that, you hold your feelings in check until you feel you are on firm ground. This sets you on a course of being clear about who you are and what you value. No one has ever accused you of being wishy-washy. You know your own mind, your own feelings, and your own intentions. However, if you feel uncomfortable or insecure, you will hide yourself, not to deceive anyone but to protect yourself. Once you've established a rapport with another, you open up and trust implicitly and without question. For you, intimacy is built on knowing that you can count on someone the way you count on yourself, without reservation and with complete faith. The key here is that love is more than a feeling to you. It's definitely an action. In your heart, how can you say you love someone, care about someone, if you won't show them, take care of them, and defend them (if necessary)? So you demonstrate, as much by what you do as by what you say, exactly what the people in your life mean to you. There really is no one as steadfast as you are. Which is why you take your time building relationships.

Values and Resources

What you stand for in life is more than just a series of words in sentences. It's a way of life. You *must* be what you say you are. It's not enough to say you stand for something if you aren't willing to demonstrate it. That's why it's almost impossible for you not to follow through, not to show up when you say you will, and not to keep the promises you make. Otherwise, you disappoint yourself, leaving a bitter taste in your mouth and a scar on your self-esteem. This isn't always the easiest path to take, but that doesn't faze you in the slightest. After all, isn't life about hard work, dedication, and trusting yourself to be your best and do your best, no matter the cost? For you, these are absolute and fundamental truths, built on that almost limitless resource of inner strength that runs deep within you.

Goals and Success

There are two distinct paths that define this area of your life. The first is to make life safe, secure, and steady. The other is to push yourself to continue to do more and be more. The reality is they often operate at cross-purposes, because the part of you that seeks stability and dependability wants sameness while the other part wants growth. Instead of trying to choose between the two, you are asked to find a way to work with them together by recognizing that moving beyond the stability you have already created doesn't equal loss and devastation. Rather, the desire to grow offers the chance to build on existing security. Success then is a process of expansion rather than denial.

Taurus Keywords for 2020
Flexibility, willingness, grace

The Year Ahead for Taurus

Inspiration, upheaval, and transformation continue to be key themes for you this year. Now, before you decide to hide under your bed or stick your head in the sand, take time to look past any unnerving or mind-blowing experiences that typified 2019 to see that you are merely stripping away the things you no longer need, so that space is created to use all those fantastic images you hold of your future and craft a more vibrant life. Granted, you probably feel like you are being forced to do this. And there is no denying those feelings. However, avoid seeing your discomfort as a sign that you need to dig in further and preserve your life the way it is. That, quite simply, will not work. Rather, it will do exactly the opposite of what you intend. It will not make you feel safer or more secure. It will actually create more turmoil, more bedlam, and more insecurity.

Instead, take a moment, breathe deeply, and realize that at the heart of change is an invitation to grow. All the things, habits, and beliefs to which you are so deeply attached are not the source of who you are.

Instead, they are merely signposts and symbols of your determination and your innate capacity to weather any storm. Use nature as your guide and see the wisdom inherent in the cycle of life, which shows you time and time again that, in order for new growth to occur, you need to be able to recognize and purge anything that drags you down or inhibits you. Use this awareness and your built-in connection to the Earth as a source of strength and insight. Everything in nature is always in a process of change, of adaptation, and of responding to the environment in order to thrive. And you are no different—whether you like it or not. The reality is that change is inevitable. Nothing you say or do can ever modify that basic truth. What is optional is whether or not to grow.

This year promises a profound opportunity to commit yourself unwaveringly to the kind of growth that gives you a deeper appreciation of your own skills, talents, and abilities at the same time it makes you feel that your life as you know it is coming to an end. This is the energy cocktail of Saturn, Uranus, Neptune, and Pluto inviting and pushing you into a space and a place you've never been in before. Will you be overwhelmed? No doubt. Will you be uncomfortable and afraid? Probably. But if you embrace the possibilities offered to you, you will initiate a cycle of becoming that no words can really describe right now. Just remember, all you really need to do is take one step.

Jupiter

As 2020 begins, you are filled with optimism on the surface and a strong feeling of apprehension directly beneath it. Of course, this is likely to make you more than a little disoriented, because you are rarely at ease with those kinds of extremes burbling around in your consciousness. Just know that you need to maintain the optimism in the face of all the deep uncertainty life is triggering in you. Optimism is the purview of Jupiter, and you need to play in his world as much as you can because, if you give free rein to your anxiety, Jupiter will abandon his push to get you to see the joy in life and amp up all the fears. This sounds like a tall order, and on some days it is. But remember, Jupiter's job in 2020 is to keep the light of hope alive. This helps you unearth long-buried aspects of yourself that you've overlooked in the grind of daily life, reconnect to all that latent energy stored within you (not the least of which is your faith in yourself), and put it to use building a new foundation in your life—one that marries all the wisdom you've accrued with the brand-new surge of energy you feel inside and out. You definitely want to push the envelope and take some chances. Trust those feelings. Then create the path that allows you to turn all that intense and wild energy into something of lasting value to you and only you. Time to stand strong and resolute, even if it looks like no one else understands what you're doing. Following that inner calling right now is the best thing you can do for yourself.

Saturn

Well, you are definitely certain that the only thing that's really kept you sane over the last twelve months is the sense that you are still standing on solid ground, in spite of that Uranian rollercoaster ride that 2019 turned out to be. Keep that feeling in mind when Saturn meets Pluto on January 12, because you'll need it as you are suddenly overwhelmed by the fear that you were just kidding yourself, that nothing in life is solid, much less stable, as everything seems to turn itself inside out. This leaves you feeling so vulnerable that you aren't even sure how to take one measly step forward, never mind make a plan or put it into action. Rather than panic and look for an escape hatch, stay present and don't jump to any hasty conclusions about you or your life.

Instead, it's time to put into practice all that deeper awareness you've accumulated since Pluto started his journey through Capricorn back in 2008. First, the awareness that life is more than running on a treadmill, doing the same things day in and day out. Second, that what truly defines security is your internal fortitude and your gut instinct. And third, that hanging on to anything and everything only weighs you down, rather than freeing you from anxiety and insecurity. Saturn is going to push you to do this. To make a commitment to yourself that leads to a totally transformed life, one whose foundation is no longer built on shaky, outdated, and limited perceptions about who you are and what your purpose is. It won't be comfortable or easy, but it is imperative. Just know that no one, but no one, has the perseverance and inner will that you do. You just have to put them to use.

Uranus

Well, the bringer of the unpredictable continues to ask you to prune the deadwood from your life. Just because something was once useful doesn't mean it needs to take up permanent residence in your life. Now, that doesn't translate into getting rid of things that are still meaningful to you. Quite the contrary. The challenge here is taking time to sort through your life on every level—physical, emotional, intellectual, and spiritual—to find what is crucial to you right now. As a Taurus, your purpose in life is always to be building a world based on what you value. That requires flexibility and a recognition that you need to be continually evaluating those values in terms of their real contribution to your life, something that you aren't always inclined to do. For example, following through is central to who you are. Once you choose a course of action, you are in it until the bitter end. There is no reassessing or recalibrating or reviewing, but just a stubborn insistence on sticking to the original commitment you made without regard to changing circumstances. This is counterproductive and counterintuitive, leaving you deflated and wondering what happened. The answer is simple. You forgot the one thing you need to value above everything else: you! Yes, you. This needs to be central to your life.

And that's what Uranus is asking you to do. Value yourself first. You need not be afraid that Uranus is asking you to abandon your core values—honesty, integrity, and keeping your word. However, he is asking you to recognize that the underpinning of your values must be a deep respect for yourself rather than a rigid adherence to a set of rules, decisions, determinations, and assessments that are decades old. Sweeping out the old to make room for the opportunity to construct your life based on who you've become is both liberating and terrifying in equal measure. However, you've got the stuff needed to take up this challenge and succeed, no doubt surprising yourself and others in the process. Just remember, you aren't abandoning yourself at all. You're just unearthing your authentic self, buried underneath the detritus everyone accumulates by living.

Neptune

The invitation Neptune continues to offer you in 2020 is straightforward: Pay attention to all those unusual senses, feelings, and insights that keep popping up in your life at the most unexpected times, when you're both asleep and awake. Your nighttime dreams take on a vivid, almost surreal quality. The key is not to take anything literally but instead to concentrate on how you respond to your dreams and to delve deeper into what stands out to you about your dreams, whether it's a feeling or an image. Your daydreams (and yes, there will be lots of those as well) offer a slightly different journey off the beaten path. You'll feel your imagination take flight, and you'll find your capacity to see all future possibilities amplified to the point where your circuits are on overload. Remember that what you are seeing is potential and that you need to exercise some caution in taking what you see literally. Neptune is not leading you to anything concrete as much as he is helping you define a vision.

Pluto

Pluto's message is clear: Time to step up to the plate and be accountable, not on the surface but deep within. You are exceptional at handling life on the external plane. Rarely does that intimidate you. But going inward? Well, that's another story. This year you simply cannot escape the demand that you give more than a passing attention to that internal push to eliminate what is no longer useful. Time to dig deep and find out whether you are ready to do what seemed unimaginable just eleven years ago, when Pluto began his assault on your beliefs, your attitudes, and your basic foundation. Time to stop clinging to the past and what you have already accomplished. There's a new day dawning and, along with it, a new you. All you need to do is let go and trust yourself. That's step one. Accept that Saturn is putting you to the test. Will you take the insight offered by Pluto and use it constructively and productively? Or will you stick to the same old thoughts and pathways? The choice is yours. One offers rust and rigidity, the other vibrancy and vitality.

How Will This Year's Eclipses Affect You?

Eclipses signal intense periods that highlight major growth opportunities for us in the process of creating our lives. They are linked to the lunar phases—specifically the New and the Full Moon—and involve the relationship between the Sun, the Moon, and the Earth. A Solar Eclipse is a magnified New Moon, while a Lunar Eclipse is a magnified Full Moon. Eclipses unfold in cycles involving all twelve signs of the zodiac, and they occur in pairs, usually about two weeks apart.

This year there are six eclipses: two Solar Eclipses (one in Cancer and one in Sagittarius) and four Lunar Eclipses (one in Cancer, one in Sagittarius, one in Capricorn, and one in Gemini). This mixed bag of energies signals a shift from last year's focus on redefining nurturing versus babysitting, obligation versus accountability, family versus career, time for self versus taking care of business, and feelings versus rational thought. Three of this year's eclipses (the Lunar Eclipse on January 10 and the Solar Eclipse on June 21, both in Cancer, as well as the Lunar Eclipse on July 5 in Capricorn) complete this cycle, while the new eclipse cycle calls on us to understand that there is no wisdom in living in an ivory tower, stuck in our belief that there is only one way to live life while cut off from that very life. Instead, we need to get down to the streets and actually experience our environment, talk to people, create a dialogue, and embrace diversity. Only then can we create a world that truly embodies freedom and opportunity. Three eclipses (the Lunar Eclipse on June 5 in Sagittarius, the Lunar Eclipse on November 30 in Gemini, and the Solar Eclipse on December 14 in Sagittarius) begin this process.

The first eclipse of 2020 takes place on January 10, and it's a Lunar Eclipse in Cancer, giving you the opportunity to more clearly define just how you nurture yourself by asking you to examine just what you think about you. This is a very important step if you are to make use of the eclipse cycles of 2020, which invite you to abandon old habits that keep you from being fully present in your life and from being fully committed to creating a brand-new paradigm for how to value yourself. Granted, that's asking a lot. It isn't easy for you to contemplate a complete overhaul of everything you've been and done, much less do it. Trust that you are ready and recognize that the key ingredient to making this transition is to accept that holding on for dear life will not solve anything. The only way forward is to embrace the internal upheaval and turmoil you are likely to feel. Whether you realize it or not, this is the right kind of fuel to break apart anything that creates stagnation, because you are poised to begin a cycle that offers passion and purpose instead of predictability and inertia.

Taurus | January

Overall Theme

The year kicks off with a shakeup that you feel right in the core of your very being, one that presages a year of profound transformation. Accept that it's likely to be unsettling and unnerving and you will be ready to tackle the kinds of challenges that you are sure indicate impending ruin. The key is to rely on what always sustains you: your fortitude and perseverance.

Relationships

Your focus is so centered on trying to figure out how to move forward without losing yourself that you aren't really paying a whole lot of attention to others. It isn't because you don't care. On the contrary, if someone asks for help or input, you are quite willing to engage. You just aren't particularly tuned in to the world around you right now. That's okay. Take care of yourself.

Success and Money

Refrain from making any life-altering decisions based on any combination of fear, panic, or paranoia. There's no avoiding the anxiety conjured up by the emotional and intellectual tsunami taking place inside you. Just don't react to it by acting in haste. Instead, use this area of your life to restore some semblance of calm by putting one foot in front of the other.

Pitfalls and Potential Problems

There's a strong probability that you are going to think you are losing everything and that life will never be the same. Well, that's true. Except for one thing. Rather than seeing this transformation as a loss, see it as a letting go. Because life will not be the same whether you choose to grow or to hang on for dear life. The first option offers a brand-new beginning, while the second one leaves you stuck.

Rewarding Days

4, 5, 13, 14

Challenging Days

10, 11, 12, 23

Taurus | February

Overall Theme

It's not so much that things settle down this month, but rather that you feel a combination of detachment and numbness. And that's so much better than the alternative nibbling at the corners of your consciousness. This is not the time to resign, give up, or throw in the towel. Not when you are actually doing some very important inner work at a level so deep that you cannot get a fix on it. Relax, trust, and breathe!

Relationships

This month you need to ask for support in keeping your feet planted firmly on the ground. So call in your support system. You have one, even if you aren't aware of it. To get the job done, set aside your fear of failing and your belief that you always need to display how competent you are. There are times when you just can't do it alone. This is one of them.

Success and Money

The very last thing on your mind, much to your surprise, is anything related to career or financial gain. You just want to hunker down and try to get your bearings before making any changes in this area. Of course, you are paying attention to matters of financial security, if only to shore up your wobbly sense of self.

Pitfalls and Potential Problems

Accept that much of what happens this month simply cannot be measured, quantified, or calculated. This, in and of itself, is foreign territory to you. So you find yourself constantly scanning the horizon of your life to find a sign, any sign, that will give you a sense of the direction you need to go in, but all you see is where you came from. Go within.

Rewarding Days

10, 11, 23, 24

Challenging Days

8, 9, 18, 19

Taurus | March

Overall Theme

Life is definitely a double-edged sword this month. On the one hand, you feel the rumblings that your life is about to be pushed to the limit for the second time this year. On the other hand, this awareness brings no comfort because you are sure you won't survive the test. First, let go of the idea that this is a test. It's an invitation to a new you, one stripped of all that is no longer relevant. Keep that in mind and you'll have the necessary courage when you need it.

Relationships

The shift happening in your life is creating a new understanding about what you seek in your relationships. As a consequence, you find yourself looking at the people in your life with a new discernment and insight. This process reveals some shocking and disappointing perceptions, leaving you uncertain about what action to take. Do nothing. Those people who no longer need to be in your life will fall by the wayside. It's just a matter of time.

Success and Money

Your value system is on the verge of the biggest overhaul you've ever experienced, and you're exhilarated and terrified simultaneously. Part of you is ready to jump in and take the risk to assess your life choices and whether you want to find a new path. The other part? Let's just say it wants to stick its head in the sand until the urge for significant change passes.

Pitfalls and Potential Problems

As hard as it's likely to be, you need to stand quietly and firmly at the crossroads of the huge shift going on in your life. This month reveals a lot more that you need to know about who you are and what's important to you. That requires stillness and awareness, not ill-considered reactions and responses. Schedule things that make you feel nurtured and loved.

Rewarding Days

8, 9, 26, 27

Challenging Days

6, 7, 20, 21

Taurus | April

Overall Theme

You are slowly finding your way back to center, even as the rollercoaster ride continues. This brings a building sense of security as you discover that the principles you so deeply honor haven't changed one bit. This revelation allows you to see that much of what you thought was a value was actually a belief or a preference. And those don't always stand the test of time.

Relationships

It's probably a good idea to take a deep breath every time someone says anything to you, because you are so keyed up that you don't have a filter or the capacity to take anything with a grain of salt. As you create your new world, you are likely to resist anything that you feel is a judgment, an attempt to control, or a lack of sensitivity. Just do it quietly. There's no sense in lighting a fire.

Success and Money

This is a great month to begin any new endeavor that leads to a happier, more content future in this part of your life. Just stick to the planning aspects of this change and begin to get your ducks in a row. The most important thing to remember is to keep your money where it is. This is a time for spending your energy and conserving your financial stability.

Pitfalls and Potential Problems

Challenges come your way both internally and externally, leaving you wondering what is going on. Well, it is always in your nature to make one last attempt to maintain the status quo before executing any major change in your world. And this is perhaps the biggest shift you've ever undertaken, so you were bound to question yourself up until and during the very last second. As for the resistance from others, ignore it. It's their stuff.

Rewarding Days

5, 6, 23, 24

Challenging Days

13, 14, 27, 28

Taurus | May

Overall Theme

There are two words that symbolize your life this month. One is caution and the other is confusion. Now, caution is something with which you are deeply familiar. In fact, it might be your middle name. But confusion, not so much. In fact, you have a deep fear of it. However, it truly is unavoidable now, so don't jump into anything, no matter how good it appears.

Relationships

You really don't ever use the words *games* and *relationships* in the same sentence, which leaves you vulnerable to having the wool pulled over your eyes. So be on alert as you are presented with a couple of people or situations that seem too good to be true. If something or someone seems off, it probably is. Bow out gracefully and quickly, no matter who is involved.

Success and Money

Neutrality is the best policy as you come in contact with a number of possibilities and potentials that offer quick rewards. Acknowledge your innate suspicion about anything easy, look past the pretty pictures being painted, and ask questions. Then decline. Now is not the time for taking this kind of risk.

Pitfalls and Potential Problems

With all the turmoil of the first four months of 2020, you yearn for something to perk you up, to give you hope, to make life look bright and shiny again. That's easily accomplished by beginning a program of doing life-affirming, nurturing, and kind things for yourself, not trying to turn a sow's ear into a silk purse with one over-the-top, questionable decision or expenditure.

Rewarding Days

2, 3, 29, 30

Challenging Days

6, 7, 25, 26

Taurus | June

Overall Theme

There's no doubt your system is on overload. Between trying to let go of the detritus in your life and initiating a new life cycle, you aren't sure whether you are coming or going. Time to recharge your batteries. Take a break and go outside. Sit and absorb all the vibrancy of renewed life. Feel yourself come alive, reenergized and ready to go.

Relationships

One area of your life that seems clearer to you than before is relationships. You've emerged from a long examination of the who, what, where, why, and how of connection with a deeper sense of the direction you want to take in the future. This fills you with optimism and hope that you can replicate this newfound joy in other areas of your life.

Success and Money

An opportunity that you thought was long gone (it seemed to disappear in a haze several months ago) rebounds back into your life. Granted it's been overhauled significantly in both intent and structure, which makes it much more attractive than it was before. Take a good, long look before you make up your mind.

Pitfalls and Potential Problems

Old attitudes, beliefs, and biases surface during the Lunar Eclipse on June 5, upsetting you and making you feel like you're taking twenty giant steps backward. This is not the case. Just know that you cannot completely erase everything you have valued, thought, been, or done. Connecting to the past is an opportunity to see just how much you've grown, not a message that you've failed.

Rewarding Days

11, 12, 26, 27

Challenging Days

4, 5, 21, 22

Taurus | July

Overall Theme

A sense of lightness permeates you, and you bask in the feeling that you've made it out of that long, dark tunnel you were convinced you were going to live in for the rest of your life. Don't let go of that feeling. You'll need it as your emotions grab hold of you and take you through a series of peaks and valleys, testing your inner resilience.

Relationships

With a new relationship manifesto in place, you turn your attention to making new connections, both personal and professional. You are definitely seeking people who expand your awareness and your life. This makes you realize just how much you are truly prepared to abandon the tried and true and make room for the wealth of possibilities just over the horizon.

Success and Money

Be careful not to make hasty decisions involving money this month. First, because this is not a time for big expenditures, since unforeseen demands suddenly crop up. Second, because you simply need to get more information before making any commitments that fall outside the financial plans you already have in place.

Pitfalls and Potential Problems

The best thing to do is enjoy the optimism coursing through your body and your consciousness without taking it as a sign that you need to push life forward right this instant. It's true that you don't like life when it doesn't look like you're doing anything. What you're doing is getting ready to merge the wisdom of your past with the potential created by your willingness to change. The result promises to be magical.

Rewarding Days

8, 9, 23, 24

Challenging Days

4, 5, 18, 19

Taurus | August

Overall Theme

Although things are quieter and sunnier, you feel something percolating just below the surface. Let it be. There's nothing you can do about stuff whirling around in your deeper consciousness. Instead, enjoy the space life has provided and be content with the blessings you see all around you. Being in the moment is not only the best course of action but also the best medicine.

Relationships

You feel all warm and snuggly, just like your favorite comfy couch that always makes you feel safe. Then suddenly the wall you've put around yourself to deal with the turmoil of the last several months disintegrates, leaving you relaxed and definitely more approachable. This leads to a happy whirlwind of a social life and a deep sense of contentment.

Success and Money

Your mind is, quite frankly, not focused on this area of life right now. You are satisfied leaving things as they are so you can truly experience the first bit of peace and quiet you've had all year. One thing you need to do is use your financial resources to treat yourself to something just because. Don't worry that you'll overspend. That simply won't happen.

Pitfalls and Potential Problems

Don't settle into old patterns because it feels like the pressure is off. That may well be, but this is a time when you must continue to honor the changes you know you need to make. Habits do die hard, especially for you, and they often continue to exercise a huge pull. Recognize that familiar call and resist it by doing whatever makes you feel new.

Rewarding Days

10, 11, 23, 24

Challenging Days

3, 4, 21, 22

Taurus | September

Overall Theme

No matter what presents itself for your consideration this month—and a lot of opportunities will—you are confident and ready to take it on. This finds you bouncing around from thing to thing. You are busy, busy, busy and you love it. Finally, life looks the way you like it. The extra added bonus to all this is that your creativity is at a maximum.

Relationships

Because you love life right now, you love everyone. That's because, when you are truly in your element, everything takes on a special glow, including the people with whom you cross paths. However, you probably will have less time to spend just hanging out. Most of your interactions with others are directly connected to you being in the throes of doing something.

Success and Money

With your engines rested and recharged, you are ready to go full steam ahead and find a new focus for all the creative energy roaring around in your brain. Before taking on anything new, make sure you run it by someone you trust, because your enthusiasm coupled with months of what you consider inertia (at least in the external world) could be a recipe for regret.

Pitfalls and Potential Problems

It definitely feels like somebody took off your shackles and let you loose. And it's exhilarating. Enjoy it. Just don't burn yourself out. Make sure you take a couple of hours every day to relax and breathe. This is just the beginning of a long period of initiating new and exciting things in your life. Refrain from thinking you have to do it all right now. Save some of that energy. You'll need it.

Rewarding Days

1, 2, 15, 16

Challenging Days

11, 12, 24, 25

Taurus | October

Overall Theme

The momentum you established in September carries you through a bunch of rough spots, helping you stay focused and undeterred by any challenges to your confidence or your plans. For the first time in 2020, you are able to ride the waves of change rather than feeling like you are on the verge of being totally inundated and unable to manage. Three cheers for you!

Relationships

Be on the lookout for unsolicited input, advice, or just plain interference. The most important thing to remember is that whatever you hear has nothing to do with you and everything to do with the person or persons deciding they just have to "help" you. The only person you need to listen to is yourself, because you are in charge of your life. No one else.

Success and Money

You may be tempted to splurge in an effort to reduce some of the stress you are experiencing. It's okay to treat yourself. After all, you work hard and you deserve to reward yourself with something that makes you feel good. Just don't go overboard. On the career front, prepare to be surprised by an unexpected offer that truly comes out of left field.

Pitfalls and Potential Problems

Of course you have the staying power to get through anything. That's a given. It's just that sometimes you get really tired of having to do that. This is one of those times. Oh, it doesn't show outwardly at all, where things continue along a good path. But internally you are pretty whiny. Let it out. Otherwise it will start to drag you down and slow you down.

Rewarding Days

3, 4, 26, 27

Challenging Days

8, 9, 17, 18

Taurus | November

Overall Theme

It's not quite smooth sailing in November, but it's extremely close. You regain your innate equilibrium, making it so much easier to implement the new ideas and the new reality to which you are now completely committed. The result is a total upswing in your attitude, so much so that you hardly notice the bump in the road that crops up at the end of the month.

Relationships

Don't be surprised if you are confronted by difficult challenges from the people closest to you. It's not that they're looking for a fight, even though it feels that way. Stand your ground, politely and kindly. And say what's on your mind without pointing fingers. If you don't like the way you're being treated, say so clearly. That's a much better strategy than being defensive or feeling like you need to explain yourself. People can't ask for respect if they aren't willing to give it.

Success and Money

You find yourself obsessed with your financial status. Can you maintain the level of security that you have? Can you create more? All this leads to the sudden revelation that it's time to reassess just what money means to you, as well as recognize that you'd like to reevaluate what you consider your resources to be. Give yourself the space and time to do this. It will be a continuing theme for the next year at least.

Pitfalls and Potential Problems

Steer clear of any inclination to criticize yourself. Instead, acknowledge the growth you've experienced in the last few months. You've started to move mountains within you, and along the way, you've discovered that doing so won't destroy you. It has actually strengthened you, helping you realize that your greatest asset is yourself.

Rewarding Days

9, 10, 22, 23

Challenging Days

13, 14, 29, 30

Taurus | December

Overall Theme

Suddenly there aren't enough hours in the day to keep all the plans you initiated in motion. Yet you don't feel you have any choice but to keep going in spite of a little bit of fatigue and a fear that nothing will actually get done. Why? Because you can't deny that invisible force or energy driving you forward. This is just the beginning of finding a deeper satisfaction in who you are and what you do.

Relationships

Life is truly in hyperdrive right now, and that includes how, when, and if you have time to stop long enough to do more than say hello to anyone. The key is not to worry but instead to actually be clear with others that time with you needs to be scheduled. That way you can pack a lot into a short period of time, rather than trying to be fluid and spontaneous, which will only lead to frustration for everyone.

Success and Money

Giving yourself permission to let go of financial expectations that only hog-tie and limit you leads to a renewal of faith in yourself and an openness to taking a look around to see if where you are career-wise is actually where you want to be. Once you get over being surprised that taking a risk is really attractive to you right now, you find yourself daydreaming about possibilities and potentials.

Pitfalls and Potential Problems

It's ironic that the prospect of liberating yourself from aspects of yourself and your life that you now realize drag you down makes you want to put on the brakes. Recognize this response for what it is: your default position. The one designed to keep you from undermining your security. Well, it can also keep you from expanding your life by convincing you that stagnation is desirable. That just won't fly in 2021. Embrace change from within and you will blossom.

Rewarding Days

7, 8, 24, 25

Challenging Days

1, 2, 30, 31

Taurus Action Table

These dates reflect the best—but not the only—times for success and ease in these activities, according to your Sun sign.

	JAN	FEB	MAR	APR	MAY	JUN	JUL	AUG	SEP	OCT	NOV	DEC
Move					2, 3			10, 11				
New romance			26, 27						1, 2			
Seek coaching/counseling				6, 7						15, 16		
Ask for a raise		23, 24									17, 18	
Vacation	4, 5						7, 8					
Get a loan						2, 3						11, 12

Gemini

The Twins
May 22 to June 21

Ⅱ

Element: Air

Quality: Mutable

Polarity: Yang/masculine

Planetary Ruler: Mercury

Meditation: I explore my
inner worlds

Gemstone: Tourmaline

Power Stones: Ametrine, citrine,
emerald, spectrolite, agate

Key Phrase: I think

Glyph: Pillars of duality,
the Twins

Anatomy: Shoulders, arms,
hands, lungs, nervous system

Colors: Bright colors, orange,
yellow, magenta

Animals: Monkeys, talking birds,
flying insects

Myths/Legends: Peter Pan,
Castor and Pollux

House: Third

Opposite Sign: Sagittarius

Flower: Lily of the valley

Keyword: Versatility

The Gemini Personality

Strengths, Talents, and the Creative Spark

For you, life begins and ends with your willingness to sample and experience everything in life that you can. After all, how can you satisfy your insatiable curiosity and a mind that requires stimulation if you sit in a corner all alone in the dark? You need to be out and about in the world, gathering whatever strikes your fancy, whether it's ideas, information, mementoes, feelings, or people, in your never-ending pursuit of the wonders of life. You live in the certainty that just around the next corner is something that will expand your world in ways you haven't considered. So there truly is no path on the planet not worth wandering down, even if it's temporary or short-lived.

This openness, this flexibility, gives you a definite advantage in being able to meet the world head-on, always with the view that you can meet the challenge of the new and unforeseen without batting an eyelash. After all, there's a nugget of knowledge or experience just waiting to be discovered. And that's something you simply can't resist. It's the light of life, the joy, even the mental and emotional candy you crave. It's also the source of your creativity, because it allows you to move the pieces of life's possibilities around in your head, thinking and thinking and thinking; trying on this potential, playing with that possibility, then sharing all that mental output with others so you can see it more clearly and play with it some more. There's nothing quite like thinking in all its forms. You can't imagine what life would be like without it. In fact, for you, it is life.

Blind Spots and Blockages

Let's face it. You like to gad about. But do you ever slow down long enough to actually appreciate the experience? Having the experience is one thing, but knowing what it's about is another. Information is not knowledge. Yes, you are meant to flit (after all, you are the reporter of the zodiac), but your fear of boredom often means you are so busy consuming facts and information that you really don't see that, all by themselves, those tidbits don't actually mean much. Knowing stuff isn't a substitute for doing something with what you've learned. Obviously, you need to be mentally stimulated. Your blind spot is that you switch your thoughts around to see what the other side of the coin looks like, not realizing you are confusing yourself and everyone who knows you.

You don't really mean to be inconsistent, but you can be, partly because you believe anything is worth trying once, whether it's going bungee jumping or considering any thought, idea, notion, or concept that crosses your path. In fact, you rarely meet an idea that doesn't grab your attention, even for a nanosecond. After all, the world of thoughts and ideas is your personal playground. It's just that you fail to let others know you are just trying something on, not committing to it for eternity. Which is fine. How can you truly know what matters to you if there are things you refuse to consider? The pitfall here is that you often forget to pledge yourself consistently to a set of guidelines or principles, thus turning flexibility into inconsistency. Ultimately, this creates huge issues for you, because, whether you realize it or not, the lack of real substance you build into your world can leave you flapping in the wind, unable to move beyond the flitting.

Intimacy and Connections

It's easy for you to meet people, to make that initial connection, because your curiosity always leads the way. There's nothing quite like the rush of new encounters and all they promise. What could possibly be more interesting than finding out the who, what, where, when, why, and how of other people's lives? Forget what makes them tick. Do they have fascinating experiences or interesting perspectives to share? In other words, do they entertain your brain? If not, they join the ranks of the acquaintances in your life. And you have plenty of those. But forging a relationship and building intimacy is a different story. The truth is you are more interested in plumbing the depths of someone's mind than plumbing the depths of their heart. At least to begin with. Quite simply, the only way to your heart is through your head. No mental chemistry automatically means no wandering down the path of emotional intimacy—which is something that makes you break into a cold sweat anyway, because your relationship to your emotional self is often quite tentative. Now, that doesn't mean you don't have feelings. You do. You just avoid building emotional intimacy with yourself, which almost guarantees that being open to others is a mountain you aren't sure you can climb. Instead, you let them into your head and you believe that's enough. The question is, are you sure?

Values and Resources

As in all other aspects of your life, this area begins and ends with your mind—the resource you count on more than any other in your life, the one that is most valuable to you. It's impossible for you to believe that anything else contributes as much to defining who you are and how you live than your mental faculties. Everything must and does pass through your brain for analysis and scrutiny to see if it passes the litmus test of how much it adds to your life. Once you've established that something is meaningful to you mentally, then and only then does it become emotionally significant. Which is the actual bedrock of how you assign value in your life. This may seem counterintuitive, but from your perspective, how can you possibly attach yourself to anything that doesn't make sense to you or fit your view of the world?

Goals and Success

You aren't always sure how to define exactly what these two words mean, never mind how to shape them as parts of your life. That's because you always want to be open to whatever may cross your path and you really don't like making decisions that you are afraid limit your possibilities. The key is for you to find a path in life that offers a constantly shifting world with variety galore and the chance to express your innate capacity to multitask. This automatically leads to success and helps you target future goals. That way you feel you are always on the verge of a new beginning rather than tied to something predictable and unchanging.

Gemini Keywords for 2020
Adaptability, strength, vulnerability

The Year Ahead for Gemini

If you are seeking a multitude of opportunities to shift your perspective and grow exponentially, 2020 is the year for you. It won't be easy, but it will be worthwhile. The key is to accept that you cannot anticipate just how or why or when life promises to take unexpected turns. Which, of course, is a difficult thing for your truly agile mind to grasp. How is it possible that you cannot conjure up the various scenarios that might crop up? The answer? What ends up on your plate is outside anything you've experienced before. The challenge is to recognize that no amount of intellectual or mental gymnastics is really going to help.

Of course, this doesn't mean you can't entertain yourself by imagining the possibilities. Just don't be shocked or annoyed or discouraged if all your musing and contemplating doesn't translate into any tangible preparation for what is likely to manifest. What you are being asked to do this year is to get past all that predictable playing around in your head to create a quiet space for your intuitive brain to communicate with you. Not so you can arm yourself against the deeper tides swishing around inside you, but so you can immerse yourself in them, thereby getting to know yourself in a whole new way. You are fond of telling others that what they see is what they get, but it truly is just camouflage, because not only do you need to protect the deeper parts of yourself, but you don't quite know what to do with them. In fact, your favorite coping mechanism is to disconnect at the mere hint of anything that cannot be handled by your cognitive brain.

Well, that simply won't work in 2020. The combination of Jupiter, Saturn, Neptune, and Pluto feels like a pressure cooker about to explode, so trying to avoid their push to get you to dive into the depths of your own psyche is futile. And dangerous. In fact, it's not unlike trying to plug a multitude of holes in a dike with a measly ten fingers. It's only a matter of time before you are completely overcome by the force of your own inner experience. Now, before you decide that all is lost, remember the key is not to resist but to take a few moments each and every day to acknowledge all that emotional material trying to find its way to the surface to be released. Then give it space to be, rather than trying to do anything with it. Feel what you feel. Refrain as much as possible to think about what's happening. Otherwise, life has the potential to get really unpleasant, engulfing you more and more in past trauma and drama. Sounds pretty intense, because 2020 will be just that. So trust yourself to ride the waves, take up meditation so you can calm your entire being, create a network of friends you know are available to listen to all the stuff emerging from the darkest corners of your being, and take that incredible capacity you have to find the light in everything and turn it on full blast as you travel through this once-in-a-lifetime opportunity to integrate some long-buried sides of who you are.

Jupiter

It's not going to be easy to assess just what Jupiter's impact is likely to be in your life this year. Will he ease your challenges and remove obstacles, or will he amplify the tests facing you? Or perhaps both? If that seems contradictory, well, it's because it is. Because Jupiter amplifies whatever is happening in your world and because this year is full of intense swings in mood and approach, you can't expect any level of consistency from this planet, other than the fact that he likes to make things bigger if not better. The key here is for you to maintain your sense of humor and find the blessings in the middle of the chaos. Of course, this requires optimism, which is definitely up Jupiter's alley. In fact, he is the conduit for the feeling that somehow, some way, things will get better. So take time every day to find something that lights you up from the inside. And above all, laugh—at a silly dog or cat video, at an episode of your favorite comedy, or at whatever makes you giggle, even at yourself. Laughter is exactly the medicine you need, and it goes a long way to creating space for positive things to begin to grow in your life.

Saturn

As Saturn joins up with Pluto on January 12, you are likely to feel like your life is suddenly so oppressive you aren't sure whether you have the strength to muddle through the swamp that has taken up residence in your entire being. Recognize that this is a temporary state of affairs designed to lighten a load you've been carrying for a very long time. But in order to do that, you must do two things. First, acknowledge what is happening. Running away or trying to hide from these profound feelings, which include loss, grief, disappointment, abandonment, fear, and insecurity, only promises to create more of those feelings. The combination of Saturn and Pluto demands that you purge and cleanse all the stuff you've socked away in your emotional dumpster. And, the more you resist, the more pressure you will be forced to confront. Second, be accountable for what rises up from the depths. It's the only way to transform your old emotional reality, full of a series of beliefs and patterns that are at the root of some very difficult and painful life experiences. Part of this process is letting go of any need to play the blame game. That's unproductive and keeps you chained to the very things you need to release, and interferes with your chance to truly gather insight and wisdom from your life experiences. Being accountable is not the same as labeling things good/bad, right/wrong, or success/failure. It is honoring you, your life, and your experiences in a way that leads to freedom from judgment and guilt, thus opening yourself up to the chance to build a new emotional foundation based on true knowledge of and respect for yourself.

Uranus

As if you weren't already feeling unsettled and overwhelmed by all the pushing and shoving going on between Saturn and Pluto, Uranus is adding to the feeling that everything in your life is one breath away from a complete breakdown. All in all, it feels like your life is being completely rebuilt from the inside out and without your permission. Uranus keeps rumbling and stirring the pot, just out of sight of your conscious mind, which normally loves to play with possibilities. But what Uranus is showing you makes you wonder if you aren't just a little bit crazy. Well, at least that's how your conscious mind interprets things. The reality is Uranus can offer you one truly magnificent gift in 2020: the chance to step outside the known quantities of your life and dream your way into a new life. To do this, you need to engage in activities that speak to your imagination. Meditate. Explore symbols and symbolic languages. Sit with nature. Listen to music. Get a deck of oracle cards and pick one every day. Uranus is asking you to get in touch with the fact that you are a multifrequency being who is being offered an opportunity to break down walls and barriers that inhibit your ability to see life and live life in a way that's totally unexpected and completely outside your comfort zone. So take a deep breath and relax. The vision of a new life is emerging.

Neptune

With all the intensity being produced by the rest of the planetary players, Neptune seems to offer some welcome relief, an escape hatch with the potential to ease your mind and lower your emotional blood pressure. And that is true, provided you don't decide to take up permanent residency in the fantastical world of lollipops and rainbows. Beware of the tendency to avoid reality in favor of some pretty picture you have every capacity to conjure up, especially in the areas of career and life purpose. Instead, understand that Neptune continues to ask you to let go of anything that no longer feeds your soul or aligns with your ideals. Granted, his method of doing so is extremely disconcerting. He makes everything kind of foggy or murky or fuzzy around the edges. This is an invitation to understand that nothing is ever as solid as we would like, that the true source of creativity doesn't come from the physical aspects of life as much as from the formless, fluid, and ever-shifting consciousness deep within us. And right now, there's a wealth of images and visions dancing around in your head. Play with them. Let them give you a glimpse of where life might be taking you as well as light the fire of hope inside you. Just understand that much of this is ephemeral, not a platform on which to build a new life. Pay attention to recurring images, dreams, or symbols. Those are the keys to the future. The rest is intended to keep you open to potentials and possibilities and to reduce stress by keeping you connected to your imagination.

Pluto

Your internal struggle to process, master, and transform the deeper aspects of who you are continues at a level of intensity that you often can't quite get your cognitive, rational mind around, which leaves you feeling totally out of your depth. And that's the point. Pluto has been challenging you since 2008 to realize there is so much more to you than curiosity, mental agility, and the capacity to entertain any thought at any time, that deep within you is a desire to assemble knowledge and wisdom that can sustain you. But that means moving into territory that scares you because it can't be quantified or measured. You just have to let go and trust—not something you see as desirable, much less possible, during much of 2020. It's likely to be far more attractive to just turn off, shut down, and build walls around the overwhelming vulnerability you feel. Resist that temptation. Instead, embrace your vulnerability and you'll find it makes you stronger than you ever thought possible.

How Will This Year's Eclipses Affect You?

Eclipses signal intense periods that highlight major growth opportunities for us in the process of creating our lives. They are linked to the lunar phases—specifically the New and the Full Moon—and involve the relationship between the Sun, the Moon, and the Earth. A Solar Eclipse is a magnified New Moon, while a Lunar Eclipse is a magnified Full Moon. Eclipses unfold in cycles involving all twelve signs of the zodiac, and they occur in pairs, usually about two weeks apart.

This year there are six eclipses: two Solar Eclipses (one in Cancer and one in Sagittarius) and four Lunar Eclipses (one in Cancer, one in Sagittarius, one in Capricorn, and one in Gemini). This mixed bag of energies signals a shift from last year's focus on redefining nurturing versus babysitting, obligation versus accountability, family versus career, time for self versus taking care of business, and feelings versus rational thought. Three of this year's eclipses (the Lunar Eclipse on January 10 and the Solar Eclipse on June 21, both in Cancer, as well as the Lunar Eclipse on July 5

in Capricorn) complete this cycle, while the new eclipse cycle calls on us to understand that there is no wisdom in living in an ivory tower, stuck in our belief that there is only one way to live life while cut off from that very life. Instead, we need to get down to the streets and actually experience our environment, talk to people, create a dialogue, and embrace diversity. Only then can we create a world that truly embodies freedom and opportunity. Three eclipses (the Lunar Eclipse on June 5 in Sagittarius, the Lunar Eclipse on November 30 in Gemini, and the Solar Eclipse on December 14 in Sagittarius) begin this process.

The first eclipse of 2020 takes place on January 10, and it's a Lunar Eclipse in Cancer, creating either opportunity or crisis or both. Most likely both, because the eclipse itself continues the challenge presented to you last year to examine any deeply entrenched beliefs you have about what is valuable to you and find a way to shift or change them completely to match your ever-expanding sense of who you are at your core. So face your fear, reluctance, and resistance head-on, no matter what burbles to the surface, no matter who or what gets in your way, and no matter how insecure you feel. This is crucial if you are to build a new foundation for your life, one upon which you can stand proudly and strongly, no matter the circumstances life dishes up. This theme repeats itself again and again each time there is an eclipse in 2020, because it's at the root of your continuing growth cycle. It's definitely crunch time. You need to be able to stand firm in your knowledge of yourself and what's important to you in order to make the best use of the year's remaining eclipses and show up with wisdom and grace as the best person you can be.

Gemini | January

Overall Theme

The year begins with a strong shock to your whole system, leaving you feeling like a bit of an emotional mess. That's definitely not your favorite place to be, because you are never really sure exactly what to do when the feeling side of life takes precedence over your mind. The gift in it, once you stop resisting, is to see this as a chance to break free from anything inhibiting your forward movement into a brand-new world.

Relationships

Your tolerance for what you consider the follies of others hits an all-time low, especially if it impacts you personally. That's because you need to find what's authentic in others in order to reinforce your deepening desire to remove anything from your life that feels or is fake. Of course, the impatience you exhibit toward others reflects your own frustration with yourself for committing similar misdemeanors.

Success and Money

This is a time of gathering your resources so you can build a new foundation based on the ongoing major shift in how you view yourself and what you value. It's definitely not a time to take any huge risks, because you find yourself unable to find a clear vision of exactly what's happening. Maintaining the status quo externally is not a failure to move forward. It's an act of conservation.

Pitfalls and Potential Problems

The pressure you feel from within and without is so intense that you aren't sure you can actually find a way to ease it. Well, you can, provided you are able to relinquish any sacrosanct ideas or beliefs you have about who you are, what you want, or where you think you should be going. Right now, all bets are off. Just be present in each day and forget trying to predict the future.

Rewarding Days

21, 22, 24, 25

Challenging Days

10, 11, 12, 19, 20

Gemini | February

Overall Theme

Things feel a lot softer and lighter, if not fuzzy around the edges. However, you are just grateful for a respite from that deep inner push to find all the answers to all of life's earth-shattering mysteries, never mind the key to figuring out whether your life is off track or stuck. It's neither. It's in transition. Relax and take time to nurture yourself. That's a conundrum easily solved.

Relationships

Your patience continues to be nonexistent when it comes to tolerating the ups and downs of connecting to others. Fortunately, you choose not to share your thoughts or opinions about what others do, because, along with feeling impatient, you really don't care enough to be bothered. Rather than being critical of yourself, recognize that part of you really does understand that the choices of other people, even those closest to you, are really none of your business.

Success and Money

Another month of caution is recommended. Take time to look at where things currently stand in your life in terms of both career and money. This leads to the emergence of a potential new path, one that builds on your current skill set and offers exciting growth for the future. Let it percolate so that the next steps you need to take are revealed.

Pitfalls and Potential Problems

You feel caught in a never-ending cycle of "things aren't the way they are supposed to be, but I don't know what to do about it." The heart of the matter is untangling all those twisty expectations you have about your life. This relieves a lot of pressure, allowing you to accept your current circumstances long enough to find the keys to the kingdom that lie within—the keys that offer an abundant future.

Rewarding Days

12, 13, 23, 24

Challenging Days

5, 6, 16, 17

Gemini | March

Overall Theme

Your brain comes alive with a series of insights and light-bulb ideas that reinvigorate you mentally, physically, emotionally, and spiritually. This lifts you up in unexpected ways and gives you the strength to begin a necessary purging and cleansing of anything in your life that is weighing you down. And you find there's quite a lot of detritus you have been hiding from yourself.

Relationships

Now that your attention is so intensely focused on cleaning out the musty corners of your life, you are kinder and gentler to the rest of the planet. In fact, you take some time to acknowledge to those closest to you that living with you or being with you hasn't been much of a picnic lately. This leads to a huge release of tension on both sides and a return to enjoying the company of everyone in your circle.

Success and Money

You continue to find the necessary pieces to create that new beginning you envisioned last month. Much to your surprise, this isn't as onerous as you thought it would be. The reason? It's exciting to pull together what it takes to make your dream come together. Plus, it's an opportunity to use your gift for multitasking.

Pitfalls and Potential Problems

It's likely to be easier to clear out your mental and physical closets because they are so much more real and tangible to you now. But your emotional closet? Now, that's like climbing Mount Everest. Oh, the pain and disappointment you've shoved in there, hoping never to see them again. Well, the time has come to face them, feel them, and let them go. Otherwise, they have the potential to hijack what you desire.

Rewarding Days

10, 11, 26, 27

Challenging Days

8, 9, 24, 25

Gemini | April

Overall Theme

A tremendous optimism clashes with a secret fear that you are sliding backward, because it suddenly feels like all the forward progress you are making is being consumed by unresolved feelings of not having sufficient gravitas to build anything, much less a new life. The key is not to blow anything out of proportion. It's not about whether you can deal with all the negative self-talk. Rather, it's about strengthening your inner self by absolutely trusting one person: you.

Relationships

As you struggle to keep your feet planted firmly on the ground, take a leap of faith by confiding in those closest to you. Much to your surprise, you discover that they can see clearly that life has been and is still pushing you into a state of overwhelm quite regularly. This allows you to further drop the pretense that all is well and find real support, alleviating a lot of fear.

Success and Money

Just when you thought your capacity to network had somehow vaporized, you find yourself making connections left, right, and center. This buoys your spirits and helps you deal with those deep insecurities continually whispering in your inner ear. And that's a definite win. At least two of the people you meet this month promise to make a big impact on your new plan.

Pitfalls and Potential Problems

The best thing to do as you swing back and forth between faith in the future and the certainty that you are doomed to be forever inhibited by the past is to treat yourself. Do as many small things or big things as necessary to bring a smile to your face. It's the most effective way of keeping your natural optimism afloat and invigorated.

Rewarding Days

6, 7, 15, 16

Challenging Days

13, 14, 27, 28

Gemini | May

Overall Theme

You are challenged by yet another wake-up call to step into the best version of yourself you can be. But wait, there's still some inner recalibration that needs doing. So you are caught between the need to push forward and the feeling that the new foundation you are building is not quite complete. Right on both accounts. Refrain from choosing one over the other and see both as necessary and purposeful.

Relationships

The most important thing you can do now is take on the role of the observer rather than get dragged into some uncomfortable situations that see you reverting to old relationship patterns. You know the ones—where you are acquiescing to the needs of others or running for the hills. Your goal needs to be to stay present. And, in this case, to remain detached.

Success and Money

The hard work seems to pile higher and higher with each passing day, leaving you with little time to focus on your new direction. This doesn't mean you are losing ground. In fact, you'll find just the opposite is true by month's end as new avenues and ideas blossom, helping you realize that your creative mind was busy moving things forward even when you weren't consciously paying attention.

Pitfalls and Potential Problems

There's a strong chance you are going to feel a lot like a cross between Eeyore and Winnie the Pooh: one minute convinced that no matter what you do, nothing good is coming your way, and the next absolutely sure that a pot of honey is around every corner. This might make you crazy, just a little. Keep physically active or sit under a tree. Or just breathe. That way, you will be more grounded and less susceptible to the inner tides of your mind.

Rewarding Days

4, 5, 22, 23

Challenging Days

10, 11, 25, 26

Gemini | June

Overall Theme

The first part of the month sees you happy and in your element. After all, it is *your* time of the year. Gather those good feelings so you are ready when you find yourself being challenged again and again to explain, explain, explain, to set some clear boundaries, and essentially to tell anyone who thinks otherwise that what you do is none of their business. Just remember to be polite.

Relationships

Indeed, it looks like anyone and everyone you know has an opinion about what you should do, when you should do it, and how you should do it. That's because you are fully committed to growing your life in a healthier direction, leaving behind old ways of being. This *is* making other people uncomfortable, because they want you to remain the same. This is likely to shock you. At the same time, you know you have no choice but to forge ahead.

Success and Money

Working on your new direction is truly your sanctuary and your happy place. What's more, you get an unexpected vote of confidence from a source that surprises you, and that support turns out to be not just emotional and intellectual but tangible as well. This makes you realize that your vision is more than a dream. It really has legs.

Pitfalls and Potential Problems

You are fond of believing that it's important to listen to the thoughts and ideas of others, partly because it can often be a source of inspiration and partly because you just love mental gymnastics. It's time to limit the amount of input from others. You are in the midst of a huge transition, and trusting yourself doesn't call for making it open season on allowing others to say whatever they want.

Rewarding Days

11, 12, 26, 27

Challenging Days

6, 7, 16, 17

Gemini | July

Overall Theme

It feels like your subconscious just won't stop talking to you. Don't ignore those deeper whisperings and the feeling that something isn't quite right, even though it might be your preference. After all, you are much more comfortable if things are what they appear to be. Set aside your uneasiness and welcome the insight and information you are tapping into. It's valuable.

Relationships

You find yourself in some hyper-alert universe of your own making, completely unsure how you got there. The result? You are suspicious and fearful of anyone and everyone, which stuns you into a weird silence where you wait to find out what others are going to do before you say anything, much less do anything. This will pass, but take time to find out what triggered your off-kilter response. A hint: it was something said to you that curbed your freedom.

Success and Money

An opportunity crops up in your current job that you definitely weren't expecting. This leads to a whole lot of confusion about what to do. Should you take it or stick with the project that you see taking you forward in your future? First, is it a case of either-or? Is it possible that growing in your job will support the long-term success of your plan?

Pitfalls and Potential Problems

It's one thing to be aware of all the nuances swirling around in your world, but it's another to create fantastical, paranoid fantasies around those nuances. If you are unclear what is happening, you can do a few things. First, don't assume that it has anything to do with you. Second, ask the questions for which you desire an answer. Third, stay centered in your reality and trust yourself.

Rewarding Days

9, 10, 23, 24

Challenging Days

4, 5, 18, 19

Gemini | August

Overall Theme

Your brain and your mouth are hard-wired to be in constant motion this month, so much so that even you wonder if you know how to be quiet. It's a reaction to months of uncertainty about what your life was really meant to be, which led to an abundance of inner reflection combined with a lot of insecurity about what you wanted to say and whether you should say it. That's no longer a problem. Go for it.

Relationships

You continue to watch the people in your life with a depth and intensity that isn't always part of your modus operandi. Gone is the paranoia and fear, and in their place is a more detached, objective approach to determining whether your relationships are healthy and growth-oriented. This, in itself, creates a happier, more optimistic feeling, both about yourself and others.

Success and Money

In spite of your promise to yourself to keep your future plans under wraps for the time being, a series of unusual circumstances put you in a situation where you feel compelled to reveal all. And then you immediately regret it. Don't worry, this isn't a lapse. It's fate stepping in. This won't be obvious immediately, but it leads to a very important door opening.

Pitfalls and Potential Problems

You really need to relax and have some fun. Things are moving along quite nicely. Even the challenges provide you with a chance to observe how good you are at solving problems. So don't complicate things, even when tempted. After all, it's been that kind of year, so why should this month be any different? Well, it is. Enjoy. Recharge. Regenerate.

Rewarding Days

8, 27, 28

Challenging Days

6, 7, 17, 18

Gemini | September

Overall Theme

That all-systems-go attitude you basked in last month starts to become a distant memory as the pace of life slows down once again. You haven't lost the fire in your belly. It's just that you need to deal with some of the challenges that cropped up, requiring you to take time out to recalibrate just how you want to move forward.

Relationships

The social butterfly in you takes the stage, front and center, and you find yourself longing for some good old-fashioned hanging out, having fun, and laughing. You are definitely in the mood to enjoy the company of others, with no other goal in mind than being lighthearted. It's a welcome break from all the unrelenting intensity defining your relationships recently, leaving no space for you to breathe.

Success and Money

Stay positive and refrain from interpreting any lack of movement as a complete standstill. The revelation you shared last month has found fertile ground, and things are shifting, just not in any obvious, external way. Unbeknownst to you, you've birthed a much larger, much grander opportunity than you ever could have imagined.

Pitfalls and Potential Problems

You can't decide whether you're glad the universe isn't pushing you this way and that or whether you're disappointed. Take a deep breath. You are coming out of that dark space you felt confined to for much of this year, and you can definitely see the light. However, that doesn't mean the transformation is complete. There's still much to be done.

Rewarding Days

1, 2, 16, 17

Challenging Days

11, 12, 24, 25

Gemini | October

Overall Theme

Your creative mind is once again in overdrive, but you're having some difficulty making sense of all the ideas bouncing around in your brain. Forget the need to quantify them. Just make note of them before they disappear, because you are trying hard to make them meaningful before you even have time to play with them or savor them or sort the wheat from the chaff.

Relationships

The number of people, old and new, who cross your path in the next thirty-one days is staggering. Every time you turn around, there's another invitation. Rather than automatically saying yes to everything, whether it's a person or an opportunity, take time to ask yourself what is in your best interest. Otherwise, you find yourself giving precious energy to people and things that drag you down.

Success and Money

Work is going to be a tough slog, as you find yourself forced to go over things you thought were done. Don't waste time resisting the turn of events or trying to figure out why this happened. Just know that as you revisit your previous efforts, a light-bulb moment makes it all worthwhile and clears up some confusion you had about your new personal project.

Pitfalls and Potential Problems

Details are not always your forte, because you definitely like to paint life in broader strokes. So when your brain is lit up like a Christmas tree, it's really annoying to find yourself stuck in a morass of picky, little factors that, in your mind, don't affect the outcome. However, it's a necessary exercise this month. It's the only way to make sure the foundation of what you are building is truly solid.

Rewarding Days

17, 18, 26, 27

Challenging Days

13, 14, 29, 30

Gemini | November

Overall Theme

Armed with a new appreciation for the rewards that accrue from a deeper, more detailed review of where you are going and what you want to accomplish, you are ready to tackle anything and launch yourself wholeheartedly and confidently into the future. If this year has shown you anything, it's that you are made of very strong stuff.

Relationships

It's not so much that you are hypersensitive as much as it's a case of waking up to find you are quite easily wounded by things that normally cause barely a ripple in your consciousness. Quite possibly, it's connected to a sudden feeling that you really don't have the desire or capacity to be tolerant. Accept this. Keep your own counsel. And examine why you are so triggered. This yields valuable insight, releasing a lot of resentment and anger.

Success and Money

An unexpected reward and some public recognition arrive on your doorstep, sparking optimism and an opportunity to truly celebrate you with a much-needed acknowledgment of just how hard you're working—at everything, not just in this particular area of your life. Take some time to treat yourself to whatever makes you feel special. It's your choice.

Pitfalls and Potential Problems

You aren't sure whether you can really trust the feeling that life is starting to ease up, that you are no longer going to be pulled through the eye of a needle. After all, it could be wishful thinking, something you worked hard to avoid this year. However, even with all that optimism coursing through your consciousness, you are exhausted. And that makes you short on faith. Well, trust that things are getting better, because they are—all because you insisted on persevering.

Rewarding Days

17, 18, 24, 25

Challenging Days

3, 4, 29, 30

Gemini | December

Overall Theme

As the year comes to a close, you don't feel any more certain about the purpose of life than you did in January. With one difference: you are now more certain about yourself. No matter the obstacles and challenges thrown at you—and there were a multitude of those—you jumped in and mastered them with more dexterity and clarity than you might have predicted. Give yourself a round of applause. You deserve it.

Relationships

The best adjectives to describe how you feel right now about anyone and everyone in your world are mellow and compassionate. Gone is your intolerance. Instead, you are aware that the healthiest way to relate to others is to let go of any notion that it's your job to meet their expectations and vice versa. And if everybody sticks to that approach, things will be just fine.

Success and Money

In the midst of your relief that the year ended better than it began, you are ready to move on to bigger and better things. And the signals you are getting certainly indicate that an abundance of support and success is on its way. Take time to examine all that you dealt with this year. It gives you that extra boost of confidence going into 2021.

Pitfalls and Potential Problems

In your haste to move on from one of the most demanding years you are ever likely to encounter, you need to slow down and be grateful for what transpired. Because in the middle of deconstructing your reality and wondering if you would survive, you emerged stronger, more resilient, and more hopeful. And that's a victory of major proportions.

Rewarding Days

7, 8, 24, 25

Challenging Days

13, 14, 27, 28

Gemini Action Table

These dates reflect the best—but not the only—times for success and ease in these activities, according to your Sun sign.

	JAN	FEB	MAR	APR	MAY	JUN	JUL	AUG	SEP	OCT	NOV	DEC
Move										13, 14		
New romance				6, 7		11, 12						16, 17
Seek coaching/counseling			12, 13		2, 3						13, 14	
Ask for a raise									1, 2			
Vacation		11, 12						3, 4				
Get a loan	4, 5						27, 28					

Cancer

The Crab
June 22 to July 22

Element: Water

Quality: Cardinal

Polarity: Yin/feminine

Planetary Ruler: The Moon

Meditation: I have faith in the promptings of my heart

Gemstone: Pearl

Power Stones: Moonstone, Chrysocolla

Key Phrase: I feel

Glyph: Crab's claws

Anatomy: Stomach, breasts

Colors: Silver, pearl white

Animals: Crustaceans, cows, chickens

Myths/Legends: Hercules and the Crab, Asherah, Hecate

House: Fourth

Opposite Sign: Capricorn

Flower: Larkspur

Keyword: Receptivity

The Cancer Personality

Strengths, Talents, and the Creative Spark

The very thing that defines you is your capacity to respond to the world immediately with a deep emotional availability. It may not always be obvious, even to you, but you are always tuned in to what's going on around you. It's impossible for you not to sense the tides shifting and moving and changing. After all, you are a Moon child and that is the gift of the Moon. You instinctively know what path to take, giving you the upper hand in being able to adapt with flexibility to what life dishes up, always being able to find the best way to feed and nurture your world and yourself to produce long-lasting and positive results. The challenge you face is accepting that the world doesn't always value your intrinsic gifts. But you can and you must. It's the only way to continue to grow in strength internally so you can be true to yourself. It really is a talent to be able to sense and feel life at a heart level and to share what that path offers. Consider the newly emerging plant seeking water so it can grow. You are the water, both in your life and in the lives of others. It is the source of your passion and your creativity. It is the spark that takes you ever deeper into the power that lies within.

Blind Spots and Blockages

It can get awfully crowded inside your shell, even if you are in there all by yourself. After all, you are surrounded by the multitude of unexpressed emotions you choose to hide from. The ones you think you can avoid, the ones you believe you can leave behind. What you fail to realize is you are actually running away from yourself, blindly and without taking into consideration the fact that you are constantly disconnecting from the core of your being. The result is you don't like the emotions that people trigger in you. What's more, you don't like their emotions, period, and you aren't particularly sure about your own either. This is largely because you live in a world that believes that feelings and emotions are inconvenient at best, leaving you deeply divided and at odds with yourself. So you go searching for your comfort zone. It could be anything from food to the doily that your grandmother made for you forty years ago. You hold things close, including yourself. You get teary-eyed. But sentimentality is rarely a substitute for real feelings. It's just a camouflage so you don't have to acknowledge, never mind express, all those less-comfortable emotions lurking just below the surface, always ready to erupt in defensiveness at the slightest provocation.

Wouldn't it be easier to pretend everything is warm and fuzzy? Well, that's easier said than done. For you, life is all about what you feel and yet you are constantly forced to live in your head rather than your feeling center. This puts you perpetually on edge, highly emotional and ready to crawl out of your skin. Time to learn the difference between feelings and emotions. Although they are lumped together and believed to be one and the same, they aren't. Feeling is a sense, not a response. Emotions are a reaction to what you feel. Give yourself space to feel. That empowers you to let go of all the emotion clogging up your life. Not only is it getting in the way, but climbing over it makes getting on with life difficult.

Intimacy and Connection

This part of your life begins with one simple desire. On the surface, it looks a lot like safety and security, but it actually goes deeper than that. What you seek is simpatico, which isn't something easily defined. Yet you know it when it shows up in your life—that moment of instant recognition that removes all your carefully constructed walls and barriers and opens up your heart without hesitation to welcome in the feeling that you are truly home. You live for that. You anticipate it every time you meet someone new. And you recoil and retreat if your antennae sense anything less than that. The walls go up, and the determination to protect yourself at all costs kicks in. The problem with that is it often leads you to disconnect from yourself, because you feel you can't trust yourself. Which is the furthest thing from the truth. Who and what other people are isn't a reflection of you. So relinquish the notion that, in order to protect yourself, you need to wall off your sensitivity and vulnerability by controlling your relationships. It doesn't work, and you really are only hiding from yourself. The best way to protect yourself is to be yourself. It's the only way to meet life and all the people in it head-on.

Values and Resources

The key here is to remain open to the changes that naturally come with the unfolding of life. Often you attach yourself to external things, because they are visible and measurable and because that's what the world tells you is important. But in your heart you know the true resources of your life are your connection to what fills your feeling center with joy and contentment. At your core, it is the simple things that light up your life, the things that others often overlook: hugging and smiling and laughing, empathizing and listening and sharing. Those bring you a sense of belonging, which is what you value most.

Goals and Success

Once you establish a sense of security, you are highly motivated to achieve the goals you set for yourself. The sticking point is defining your goals. You have all the necessary determination and commitment to create success, but your goals must be tied to a deep feeling that what you pursue nurtures you. It *has* to feel right, something that isn't always easy for you to claim as your truth. Plus, it often puts you at odds with the world at large, where the practical and logical is valued above creating success that feeds the heart and soul. The challenge is to recognize it's not a case of either-or. If you put heart and soul first, the rest will follow.

Cancer Keywords for 2020
Passion, preparation, courage

The Year Ahead for Cancer

The year begins with an overwhelming sense that you are not safe anywhere because the prevailing energies represented by the combination of Jupiter, Saturn, and Pluto are pushing you so far outside your comfort zone that you feel totally unanchored. The purpose behind this is at once both simple and complex. Simple because the message is that old patterns and approaches to life are no longer effective. Rather, they are keeping you stuck in an ongoing confrontation with fear. Complex because, in order to truly grow, you need to recognize that dissipating that fear and freeing yourself from the self-imposed restrictions resulting from that trepidation requires a deep dive into the core of your being to find that inner strength that you often overlook.

And what, you may ask, is that strength? Your capacity to feel, to sense, to be tuned in to the tides of life as they constantly shift and change. After all, your avatar, your guide, your angel, is the Moon, whose very nature is to be fluid and adapt to life's changing circumstances by going with the flow. You instinctively know how to do this. However, you ignore it because operating from that space is not seen as valuable by the outer world, leaving you feeling disconnected and at war with yourself and the outer world as you struggle to find a way to be your essential self. This year offers a once-in-a-lifetime opportunity to break free from that particular contretemps, reclaim your fundamental nature, and blossom into someone who is anchored from within, who totally embraces the length and breadth of their connection to the feeling realm, and who knows that their strength is limitless as long as they live life from the inside out. The key to being able to do that is to accept that life is uncertain. Not an easy task by any stretch of the imagination, especially when it feels like the whole foundation of your life is on the verge of imploding as you resist the need for transformation at the same time you long to free yourself from anything that keeps you feeling trapped.

It really feels like a never-ending game of internal, emotional ping-pong, with no apparent winner in sight. Recognize that welcoming deep change is not a recipe for destruction but rather a chance to create a new foundation based on a healthier, clearer picture of who you are and where you are going. And recognize that you do have some cosmic help to guide you through this really intense period. Uranus invites you to toss out any outworn values that cloud or interfere with your hopes and your future, while Neptune continues to push you to broaden your understanding of the spiritual part of your life. Tuning in to those energies alleviates much of the tension you experience and gives you space to contemplate the rewards that await your willingness to change. But first you really do need to let go and stop holding on tight. The past is just that—the past. You can carry forward anything from your life's experiences that is truly meaningful to you while relinquishing anything that inhibits the creation of a truly authentic life. And that, in a nutshell, is the gift and the challenge of 2020.

Jupiter

The simplest way to understand what Jupiter brings to the table is to recognize that he amplifies whatever is currently going on in your life. So if you are fearful, he can take you to the stratosphere of dread and anxiety. If you are happy, joyful, or content, he can expand that until you feel you are going to burst. This is the conundrum that faces you this year: do you drown yourself in the negative or do you reach for the positive with all the faith you can muster? At the root of this challenge—which you experience at depths you didn't know you had—is the need to reexamine what is truly meaningful to you. This requires the willingness to take a good, long look at all you hold sacred and ask yourself whether your life is nurtured and supported by what you believe or whether it's starved and diminished. This is an important process if your intention is to grow beyond the current state of your life, which Jupiter is more than ready to help you do. He is, after all, the quintessential optimist, and in 2020, the more you cultivate an optimism and an openness to the possibilities of life, the easier it is to overcome anxiety and feel that you truly can create a life full of what actually nurtures you.

Saturn

You are definitely going to feel that Saturn is the thorn in your side in 2020, constantly reminding you that there are limits to what you can and cannot do. That you not only should but must maintain your commitment to the tried and true, to your duties and obligations, and to the life you've already established. This may seem in direct opposition to a deeper need to transform your life by letting go of anything that feels like nothing but an empty shell. In fact, it's likely that you find yourself wondering if you yourself aren't empty. Such is the weight that Saturn is going to bring to bear on you. Before you jump to any pessimistic, life-is-terrible conclusions, take time to consider that there is an upside to being weighed down. Quite often you avoid changing things in your life because you persuade yourself that life is safe only if you maintain consistency. Saturn's apparent demand that you continue to do this actually forces you to rebel against a self-imposed tyranny whose roots are in your willingness to repress yourself in the name of security. Once that awareness sinks in, you are then free to transmute that heaviness into a new life foundation, one that reflects the wisdom you've gained from confronting the limitations you've imposed on yourself. Saturn's message is always the same: Be accountable for yourself. No matter what you do with your life, true security, true accomplishment, and true integrity come from that singular principle. If you honor that, the depressive nature associated with Saturn dissipates.

Uranus

Don't be surprised if you are suddenly struck by a powerful urge to simplify your life by clearing out anything and everything in your physical environment. The things you once took comfort in now seem totally unnecessary and extraneous to the essence of who you desire to be and what you see as essential to your life. Of course, this is a bit of a shock to your system, but the reality that you have hung on to stuff because you thought it defined you or your life, even if you haven't paid much attention to it in a very long time, is also staggering. As liberating as this is, be careful not to be so intent on getting down to the bare bones that you fail to pay attention to what you are purging. Not everything connected to your past is destined for the recycle bin or the garbage can. Some of it is worth keeping, especially if it strengthens, supports, or inspires you. This is all part of a huge shift in reevaluating where you are in your life and where you might wish to go. There's no doubt it feels chaotic at times, but underlying that is a profound feeling of excitement and anticipation. Accept it. Life promises to be so much better if you do.

Neptune

Neptune continues the overall trend of 2020 where everything truly feels like an either-or choice. So what's behind Neptune's Door Number 1 and Door Number 2? Well, behind Door Number 1 is dreams, clarity, vision, faith, and truth, while behind Door Number 2 is fantasy, illusion, delusion, doubt, and lies. Or is it the other way around? Welcome to the world of Neptune, where things are never quite what they seem and it's difficult to completely nail anything down. It's not always easy to tell the difference between a dream and a fantasy, clarity and illusion, and vision and delusion, because they simply don't come with clearly defined boundaries, which is both a blessing and a burden. So how can you use his energy effectively in 2020? First, recognize that Neptune communicates in images and symbols. So trying to use your conscious, logical mind to deal with his energy is likely to leave you dazed and confused. Instead, keep your connection to your feeling center open. Allow yourself to daydream, to follow your imagination wherever it takes you, and to be receptive to any internal call to take your life in a completely new direction. It really does take courage to let go of habit patterns and deeply- imbedded beliefs. Neptune's gift in triggering this process is his capacity to blur the edges of everything he touches so you are forced to ask yourself whether your attachment to the various aspects of your life actually inspires you, fires up your imagination, and invites you to live creatively rather than predictably. This may seem overwhelming, but using Neptune's energy in this way alleviates much of the anxiety that feels like your constant companion in 2020.

Pluto

If you thought that you had come to grips with Pluto's push to go deep into your psyche to find what you've buried, excavate it, bring it into the light, and release it so that there's space for you to breathe and contemplate a new beginning, think again. Things are about to go up a notch or two in intensity, leaving you feeling that you are going to either implode or explode. Neither is likely to happen. However, knowing that isn't likely to change your sense that you are standing on the precipice of the biggest shift you are likely to experience in this life, and you have no idea whether it leads to the best things in life or the worst. Yet that's the risk that Pluto has been preparing you for since 2008. And now that he has come face to face with Saturn, there is no backing away from the invitation and the need to actually rebirth yourself in real, tangible, and practical ways. There is no new beginning unless you actually live it. So the time has come to put up or shut up. Will it be easy? Probably not. But trust the inner knowing, the expanded ability to tune in to life, and the commitment you made to let go of the detritus of your life that Pluto offered you. After all, you took up the challenge. Now you have the chance to ground it in your life in a multiplicity of ways that will surprise and delight you.

How Will This Year's Eclipses Affect You?

Eclipses signal intense periods that highlight major growth opportunities for us in the process of creating our lives. They are linked to the lunar phases—specifically the New and the Full Moon—and involve the relationship between the Sun, the Moon, and the Earth. A Solar Eclipse is a magnified New Moon, while a Lunar Eclipse is a magnified Full Moon. Eclipses unfold in cycles involving all twelve signs of the zodiac, and they occur in pairs, usually about two weeks apart.

This year there are six eclipses: two Solar Eclipses (one in Cancer and one in Sagittarius) and four Lunar Eclipses (one in Cancer, one in Sagittarius, one in Capricorn, and one in Gemini). This mixed bag of energies signals a shift from last year's focus on redefining nurturing versus babysitting, obligation versus accountability, family versus career, time for self versus taking care of business, and feelings versus rational thought. Three of this year's eclipses (the Lunar Eclipse on January 10 and the Solar Eclipse on June 21, both in Cancer, as well as the Lunar Eclipse on July 5

in Capricorn) complete this cycle, while the new eclipse cycle calls on us to understand that there is no wisdom in living in an ivory tower, stuck in our belief that there is only one way to live life while cut off from that very life. Instead, we need to get down to the streets and actually experience our environment, talk to people, create a dialogue, and embrace diversity. Only then can we create a world that truly embodies freedom and opportunity. Three eclipses (the Lunar Eclipse on June 5 in Sagittarius, the Lunar Eclipse on November 30 in Gemini, and the Solar Eclipse on December 14 in Sagittarius) begin this process.

The first eclipse of 2020 takes place on January 10, and it's a Lunar Eclipse in Cancer, creating a maelstrom of internal and external turmoil, leaving you unnerved and knocked off balance. Don't resist these feelings. They are old and dusty and are getting in the way of the final steps to a complete restructuring of your life. And you are so close to doing that. However, you need to take your emotional shovel and dig out the last of your fear from deep within, fear that has dogged you for much of your life, much of it connected to the need to please everyone but yourself. It truly is time for liberation and transformation.

The remaining eclipses of 2020 connect you to a faith and determination that often overwhelms you at the same time that it uplifts and inspires you. This is a year when you emerge from your cocoon and find your place in the sun, confident in the knowledge of who you are and trusting your inner compass to guide you through whatever you need to tackle in life. You are finally in touch with the inimitable you.

Cancer | January

Overall Theme

You really aren't sure whether you are going to come crashing to the ground or soar to new heights as the push to reinvent your whole life (the irresistible force) meets the need to maintain the status quo (the immovable object). As you work to resolve what appear to be irreconcilable differences, the key is not to choose either path but to recognize you need both—a shift and a foundation. Trust yourself to find a solution.

Relationships

Expect that you are likely to experience quite a bit of this month's inner conflict in some very external ways, most particularly in your connection with others. Why? Because you are changing the very fundamental nature of the way you live your life, and not everyone around you thinks it's a good idea. All this may lead to some classic projection, both on your part and theirs. Relax. Listen to yourself and them. And refrain from defending yourself.

Success and Money

You definitely think this is the only part of your life where you are safe this month. Just put your nose to the grindstone and work hard, and all is well. And you are right. At least a little bit. Until you discover that no part of your life is exempt from the need for an overhaul. However, making change here feels a whole lot easier to you, even though you don't know why. Never mind. Enjoy.

Pitfalls and Potential Problems

Nothing was ever built in a day, and certainly not the biggest transformation of your life. The key is to welcome the discomfort arising from the purging and cleansing that accompanies this shift. It's a sign that you really are changing, not just settling into the same old same old. Of course, you aren't going to like this whole process. Not even a little bit. But the results? Well, they make it all worthwhile.

Rewarding Days

13, 14, 27, 28

Challenging Days

9, 10, 22, 23

Cancer | February

Overall Theme

The pressure eases up and you feel like you can breathe again. The only problem is this leads to a resurgence of anxiety. It's not a sign that things are going sideways. It's just that ingrained response you have when you are worried things are changing too rapidly. Rest assured they aren't. So take it easy and don't push yourself too hard.

Relationships

It's a good time to take charge and establish some new boundaries in your relationships with others. One of the biggest shifts you are going through is the awareness that you are not responsible for how others feel, nor is it your job to fix their lives. In fact, you now realize you simply can't mend what you didn't break.

Success and Money

The spotlight is yours—provided you want to claim it. So put forward any creative ideas or plans about how more could be done with less in your work environment. It might just lead to a complete change in your position or your purpose, all with the promise of better things to come. You just have to step up to the plate.

Pitfalls and Potential Problems

You aren't really sure whether you should be a couch potato or a dynamo this month. Part of you desperately wants to hide in a corner and recalibrate, while the other part is determined not to let the grass grow under your feet. You can probably do both, provided you let go of the need to label one as better than the other. After all, life is ebb and flow.

Rewarding Days

10, 11, 23, 24

Challenging Days

6, 7, 18, 19

Cancer | March

Overall Theme

A clearer sense of where you are going takes shape and lifts your spirits, even though things continue to rock and roll. Life feels less challenging because you feel an inner strength and determination that you are finally willing to embrace. You now realize that being fluid and adaptable is not the same as being weak and ineffectual. It's actually the opposite.

Relationships

You find yourself much more charitable toward the entire population of planet Earth, including those nearest and dearest. It's amazing what happens when you decide you are number one in your life, rather than everyone else who has ever crossed your path. You are actually more present. After all, you aren't really in a relationship if you don't include yourself in the equation and you focus solely on others.

Success and Money

Don't worry too much if you don't feel highly motivated to move a molehill, much less a mountain. You need a break. Making big changes calls for regular downtime. This is not something that's been high on your list of priorities, partly because life seems to intensify every time you consider taking a breather. Well, now's your chance. Go on vacation.

Pitfalls and Potential Problems

Stop waiting for life to slow down, calm down, or even stop altogether. It's not going to happen. Quite simply, 2020 is a pushy year, a demanding year, an unrelenting year. Just know you have what it takes to do more than cope. You will come out shinier and newer and stronger. So give yourself permission to take time out whenever it suits you. Otherwise you are in danger of burning out.

Rewarding Days

8, 9, 26, 27

Challenging Days

2, 3, 24, 25

Cancer | April

Overall Theme

You feel like you are running as fast as you can, but you aren't getting anywhere. That's because the urge to get moving is overshadowing any sense of direction you cultivated. Slow down—just a little—and focus. That way you can combine this surge of energy with a concrete target. It doesn't have to be a big one. The key is to start with something tangible and go from there.

Relationships

Your interest in other people is at an all-time low. And that surprises you. Generally, you make yourself available to anyone who needs you or wants you. So when the thought of spending any amount of time with others makes you queasy, you wonder what's wrong with you. The answer? Nothing. You just want to spend time with yourself. And it's exactly what you need.

Success and Money

Refrain from making any hasty decisions about your career, your future, or, most especially, your money. This isn't the time to give in to any demands or requests (whether they come from others or are self-generated) to take a risk. Being antsy and needing to do something isn't the best or the most prudent reason to take action.

Pitfalls and Potential Problems

Pay attention to what your body is telling you. Right now, your logical brain is making a play to run your life by pushing you to keep moving and not slow down, while your body is approaching burnout. This doesn't mean you have to come to a standstill. Rather, you need to find new ways to nurture your body. Exercise, massage, eating properly, and spending time in nature are all things you can do to pamper yourself and still meet the goals you set for yourself.

Rewarding Days

8, 9, 22, 23

Challenging Days

2, 3, 13, 14

Cancer | May

Overall Theme

A major change in the energetic landscape of your life relieves some of the internal pressure that's been a constant companion for the past eighteen months. Your mood lightens and life begins to feel less like a constant test of your capacity to get from one day to the next and more like you can master the challenge of creating a new life for yourself. This, in turn, gives you a much-needed boost of optimism.

Relationships

Nobody can rattle you, no matter how hard they try. You are finally certain that you don't owe anyone anything, and this leaves you mellow and calm. Of course, you still listen to what others need to share with you and support them as best you can. It's just that you are no longer willing to babysit or prop up anyone who isn't prepared to accept responsibility for themselves.

Success and Money

You are content to watch things unfold this month so you can get a clearer idea of exactly what your next steps should be. It's not that you are planning any huge changes in the status of your work life or your bank account. You are aware that change is in the wind, and you really want to make sure you don't overlook anything that might assist you in embracing the new, even though you aren't sure exactly what that is.

Pitfalls and Potential Problems

You'd really like to believe that you made it through that long, dark tunnel to the light. Accept that you can see the light but you still have a distance to go, incrementally small though it may be, before you are done making the deepest change you are likely to ever experience. Once you do that, you find yourself liberated in a different way, because you now have an appreciation of just what you have already accomplished.

Rewarding Days

2, 3, 15, 16

Challenging Days

10, 11, 25, 26

Cancer | June

Overall Theme

You wonder if you aren't walking a tightrope with no net underneath you. It's the ultimate test of your commitment to let go of the security blanket you've developed, always doing what is safe and what is expected. Instead, it's a bridge between the past and the future. One that flows over a small creek, not the skinny cable over the Grand Canyon you picture in your imagination. Which means you did the work necessary to let go of anything holding you down. Celebrate.

Relationships

Overcome with the worry that perhaps you pushed everyone far, far away, you find yourself enmeshed in an unnecessary emotional drama. What you are experiencing is healthy space between you and the people in your world. But because you are used to people camping out in your consciousness, things feel empty. Time to fill your life up with you and what nurtures you, and you will discover that those who truly love or appreciate you are still there.

Success and Money

You are still calibrating all the information you gathered last month, so recognize the need to set aside any impatience you have about getting the job done, the plan initiated, or the goals set. This is a life-altering intention you are in the process of setting, and being highly reactive only inhibits and interferes with what is in your long-term best interest.

Pitfalls and Potential Problems

The heat in your life is set on high and you are sure chaos is about to ensue. Yet somewhere inside you, you are serene and confident. This dichotomy drives you crazy, and there really is nothing you can do about it. You are between two different states of being, one ready for the new and the bold and the other hanging on to the familiar. Honor both. That way you have the best chance of emerging triumphant and whole.

Rewarding Days

16, 17, 25, 26

Challenging Days

4, 5, 21, 22

Cancer | July

Overall Theme

A few niggling doubts remain, but it's a far cry from the anxiety, worry, and fear that seemed to encircle your life any time you thought yourself ready to move forward. So you are content and ready to go, ready to grab life with passion and intensity, and ready for whatever comes next. You finally know where your strength and tenacity come from: deep inside you, rather than any external set of circumstances you rely on.

Relationships

You just aren't in the mood for anyone to rain on your parade, partly because you know how much effort you put into calling to a halt your tendency to get in your own way, and partly because there's just too much to do in taking those first wobbly steps into your new future to entertain negativity. Only one thing is required of you in this area of your life: be polite. It creates less drama than frustration.

Success and Money

Finally a picture of where you might be going emerges, and you are shocked to realize that you don't need to completely reinvent yourself, that you have a lot of skills already in place to facilitate a new beginning. This comes as a huge relief. You really didn't want to think you had to start from scratch. Plus it truly allows you to see just how you can use the experience you've already accumulated.

Pitfalls and Potential Problems

When the push to reinvent yourself began, it triggered a fear that nothing you'd already done in your life had any cache, any meaning, or anything to contribute moving forward. You will confront this insecurity one more time, precisely because the moment of truth has arrived. However, this time you aren't overwhelmed by it. Rather, it's become just a pebble on the road of your life, rather than Mount Everest.

Rewarding Days

13, 14, 23, 24

Challenging Days

4, 5, 18, 19

Cancer | August

Overall Theme

You are more comfortable in your own skin now than you have been all year, even if that skin feels entirely new. In fact, much to your surprise, you are thrilled by the new you. All of life feels shiny and fun and joyful, so much so that any challenges that crop up barely ruffle the inner confidence that is now second nature to you.

Relationships

You do wonder if you lacked your usual sensitivity during much of this year. So you turn to loved ones and friends and colleagues to make sure they know how grateful and fortunate you are for their presence in your life. It really is a case of hugs all around. And if you meet with resistance from anyone, know it's a sign that perhaps they belong to the past, not the future.

Success and Money

Seeds that you planted six months ago come to fruition in your career or job. Not only is it time to take a bow, it's time to ask for a raise or a promotion. Or both. You deserve it. And the best way to secure this double blessing is to come to the table with even more new ideas. You are no longer willing to be reliable. You want to be creative, innovative, and perhaps a little avant-garde.

Pitfalls and Potential Problems

Now that you are basking in the light, you notice that others around you are struggling. And it's not your problem, even if they think it is. Part of this new path in life is a commitment to always doing what's best for you. You didn't do all the work of the last eighteen months so you could slide backward by putting everyone and everything else first. Recognize that making yourself number one is the healthiest, most inspiring thing you can do for others.

Rewarding Days

7, 8, 23, 24

Challenging Days

12, 13, 27, 28

Cancer | September

Overall Theme

Your optimism remains high, and you are going to need it. There's a tremendous push-pull between full-speed ahead and stop right there. For once, it's not coming from you but from external circumstances. It seems no one can make up their mind about what needs to happen but you. Carry on doing what you are doing. Detach from the trauma and drama being generated by others. That way you end the month on a high note.

Relationships

You really question what the heck is going on with people, both those close to you and those not. Did they drink some weird potion? Because it seems that everyone is just a little crazy and either staring incessantly at their navel or complaining about, well, you name it. Meanwhile, you feel lighthearted and ready for fun. This is your chance to lead by example. Be the life of the party. Everyone will thank you for gently kicking them out of their funk.

Success and Money

There's a strong urge to spend money. Don't resist it. Just make sure you spend it on yourself or on things that make you smile. This is part of the process of valuing yourself rather than always taking care of business. And it energetically signals to the world at large that you are no longer willing to be undervalued at work or at home.

Pitfalls and Potential Problems

One of the results of paying more attention to your feeling center is that you are now even more aware of what the rest of the world is going through. It can overload your circuits, especially this month. Spend time in nature or do whatever brings you back to yourself. Play. Sleep. Meditate. Put a bubble of white light around yourself. Otherwise, exhaustion is likely to set in and rob you of all that newfound pleasure and excitement.

Rewarding Days

1, 2, 19, 20

Challenging Days

11, 12, 24, 25

Cancer | October

Overall Theme

A number of challenges find you drawing on the deep resources you cultivated during much of 2020. As always, you are surprised at your own capability, which, in this case, is your strong feeling core. Not only does it alleviate any internal distress you experience, but it shows you exactly what to do to turn disaster into success, allowing you to see firsthand just how much you have changed.

Relationships

Expect the unexpected. That's the best way to approach your relationships this month. It doesn't mean you won't be surprised by some unwanted input, but you will be prepared. Prepared to ignore words and actions that could undermine you, hurt you. It's not intentional. The person or persons who dump on you are acting out their own demons. The solution? Set clear boundaries and walk away.

Success and Money

A new opportunity comes knocking on your door and you are truly excited, until you realize that it takes you outside an old comfort zone, one that has limited you in the past. Rather than backing away from this golden opportunity, confront the part of you that thinks doing less than you are capable of is safer than taking the risk to do more.

Pitfalls and Potential Problems

Life is going to be like living on a swinging pendulum this month, highs and lows, and all in the same hour. It's just part of the next stage of your transformation, where you experience the new and the old simultaneously. At least you experience it that way. However, what's truly important is that you come back to center every time with a trust in yourself that runs deep.

Rewarding Days

3, 4, 25, 26

Challenging Days

11, 12, 28, 29, 30

Cancer | November

Overall Theme

You are definitely in the mood to be combative if anyone even looks like they are going to get in your way. Don't be alarmed. What you consider combative is actually assertive. What is more problematic is that your patience is running low at the best of times. Which is to say it's non-existent most of the time. Finding a creative or physical outlet for the frustration feeding that lack of patience is essential if you don't want to find yourself *really* looking for a fight.

Relationships

You want what you want, when you want it. And if you don't get it, well, you won't answer for the consequences. Welcome to your modus operandi for November 2020. You can't seem to stop yourself from being demanding, pushy, and possibly even a little manipulative. Yet inside, you are more than a little embarrassed. There's nothing wrong with what you desire. Just find a kinder, politer, and more straightforward way of asking for it.

Success and Money

A number of possibilities regarding your future suddenly converge, and you are overwhelmed. First, you didn't think anything was going to come of any of them. After all, they seemed stuck in limbo. Second, you already started formulating a plan to move things along yourself. Now you aren't sure what you should do. Don't rush into anything, and let your intuition guide you.

Pitfalls and Potential Problems

You really are tired of working so hard at everything. Time to look at your life from a different perspective. What truly inspires you, nurtures you, and satisfies you? Answering that question will lead you out of the quagmire of believing that life is a series of tasks. Find something that lights you up.

Rewarding Days

13, 14, 22, 23

Challenging Days

5, 6, 17, 18

Cancer | December

Overall Theme

You find yourself in a reverie, reminiscing about 2020 and readying yourself for what is coming next. But rather than try to anticipate what is going to happen in concrete terms, you opt to visualize your hopes and dreams. This reflects just how much the foundation of your life has morphed from focusing on safety and security to trusting your inner guidance system to create a life full of passion and joy.

Relationships

Last month's immaturity gives way to a more mature approach to relationships. You now realize that being demanding was an unconscious attempt to redress the imbalance you experienced by always meetings the needs of others. As you abandon self-imposed expectations, you feel freer and wiser, and ready to create relationships based on a respect for yourself rather than service to others.

Success and Money

You are ready for a new adventure. What that looks like exactly is yet to be determined. But you are clear that it's your decision and yours alone, so you find yourself immune to any emotional push from others. Oh, you are listening to what is being said and what's not being said, and then filing it away for further inspection, knowing that your new direction will reveal itself when the time is right.

Pitfalls and Potential Problems

It's an understatement to say you are eager to start 2021. You can feel so many new things percolating just below the surface, and you are so ready to tackle them using your newfound sense of your own authenticity. Remember, you still need to take care of life this month. You don't want to start your new year with unfinished business.

Rewarding Days

6, 7, 24, 25

Challenging Days

2, 3, 29, 30

Cancer Action Table

These dates reflect the best—but not the only—times for success and ease in these activities, according to your Sun sign.

	JAN	FEB	MAR	APR	MAY	JUN	JUL	AUG	SEP	OCT	NOV	DEC
Move	17, 18											
New romance					17, 18		14, 15				13, 14	
Seek coaching/counseling						19, 20						6, 7
Ask for a raise				23, 24						4, 5		
Vacation			8, 9						1, 2			
Get a loan		1, 2						10, 11				

Leo

The Lion
July 23 to August 22

♌

Element: Fire

Quality: Fixed

Polarity: Yang/masculine

Planetary Ruler: The Sun

Meditation: I trust in the strength of my soul

Gemstone: Ruby

Power Stones: Topaz, sardonyx

Key Phrase: I will

Glyph: Lion's tail

Anatomy: Heart, upper back

Colors: Gold, scarlet

Animals: Lions, large cats

Myths/Legends: Apollo, Isis, Helios

House: Fifth

Opposite Sign: Aquarius

Flowers: Marigold, sunflower

Keyword: Magnetic

The Leo Personality

Strengths, Talents, and the Creative Spark

You live with the certainty that no matter what comes your way, you have what it takes to meet life's challenges without flinching, without looking for a place to hide, and without running away. In fact, all of the above are unthinkable. They are a total betrayal of your innate strength, dignity, and integrity. Any Lion worth their salt always stands strong and determined. This doesn't mean you are without fear or insecurities or that you must succeed at all costs. It just means you must always honor the standards you set for yourself, which essentially boil down to you being the best person you can be. Someone truthful, intrepid, kind, generous, and faithful. Someone who always keeps promises and does what they say they are going to do.

After all, your word is your bond. Not only is it the cornerstone on which you express who you are, it's what makes you trustworthy and earns you the self-respect that you need in order to feel grounded and at peace. And it's the source of the creative spark that fuels your life. How could you possibly create anything of value if you can't honor your commitments? There's nothing more challenging or damaging to you than coming face to face with the knowledge that you didn't act within the set of standards and principles you espouse, that you didn't do what you pledged to do. It may not always be obvious to everyone else, but coloring outside the lines of your deeply held expectation that you will always do the honorable thing can slowly and surely diminish who you are from the inside out. And that is simply unacceptable.

Blind Spots and Blockages

It's hard to believe you have a blind spot. Yours may be that you are so dazzled by your own brilliance that it doesn't occur to you that other people are not as enamored with you as you are with yourself. It's not that you mean to be overwhelming, but sometimes you can be too much of a good thing. All that nobility, all that charm, all that swagger, and all that confidence can be a little unnerving for the mere mortals around you. They are always trying to figure out what your secret is. You, on the other hand, don't think it's a secret. In fact, the key to your life is pretty simple: you like yourself, you trust yourself, and you celebrate yourself. Doesn't everybody? Well, as a matter of fact, no, they don't. This always comes as a shock to your system. Even in the face of the worst adversity, you draw on some indefinable power to carry you through. And you naturally assume this is as easily available to everyone else as it is to you. Again, no.

So in asking for the Sun, the Moon, and the stars from others, you need to realize they don't always feel as capable as you do. The irony is that you do have doubts and fears and anxiety. You just don't show them or share them. Instead, you stare them down and carry on, all the while looking like you know exactly where you are going and what you are doing. This is your blind spot, your blockage—the certainty that it's inappropriate to let anyone see that side of you. Not only does this isolate you, but it turns your pride into a difficult and unforgiving taskmaster. Which then makes it seem like you are arrogant. And that offends you. Set that aside. Be generous. Let people know you are human by stripping away that I've-got-it-covered mask to reveal your uncertainty. No matter what you tell yourself, it's there.

Intimacy and Connection

Ah, love. The one thing that can rearrange your whole life, in both wonderful and difficult ways. You are an open-hearted person who really does believe that love is an elixir. And, as long as the people you get close to operate from that same framework, you commit yourself totally to building deeper and deeper intimacy. The kind that expands you, energizes you, and helps you reach your potential as a human being. However, if you discover that not everyone else's definition of love is idealistic, selfless, or even kind, your world implodes, leaving you devastated, grief-stricken, and determined never to love again, never to be vulnerable or intimate with anyone ever. So you build walls and try to make yourself hard and unapproachable. You arm yourself with anger and bitterness. But no matter how hard you try, this approach never really works, although it is a necessary part of moving beyond what you feel is a profound betrayal of everything you value to a wiser, more realistic understanding and tolerance of what it is to be human. You may no longer be the romantic you once were, but you are now ready to love and to build intimacy once again. You truly are built to love. It's as essential to who you are as breathing is to being alive. You can never truly give it up, since doing so is the same as giving up on life.

Values and Resources

It confuses you to think of these things as separate aspects of your life because they are so intrinsically fundamental to how you are. You absolutely believe that every action you take clearly demonstrates your values as well as the resources you know are waiting inside you to be tapped into. Truly, there's no camouflage or dissembling or embarrassment about what is most valuable to you. It's obvious: yourself. Everything stems from that. But with this comes an unfailing perfectionism. And that equates to deep disappointment and criticism if you fail to do the very best that you can in any and all circumstances.

Goals and Success

A life without something to strive for is totally incomprehensible to you, not because it gives you prestige or honor or even money but because you get to follow your heart, do something you love, and show just what you are made of. Therefore, a goal must be something you see as worthy of your time and energy, and your success must completely reflect everything you stand for. This might seem a little excessive to others, a little over the top, but that's because they fail to see that what motivates you comes from within rather than a need to prove anything to anyone.

Leo Keywords for 2020
Compassion, play, self-nurturing

The Year Ahead for Leo

This is likely to be a year when it feels like the work never ends. And this doesn't just mean your job or other external demands on your time. It also includes making sure you take time to process frustrations, take care of your health (whether it's physical, emotional, intellectual, or spiritual), and honor all the unexpected fears and anxieties as well as long-held hopes, wishes, and dreams now surfacing from the places where you hid them so carefully that you forgot they even existed. There's no doubt this is overwhelming for you, because you are certain that nothing ever escapes your attention and that you are always on top of everything. Welcome to 2020, where it becomes obvious that that isn't true, requiring that you acknowledge you are, after all, human. Don't be alarmed. The prevailing energies of 2020 are designed specifically to push you in that direction through an overwhelming feeling that you haven't taken out the garbage for a very long time, and now it's piled so high it threatens to obliterate your capacity to see the path immediately in front of you, never mind being able to make any real plans to shift your life. What you need to do is face the challenge this represents. And to do this, you need to dig deep into that intrinsic faith you have in yourself.

There's no doubt that, whether you recognize it or not, you are tremendously gifted at setting aside or ignoring anything you feel has the potential to undermine your belief in yourself, make you feel inadequate, or threaten to interfere with the task at hand. But doing that in 2020 only yields more problems, because there is little doubt that your circuits are definitely on overload and there's no space left in your world to disregard anything. You simply have to engage your infamous determination and set about a major purge of anything complicating your life and turning it into a circus of chaos, one with the long-term potential to damage both relationships and career. Be straightforward and honest with yourself. Acknowledge anything you avoided or buried. This is necessary if you want to lighten the load you are carrying and liberate yourself from the need to be the answer to everyone's prayers.

You may indeed have the nobility and strength to be the one who leads others to the Promised Land. After all, isn't that the responsibility of the Queen or King? However, the time has come to resign from that self-imposed position and let others develop a capacity to take care of themselves so you can take care of yourself. Of course, it's not easy for you to realign your purpose in life, largely because you think it means abandoning the very things you feel define you. Nothing or no one is asking you to do that. Rather, you are being called to change exactly how and why you express your substance, your authenticity. Who you are is truly a gift, and you can create healthier ways of showing it. This year offers a lifetime's worth of opportunities to do that.

Jupiter

The path Jupiter offers this year is twofold, as usual. To begin with, he really believes it's his job to guide us toward experiences that illuminate what is meaningful to us. How exactly that happens isn't really his concern. He just wants to expand your reality, and because you hang out in a dualistic world, what he amplifies can be hugely positive or, conversely, hugely undesirable. It is your choice. Because Jupiter knows that in the seeds of each experience is the potential for evolution. One choice is likely easier to experience, while the other forces a confrontation with anything that is self-defeating. At no time will this be more obvious to you than this year, as Jupiter gives you a glimpse into the kind of transformation that liberates you from deep insecurities and painful experiences at the same time he takes you to the brink of being absorbed by those very same things. He is, by turns, showing you the challenge of not just living through the Saturn-Pluto convergence but using it as raw material to deepen your life, purge the unnecessary baggage you've accumulated, see yourself clearly and without prejudice, and value who you are, not what you do. This, in turn, reignites your optimism and joy and leads you to choose a new path—internal, external, or both—that reconnects you to the intrinsic need you have to celebrate your life force by doing what you love. No more doing for the sake of doing or out of a misguided sense of honor. Instead, it's time to act for the sake of love, which for you is being you at your very finest.

Saturn

You aren't always sure you need Saturn in order to be prompted to do your duty, because you are convinced you were born with that already deeply ingrained. What you often overlook is that, in your world, Saturn sees his job as teaching you the value of modesty and restraint. These are not always your primary objectives because you are not hard-wired to recognize that you can overstep boundaries in the name of nobility of purpose. And there's no doubt you are honorable, principled, and magnanimous and your intent is unfailingly positive. Whether the rest of the world sees your contribution that way is quite another story, one that you are likely to come face to face with throughout 2020, as Saturn introduces you quite forcefully to the reality that you need to listen and support rather than assume and take over. The underlying purpose of this is straightforward. Time to understand it's not your job to save the world. You are not a superhero. You are a human who needs some time and space to enjoy the simple pleasures of life.

Every Lion needs to sit in the sun, and it's your turn. And, yes, whether you believe it or not, it's Saturn delivering the message. Why? Saturn is about more than just hard work and ambition. His deeper intent is to remind us to be accountable for ourselves, no matter the details of the situation. In your case, he is here to help you resign from an overwhelming compulsion to make sure you are always ready, willing, and able to do whatever is required to take care of business. But the question is whose business? This is something Pluto has been nagging you about and Saturn is asking you to finally define before you completely lose sight of all the other parts of yourself. Doing one's duty is not honorable if it's based on obligation and not choice. Rather, it's slavery. And you can end it yourself when you realize that you are the one who chose this path and it's okay to shift gears. What's more, you have all the courage, determination, and audacity to do it.

Uranus

Yet another planet whispering in your ear, telling you to change. Sigh. When will it stop? Not for a while. Uranus is in the middle of his seven-year plan to turn upside down anything connected to your previous unwavering sense of purpose so you can find a new, life-affirming way to shine. Otherwise, life is going to look a lot like somebody threw up on it. Definitely not appealing to you in any way, shape, or form. Sure, you feel all that rumbling going on inside you, and it's competing with a weariness you know is new as well as unnerving. The question then becomes how can you take any steps toward a new beginning when you feel weighed down by everything you have ever done? Time to realize that's not generating the ennui. Rather, it's a not-very-subtle awareness that you lost sight of some very valuable parts of yourself along the way. Remember joy and fun and feeling light? They are still there. You just need to unearth them by letting go of what no longer makes your heart sing. You may not know exactly what that is in real and practical terms just yet. The first step is to identify everything in your life that frustrates you, hurts you, or diminishes you. Then you will be able to identify, at your very core, what you value right now. This automatically initiates a purging, a releasing, a letting-go, creating space for you to embrace the next phase of your life. Only then will you be able to craft a new purpose.

Neptune

The best way to make use of Neptune's energy is to immerse yourself in the deep feelings, the unquantifiable feelings, emerging from a place in your psyche that has no boundaries and no real location. It just is. The gift in this is connecting to a wealth of symbols, imagery, and material that may or may not end up in a tangible form in the third dimension. And yet it offers a powerful and profound opportunity to recharge your batteries, feed your soul, and bring you to the center of yourself, something you truly need right now. It helps you to free yourself from the idea that the only things that really matter are the things that can be measured, analyzed, and manifested. You are and always have been motivated by what is in your heart and what can be created by the human spirit. Neptune is your path back to that part of you.

Pluto

Just when you thought you had a handle on Pluto's extreme, life-or-death approach to life, he kicks it up another notch in 2020. This is in large part because Saturn arrives on the scene and their combined energies ignite an internal power struggle that leaves you reeling. Well, once the room stops spinning, recognize that Pluto's intent is the same as it was when he first entered Capricorn in 2008: to transform the structures and plans and ambitions that have formed the central focus of your life so you can heal and release any fear that you are never enough. That hasn't changed. The key is whether you choose to back off from the final steps of that process or to use Saturn's purposefulness and accountability to finish it. Will this feel like pulling yourself through the eye of a needle? Possibly. However, trying to revert to old ways of being is likely to cause far deeper damage than wrapping yourself in the hope and optimism that live at the core of who are you.

How Will This Year's Eclipses Affect You?

Eclipses signal intense periods that highlight major growth opportunities for us in the process of creating our lives. They are linked to the lunar phases—specifically the New and the Full Moon—and involve the relationship between the Sun, the Moon, and the Earth. A Solar Eclipse is a magnified New Moon, while a Lunar Eclipse is a magnified Full Moon. Eclipses unfold in cycles involving all twelve signs of the zodiac, and they occur in pairs, usually about two weeks apart.

This year there are six eclipses: two Solar Eclipses (one in Cancer and one in Sagittarius) and four Lunar Eclipses (one in Cancer, one in Sagittarius, one in Capricorn, and one in Gemini). This mixed bag of energies signals a shift from last year's focus on redefining nurturing versus babysitting, obligation versus accountability, family versus career, time for self versus taking care of business, and feelings versus rational thought. Three of this year's eclipses (the Lunar Eclipse on January 10 and the Solar Eclipse on June 21, both in Cancer, as well as the Lunar Eclipse on July 5

in Capricorn) complete this cycle, while the new eclipse cycle calls on us to understand that there is no wisdom in living in an ivory tower, stuck in our belief that there is only one way to live life while cut off from that very life. Instead, we need to get down to the streets and actually experience our environment, talk to people, create a dialogue, and embrace diversity. Only then can we create a world that truly embodies freedom and opportunity. Three eclipses (the Lunar Eclipse on June 5 in Sagittarius, the Lunar Eclipse on November 30 in Gemini, and the Solar Eclipse on December 14 in Sagittarius) begin this process.

The first eclipse of 2020 takes place on January 10, and it's a Lunar Eclipse in Cancer, highlighting the need to stop hiding from the deep-feeling nature that fuels you from just behind the wall you've constructed to make you look invincible and indestructible. You are deeply sensitive. You just don't like to show it, not even to yourself. This eclipse signals that it's no longer the wisest course of action to perpetuate that approach. This year's powerful energies require you to be tapped into that vulnerability in order to grow, transmute, and transform any facet of your life that your experience shows you has gone stale, deteriorated, or completely disintegrated. Not only can you no longer avoid your feeling nature, but you must do a major emotional house cleaning. This clears the way for a refreshed and rejuvenated you, one who is open and vulnerable and who knows how to engage with the world without the pretense that you are always in control. Of course, this is likely to feel like jumping into the unknown without a clue. But that's precisely what the remaining eclipses of the year are about: leaping into the future and completely trusting yourself even when you don't know where you will land. Take a deep breath and fly!

Leo | January

Overall Theme

It's not like you to hide, but that is exactly what you take the most comfort in as you feel like you are being pushed, pulled, bombarded, and blitzed by a never-ending onslaught of pressure being brought to bear not just on your human self but on your soul. Take charge of what belongs to you, cast aside the demands of others, and find a place that nourishes you inside and out.

Relationships

This is the month when you realize you can't run away forever from lifelong relationship patterns and expectations. Time to use your innate nobility to honor yourself first and foremost, something you don't do if you truly love or respect someone. They always come first. Granted, it gives you great satisfaction to cherish and to love. However, you need to include yourself in the equation.

Success and Money

Here's another facet of your life that you think might belong on a garbage heap somewhere. But before you do anything precipitous, take a deep breath. It's not that you shouldn't initiate change. You just shouldn't do it on impulse. Take stock of everything you've accomplished, how much you've grown, and the true value of this part of your life. Then use it to build something new.

Pitfalls and Potential Problems

This is definitely not the time to find fault with yourself. It will lead you nowhere but down a dark road of self-disdain, and that won't inspire you, support you, or help you create a new future. Instead, honor your life. That way you can find a way to take all your experience and shift in a more fulfilling direction. Burning yourself to the ground is not only a waste of time but also a waste of the life you have already lived.

Rewarding Days

4, 5, 17, 18

Challenging Days

9, 10, 11, 12

Leo | February

Overall Theme

Fresh from a deep dive into every aspect of your life and the recognition that you feel overwhelmed and underappreciated, you bounce back with determination and enthusiasm. This allows you to put everything into proper perspective, which in turn reconnects you to the core of who you are. That's when your mojo kicks in and you push forward with equal parts strength and gusto. Watch out, world!

Relationships

You really want to push the limits of your relationships. Or is that knock over the walls? Probably both. You are on a mission to find out what those closest to you really expect from you. Not that you don't have an idea. You just want to hear it from them, so a healthier relationship can develop. You are tired of being all things to all people.

Success and Money

Use caution when considering any large financial moves. It's a time for conservation as you review your commitments and whether they reflect what you truly value. It's not unusual after a month of turmoil to look for some way to feel more secure. That will not come from any large outlay of money. As for career, the same approach applies. No sudden moves and no acting from impatience or fear.

Pitfalls and Potential Problems

Just because you have a better handle on what needs to be done to transform your reality so there is more joy and less stress doesn't mean you can do it all in the blink of an eye. You still need to rest and rejuvenate. Resist the temptation to try to heal, to fix, to shift everything you know is weighing you down. That's not taking care of yourself. Rather, it's backing yourself into the same corner you are trying to escape. The better solution? Have fun and play.

Rewarding Days

14, 15, 23, 24

Challenging Days

5, 6, 18, 19

Leo | March

Overall Theme

There's no doubt you are on high alert. In fact, it feels like all the hairs on your body are standing on end all the time. It's because your deeper consciousness is aware of shifting tides and a powerful reckoning between the need to hang on to who you are now and who you can be in the future. Time to let go of your fear, embrace your innate bravery, and just go for the gusto.

Relationships

No sense in trying to anticipate exactly what is likely to happen between you and anyone significant in your life, whether it's your partner, your family, your friends, your boss, your peers, or even the person at the cash register. Everyone, including you, is unpredictable. Just take things as they come and refrain from doing anything hasty.

Success and Money

You are fairly certain that something has got to change in how you approach what success means to you. Take time to examine the path you are on from an objective and detached point of view, so that you can ascertain what is working and what isn't. This leads to a renewed sense of purpose in this area and potentially a new direction.

Pitfalls and Potential Problems

The energetic forces pummelling you from the inside and outside are likely to overwhelm you. Take heart. When all is said and done, you will feel a kind of liberation that leaves you breathless—and joyful. That doesn't mean that your world is suddenly complete, settled, or even quiet. Far from it. And that's okay. Because the upheaval is somehow exhilarating at the same time that it's challenging, leaving you more alive than you've been for a long time.

Rewarding Days

12, 13, 24, 25

Challenging Days

4, 5, 16, 17

Leo | April

Overall Theme

The feeling of urgency that has been your constant companion since the beginning of the year suddenly dissipates, leaving a huge empty space. At first, you aren't sure just what to do with it. The answer is nothing. Enjoy the space. Let it be. After all, it symbolizes freeing yourself from some heavy burdens. Relax. The time to create something will arrive, and you deserve a break.

Relationships

Gone is the slightly out-of-sorts, slightly suspicious, and slightly unforgiving Lion. You are now ready to hang out, socialize, and rejoin the human race. The truth is you don't really like setting yourself apart. This is something you found yourself doing a lot, not because you stopped caring or thought you were better than everyone else but because your circuits were overloaded and you needed a reboot.

Success and Money

Some unusual opportunities pop up toward the end of the month. You feel like someone must have been reading your mind because they fit right in with the decisions you made in March to forge a new beginning. Decisions you had yet to share with anyone because you thought they still needed refining. Guess not.

Pitfalls and Potential Problems

As you emerge from the deep emotional pit you thought your life was becoming, be careful not to back-pedal by setting out to apologize to all and sundry for your failure to perform your usual duties in taking care of their realities. You know how much you trust yourself with your life. Well, it's time to let them do the same, and the way to do that is simple. Tell them you trust and support them to do what is in their best interest.

Rewarding Days
15, 16, 23, 24

Challenging Days
2, 3, 13, 14

Leo | May

Overall Theme

Your worries about what comes next—and you have been worried, no matter how you appear to the rest of the world—finally take a back seat as your whole being comes alive with a fresh set of eyes and inspirations. This gets your engine purring and your optimism humming. And it couldn't come at a better time, because you were on the verge of throwing in the towel, scaring you in a way you've never felt before.

Relationships

Your social calendar is packed with invitations and you are more than a little baffled. It seems like a long time since there was such an influx of people actively seeking your presence. The truth is you were deep in your own process and those around you recognized that you just wanted to be alone. So set aside your consternation. It really is time to have fun and fill your heart with the joy of connection.

Success and Money

As usual, once you decide to get moving, you expect the rest of the world to catch up in less than a nanosecond. Put your impatience on hold. Take time to plan exactly where you are going and why. Otherwise, there's likely to be a misstep or two that could knock you off balance, although it won't halt your forward progress in any meaningful way.

Pitfalls and Potential Problems

You are likely to wonder just how many people are living inside your consciousness, largely because you are still trying to build a foundation that can sustain you going forward. One minute, all is bliss and joy and your optimism is stratospheric, and the next, you are fighting to stay one step ahead of the gloomy and disheartening feelings you've been playing chicken with for months. Accept this ebb and flow. Both are necessary to the future you are creating.

Rewarding Days

2, 3, 15, 16

Challenging Days

10, 11, 22, 23

Leo | June

Overall Theme

Life is something of a mixed bag with old, unresolved stuff bumping up against sky-high enthusiasm, a repeat of last month's challenges (or is that a continuation?). The difference right now is that the hopes and dreams are more prevalent than the fear and anxiety, which means you feel less like you are losing a battle and more like you are creating a future.

Relationships

After spending May reconnecting with a wide spectrum of people who have played significant roles in your life, you find yourself recalibrating what kind of relationships really add substance to your world. Of course, this puts you in the slightly uncomfortable position of deciding what to do with your conclusions. Nothing. Anyone who no longer resonates with who you are becoming will naturally fade away.

Success and Money

So many people floated in and out of your life recently that you may have overlooked a golden opportunity that presented itself in a brief conversation. Don't worry! The individual who dropped this in your lap is going to follow up. Pay attention. It may not fit in your life right now, but the space for it will open up, provided you don't dismiss it.

Pitfalls and Potential Problems

Stay grounded and realistic. Otherwise, all that bouncy, happy energy exploding from all parts of your being is going to push you to jump with no safe place to land—not your idea of the way things are supposed to be. Yes, you are a fire sign, but you are the one fire sign that requires a sense of where you are going when taking a gamble. Remember that. It will make you create a focus for that gusto.

Rewarding Days

4, 5, 14, 15

Challenging Days

6, 7, 21, 22

Leo | July

Overall Theme

Remember that Boogey Man you banished? Well, he's back. Or at least it feels like it. Take solace in knowing he symbolizes the final chapter in letting go of some old, old, old detritus you set aside to be healed when the time was right. Whether it's emotions, self-criticism, past disappointments, childhood wounds, or unrealistic demands of yourself, you can let go now.

Relationships

With all the inner turmoil you are feeling, reach out and talk to those you trust. It's definitely in your nature to handle things on your own. However, self-reliance isn't always the answer, especially right now. You really need to share all that you are going through so you can clear the decks. Plus it will deepen your relationships in profound and happy ways.

Success and Money

This part of your life hums along without much input from you, which surprises you. Just know that you can and should let go, that you can trust that what you have done is enough, and that success is created by giving your creations space to grow. The results not only will impress you but will give you the confidence to move to the next stage of your plan.

Pitfalls and Potential Problems

Because so much of the last year or more has brought you face to face with unresolved aspects of your life, overwhelming you and making you question everything, you are still unsure about trusting yourself. The purpose of all this dissonance wasn't to reduce you to a pile of rubble. Rather, it was intended to clear away the internal gunk interfering with you being your whole self.

Rewarding Days

13, 14, 29, 30

Challenging Days

4, 5, 20, 21

Leo | August

Overall Theme

Your engine is revving and for the first time this year, your energy level matches your enthusiasm, giving you the confidence to push forward without hesitation. Any obstacles that you encounter are quickly overcome and the results are amazing, not just in physical, practical terms but also in personal, inner terms. For the first time in a long time, you know you can prevail.

Relationships

Strangely, the one area of your life where you feel yourself retreating rather than moving forward is this one. Well, it's not as simple as that. What you are actually doing is including yourself in your life, making your relationship with yourself valid and valuable, which it hasn't been. You can't have healthy relationships with others if the way you treat yourself isn't nourishing and respectful.

Success and Money

Time to take a close look at your financial commitments, because you have big decisions to make in how you wish to go forward, whether that includes investing in yourself or finding new ways to spend, save, or invest your money. This process is not as much about long-term security as about creating the proper foundation for what you value.

Pitfalls and Potential Problems

Stop looking over your shoulder, waiting for life to sneak up on you and knock the stuffing out of you. It's not going to happen. Well, at least not this month. Trust that joy you feel each and every day. Use it to open your heart to life once again. Remember, nothing ever gets the Lion down permanently. All bumps in the road are just an opportunity for you to show how good you are at mastering life's challenges.

Rewarding Days

7, 8, 23, 24

Challenging Days

15, 16, 27, 28

Leo | September

Overall Theme

Plans take shape, you feel you are in the zone, and all is well. Truly. Nothing is going to disturb your equilibrium because you are at peace with yourself. This makes you impervious to any and all irritations, frustrations, and provocations. In fact, you eye them with some amusement. After all, they are nothing compared to the challenges you've overcome this year. And you can finally see that.

Relationships

You feel really cuddly and loving and caring, and definitely ready to play and create space for romance, much to your amazement. You haven't felt the least bit romantic much of this year. That doesn't mean you haven't yearned for it in some deep, dark cavern of your heart. You just weren't sure you could pull it off because you were so focused on healing yourself.

Success and Money

You are ready to step into the spotlight again, ready to build a stronger, revitalized presence in your work world. After all, there's no doubt you believe you took a timeout, which can mean only one thing: you dropped the ball and your reputation suffered. Guess what? You are the only one who sees it that way. This buoys your spirits and leaves you with one less problem to solve.

Pitfalls and Potential Problems

You know things are on the upswing—finally. Just remember that the last few months really pushed you to the limit and you still need to give yourself space to breathe. The temptation to return to old ways of being is likely to creep up on you, so make sure you schedule fun, play, rest, and relaxation. Otherwise, your schedule will once again be crammed with obligations rather than choices you consciously made.

Rewarding Days

1, 2, 19, 20

Challenging Days

11, 12, 24, 25

Leo | October

Overall Theme

Expect a few minor bumps in the road, largely due to misunderstandings and bad communication. It's not that you or anyone else intends to be unclear, combative, or suspicious, but this is a month when the intensity of events triggers deep reactions in everyone, leading to questionable communication. The one thing you can do is be accountable in the moment. That way a gaffe doesn't become a long-term problem.

Relationships

Your ongoing shift in what you value in yourself turns to a further evaluation of what you desire from your connections to others. This leads to the recognition that you really do take people at face value rather than actually examining how they conduct themselves. This is directly connected to your belief that the rest of the planet cares about what they do to the same degree you do.

Success and Money

This is not a good month to choose to partner with anyone on a project, an investment, or a business. The information you need is not available, either by design or by default, neither of which works for you. The bottom line is there isn't enough clarity from a practical point of view for you to take risks. If something looks too good to be true, it is.

Pitfalls and Potential Problems

You do so love to believe that everyone's intentions are as honorable as yours. Well, before you jump on that bandwagon, take a deep breath. This is likely to be a month when no one really knows what they are saying until it falls out of their mouth. And then they may be too embarrassed to take it back or they simply don't care whether it's true or not. So take any commitments, promises, insights, or behind-the-scenes information with a large lump of skepticism.

Rewarding Days

19, 20, 25, 26

Challenging Days

1, 2, 15, 16

Leo | November

Overall Theme

Things feels a little muddy and murky, gooey and yucky, to start the month off. Relax. It dissipates quickly, once you take matters into your own hands and set about rectifying any confusion resulting from the craziness that passed for communication in October. Be polite but firm, and you get the answers you want. That way you are ready to take advantage of the burst of energy that arrives full-blown in the middle of the month.

Relationships

Oh, what you wouldn't do for things to be as nice as they appear to be. It's tiring to always have to dig deep to find out what people are really made of, past all the subterfuge and the game playing. Why can't relationships just be straightforward? Good question. One that you are going to ask again and again this month, and one that will show you what you need to know, whether or not people actually answer it.

Success and Money

You can take a big step forward in manifesting a long-term goal you set for yourself earlier this year. At this point, it has more to do with personal development and redefining your purpose than with immediate accomplishment, but it has the potential to set in motion creating and building future success. Stick with it.

Pitfalls and Potential Problems

There's a definite possibility that you are running out of the capacity to be tolerant. The irony is that it's not because people are any more problematic than they ever have been. It's more a case that you can no longer hide from the fact that not everyone is motivated by the same need to be honorable and principled as you believe you are. Be kind to yourself.

Rewarding Days
15, 16, 24, 25

Challenging Days
4, 5, 17, 18

Leo | December

Overall Theme
You feel a big shift coming, one that will end the year with your hard-won optimism intact and your capacity to create a better future for yourself deeply strengthened. And you are right. What you know goes from a hope to a certainty. Trust your heart. Grow your enthusiasm. That way you can birth a new year with the best of who you are.

Relationships
The cynicism you harbored about other people finally gives way to a deeper understanding of how difficult relationships are for everyone. You realize that examining your relationships and how they work doesn't require a full-scale rejection of everyone you know just because they are different from you. In fact, you now see very clearly that you had your own set of demands that caused as many problems as other people's expectations of you did.

Success and Money
As 2020 comes to a close, this area of your life is still very much a work in progress. This is faintly disturbing until you realize the source of the uncertainty you feel is an infusion of creative energy that you need to truly change direction with confidence and determination. At that point, you relax and your brain explodes into a thousand new ideas.

Pitfalls and Potential Problems
If there's one thing obvious from your journey through 2020, it's this: You need to do a better job of taking care of yourself, of nourishing yourself, of truly making yourself number one in a healthy, life-affirming way. This year showed you just how often you set yourself aside to take care of the needs of others. After all, who is stronger than you? Probably no one. But that shouldn't translate to you ignoring yourself.

Rewarding Days
13, 14, 24, 25

Challenging Days
2, 3, 15, 16

Leo Action Table

These dates reflect the best—but not the only—times for success and ease in these activities, according to your Sun sign.

	JAN	FEB	MAR	APR	MAY	JUN	JUL	AUG	SEP	OCT	NOV	DEC
Move			8, 9							3, 4		
New romance					22, 23						22, 23	
Seek coaching/ counseling	13, 14						8, 9					
Ask for a raise		1, 2						3, 4				
Vacation				15, 16								17, 18
Get a loan						2, 3			1, 2			

Virgo

The Virgin
August 23 to September 22

♍

Element: Earth

Glyph: Greek symbol
for containment

Quality: Mutable

Anatomy: Abdomen,
gallbladder, intestines

Polarity: Yin/feminine

Colors: Taupe, gray, navy blue

Planetary Ruler: Mercury

Animals: Domesticated animals

Meditation: I can allow
time for myself

Myths/Legends: Demeter,
Astraea, Hygeia

Gemstone: Sapphire

House: Sixth

Power Stones: Peridot,
amazonite, rhodochrosite

Opposite Sign: Pisces

Flower: Pansy

Key Phrase: I analyze

Keyword: Discriminating

The Virgo Personality

Strengths, Talents, and the Creative Spark

Taking the less-than whole, less-than-perfect, and turning it into something strong and resilient underlies everything you do, even if you aren't completely aware of it. In a deeper part of your being, you are seeking to master the various pieces and parts of yourself and then bring them together to create a foundation that allows you to respond to life with grace and receptivity. At the heart of this intention is a powerfully practical inclination to understand how things function. It's not details that interest you as much as the role they play in bringing things to fruition. You simply cannot grasp how it is that you can get anything done if you are not oriented appropriately toward the process required to get there, which means knowing and comprehending all the moving parts. And because of that focus, that desire, you are unlikely to throw your hands up in despair and give up at the slightest sign that things are not going the way you planned. Of course, you hate any deviation from your strategy, but the only thing that could possibly make it worse is regressing into helplessness. That is totally unacceptable. Besides, you are already sorting out what to do about life going sideways while resisting the necessity to do so.

Whether you like the state of affairs is immaterial in the end. In your heart of hearts, you have no choice. You must adapt and find a way to achieve the goal you set for yourself. Otherwise, all will be for naught. Therefore, you simply don't know how to stop yourself from taking what is thrown at you and finding a way to make it work. It's the only way you know how to be. It's what sparks your creative drive. It's what exemplifies who you are.

Blind Spots and Blockages

Your motto? Be prepared. Even if it kills you. You are always taking stock just in case. But your blind spot is your refusal to acknowledge that twenty-five meetings a month of the What-If Club cannot, and I mean cannot, make life run smoothly. Life is messy. It has uneven edges, out-of-whack challenges. You name it. Life will throw it at you. And no matter how prepared you are or what you do, some of that gooey, icky, crappy stuff will stick. Of course, you don't like it. Not because you can't handle it but because it means you weren't right. And that's hard to swallow. But—and you know this deep down—every experience contains a purpose, a gift, an opportunity that leads to growth, expansion, and evolution. Where would the human race be if everything was predictable, if everything could be planned, if everything could be anticipated?

Of course, I can hear you sputtering and saying *but, but, but*... because it's hard not to deny your fundamental expectation. Why can't life follow the plan you make for it? How hard can that be? Quite, actually. And that is the source of most of your inner angst. Because life goes left when you planned for it to go right, leaving you trying to decide whether to have a temper tantrum or get on with it. Usually you pick the second option, because having a temper tantrum is neither useful nor helpful. Well, who said? It might help relieve all that internal pressure you put on yourself, because, when life does blow a hole in your carefully laid plans, you label yourself a failure. After all, you must have overlooked something. Well, maybe you did, maybe you didn't. So what. Will chastising yourself over and over again change what happened? Will the constant need to find perfection both in yourself and in life actually lead to a happier, healthier you? Rather than using your tremendous problem-solving skills to cover up perceived mistakes, use them to expand your mastery of your life. It's not the experience that matters as much as what you do with it. That's the alchemy at the heart of who you are.

Intimacy and Connection

How you long for connections that transcend all the common, everyday experiences of life. Ones that arrive and are perfect and don't require anything but your presence. Which is ironic since it actually runs counter to what you actually believe about life in its entirety. And you know what that is—everything in life requires effort. The truth is that what you seek in relationships is a deep reflection of your desire to relinquish the never-ending quest for that elusive feeling that you are whole and somehow not missing anything, even though you are pretty sure you are missing something essential. This is the ultimate source of your compulsion to keep doing and trying. After all, you are unable to persuade yourself that you are complete as you are. So, what's the next, obvious step? Find a someone or a bunch of someones who will see what you have trouble seeing: that you are a human being, not a human doing. This is a reality that you must find within so you can actually create the kind of intimacy where you feel totally at home, totally safe, totally loved, just by showing up, not by doing anything.

Values and Resources

This part of life can be a bit of a mixed bag for you because you set yourself up to do the impossible: meet the expectations you have of yourself at the same time that you meet everyone else's. This is bound to create conflict, internally and externally. First, because how you value yourself is determined by how you perform the tasks you set for yourself and whether that meets the tremendously high standards that are deeply ingrained in you. Second, because although you seek a pat on the back, you don't like anything that looks like criticism, which in your world is almost anything. The key to valuing yourself and embracing the wealth of inner resources you have is to let go of that deep fear you have that no matter what you do or how you do it, you have to keep proving yourself over and over again. Life doesn't have to be a case of what-have-you-done-for-me-lately. It really can be rites of passage that show you that who you are is as important as the very last thing you did.

Goals and Success

At the core of everything you do is one simple goal, one that completely defines success for you: Do the job and do it right. And there is no negotiating that. Not now, not ever, never. So you put everything you have into everything you do. This can be tremendously exhausting and not always the most satisfying, not because your underlying motivation is wrong but because you don't always know when to quit. There really are times when you need to understand that you can't turn a sow's ear into a silk purse, no matter what you do. It's okay to redefine your standards to incorporate the things life shows you, instead of continually trying to defy what is quite obviously true. Not everything can be fixed or resolved. Nor is that your job. All that is really required is what you already give—your best.

Virgo Keywords for 2020
Openness, willingness, self-esteem

The Year Ahead for Virgo

Although your relationship with Jupiter, Saturn, and Pluto offers the potential for significant accomplishments in 2020, you must remain alert to the possibility that you will, in fact, use the energetic support they offer (by being in the compatible earth sign of Capricorn) to get lost in an endless loop of figuring out what isn't working, why it isn't working, and how could that possibly be since you are sure you did everything possible to plan the proper outcome. This is your default position, the one thing you consistently do to undermine yourself because it's a sure-fire way to avoid making another mistake. After all, if something isn't working, you automatically conclude that you made a mistake rather than realizing that sometimes stuff just doesn't turn out. This, of course, is totally unpalatable to you, even though life consistently serves up this truth on a silver platter.

Well, these three planets are offering you the chance to short-circuit this standard approach long enough to see, grasp, and accept the talent you have for problem solving with a creativity that is both practical, workable, and astounding. This is you at your very core. This is the gift of being authentically yourself. What you seek always is to make things work, which is often misinterpreted—by you and everyone else—as perfection. This is a trap, something you know at your core but often ignore out of a fear of possibly being wrong. Well, in 2020 you will be offered a multitude of opportunities to confront this pattern and release yourself from its grip, but not before you try it on for size a few more times. Just don't be discouraged if this happens. It's not easy to transform old behaviors instantly. The key is to recognize that you are in familiar territory and then find a way to shift toward a healthier response. Turn to Uranus for help in doing this. After all, his sojourn in Taurus is designed to break up old, tired, and worn-out beliefs you are still convinced hold value for you, even though they fail to truly support you at your core. In other words, they don't work for you. Once you accept that, it is much easier to see clearly that not only do you need to move away from any compulsion to be perfect but it is imperative that you do so.

It's never easy to acknowledge just how much you get in your own way. But it is time to disrupt and dissolve anything that keeps you from the joy and satisfaction of just being. After all, doing comes naturally to you, being useful comes naturally to you, and reaching goals comes naturally to you. The one thing missing, the one thing being offered to you in 2020, is opening up to the truth that you don't need to continually prove yourself. You are fine just the way you are.

Jupiter

By the end of 2020, you may or may not consider Jupiter to be your best friend. It all depends on you and the choices you make and how you choose to respond to his input. Of course, Jupiter expands everything he touches. So if you are living in a swamp of self-criticism and fear of being wrong, he is going to amplify that until you feel like crawling out of your skin. On the other hand, if you are committed to growing a healthy appreciation for who you are and what you bring to the table, he will happily magnify that and you can tap into a well of creativity inside you that you didn't know existed. This has the potential to fuel your life in ways you cannot comprehend at this point. Embrace this and 2020 is going to be a tremendous launching pad for the future.

Saturn

The message Saturn has for you is simple and straightforward. Step up to the plate and claim what truly belongs to you. Recognize the hard work you put into your life and the experience you've gathered. Now use all that to put your creativity to the truest test of all: trusting that you can and will take a leap forward in removing any artificial limitations to your future success. Too often you diminish what you do, believing it to be less valuable than what others do. Ironically, you aren't always clear why you do that. It just seems to come naturally. The truth is that this is self-imposed. First, you judge yourself as inadequate when things don't work out. Second, you believe wholeheartedly that there is *always* room for improvement. Third, you think success is predicated on perfection and getting things right the first time. All this leaves you struggling to see your life in its true light. Remove the shackles. You have the key. Of course, you will come face to face with a number of false assumptions you have about yourself, and you will be overcome at times by fear. That is to be expected. But when you draw on what you have done with your life, you will see a more positive and more complete person. Have you been perfect? No. But you will finally see that has nothing to do with becoming all that you can be.

Uranus

Whatever it is that you think you believe, think again. And again. And again. It's ironic that you base your life on what is effective (at least in your outer life) without considering whether your principles, your ethics, and your standards also meet that criterion. Time to take stock of what you hold dear in this area of your life to see if it reflects where you are today. Part of the purpose of life experience is not only to mature in how you do what you do but also to grow in how you approach your life from a spiritual perspective. In order to do that, you must be willing to let go of anything that runs counter to who you are and wish to be. It really is a case of walking your talk, and when you find that those two things are incongruent, the only thing that is going to please you is to change either your talk or your walk. Or both. Well, Uranus is more than happy to assist you by shaking things up, both from deep within or in your outer world. Expect to find yourself in conflict with your own thoughts about what is appropriate as well as challenged by situations you find yourself in. Of course, it feels chaotic. That's a given. However, the end result is a renewed faith in yourself and a clearer understanding of how your life experience is actually useful in defining what you truly stand for.

Neptune

This is the energy you find most difficult to manage this year, because it's nebulous, immeasurable, and simply weird until you understand what Neptune's role really is. But first you need to know he isn't trying to make you or your life dissolve into a puddle on the floor. Hard to believe, but true. The best use you can make of his energy is to pay attention to those inexplicable feelings that just don't seem to fit any known situation or experience in your life, now or in the past. Move past the need to quantify them or try to make rational sense of them. Write them down. These are seeds for the future, not literally but figuratively. Note anything that stands out to you, whether it's an image or a symbol. These experiences may come to you while you are conscious, in meditation, or in a dream state. You need to open up to them because you need inspiration. Part of you is tired of the logical, the manageable, and the measurable. Inspiration really does want to float free. Neptune is the perfect conduit for that. He knows life is so much more than what you can wrap your mind around, and he is inviting you to see beyond what you know. So much awaits you there.

Pluto

It's true that Pluto has been pushing your buttons for almost twelve years now. However, this year brings a deeper crisis simply because it really is time to make up your mind. Are you going to completely commit to the transformation of who you are from the inside out? Are you going to be accountable for what you truly desire? Are you going to do what works for you? Are you going to give yourself permission to see yourself as the talented, skillful being you truly are? Are you going to finally honor the core of who you are and take the risks you have the capacity to take? Or are you going to stick to what you know, believing that it is better to hang on to the status quo rather than relinquish outdated, rigid, and self-deprecating ideas about you and your life? All in all, it's more than a little overwhelming and terrifying. Just remember that you have been laying the groundwork for this since Pluto entered Capricorn in 2008, slowly but surely. And you have no doubt changed since then, even though you may not be aware of it. So take some time and sit with the challenge that 2020 presents to you and you will find untapped resources that will carry you through this year with grace and courage.

How Will This Year's Eclipses Affect You?

Eclipses signal intense periods that highlight major growth opportunities for us in the process of creating our lives. They are linked to the lunar phases—specifically the New and the Full Moon—and involve the relationship between the Sun, the Moon, and the Earth. A Solar Eclipse is a magnified New Moon, while a Lunar Eclipse is a magnified Full Moon. Eclipses unfold in cycles involving all twelve signs of the zodiac, and they occur in pairs, usually about two weeks apart.

This year there are six eclipses: two Solar Eclipses (one in Cancer and one in Sagittarius) and four Lunar Eclipses (one in Cancer, one in Sagittarius, one in Capricorn, and one in Gemini). This mixed bag of energies signals a shift from last year's focus on redefining nurturing versus babysitting, obligation versus accountability, family versus career, time for self versus taking care of business, and feelings versus rational thought. Three of this year's eclipses (the Lunar Eclipse on January 10 and the Solar Eclipse on June 21, both in Cancer, as well as the Lunar Eclipse on July 5 in Capricorn) complete this cycle, while the new eclipse cycle calls on us to understand that there is no wisdom in living in an ivory tower, stuck in our belief that there is only one way to live life while cut off from that very life. Instead, we need to get down to the streets and actually experience our environment, talk to people, create a dialogue, and embrace diversity. Only then can we create a world that truly embodies freedom and opportunity. Three eclipses (the Lunar Eclipse on June 5 in Sagittarius, the Lunar Eclipse on November 30 in Gemini, and the Solar Eclipse on December 14 in Sagittarius) begin this process.

The first eclipse of 2020 takes place on January 10, and it's a Lunar Eclipse in Cancer, inviting you to finally stop ignoring the hopes and wishes you keep so carefully hidden behind all the hard work you believe needs to be done before you earn the right to follow your bliss. In fact, you are so used to taking care of business that you aren't always sure exactly what that is. Well, this eclipse and the solar one in June are telling you to recognize that you have the proper foundation on which to build whatever your heart desires. Your immediate task is to realize that you have paid your dues. That is what the eclipse cycle of the last eighteen months has been all about: clearing away limitations you place on yourself so you can see that you are more than ready to make your true desires your number-one priority. That way you can set aside the belief—or is that the fear?—that you still haven't done quite enough to move beyond obligation to the freedom to choose. Well, you have. And the opportunities symbolized by the remaining eclipses of 2020 open up the chance to take some truly exciting risks.

To facilitate this reality, it's time to make a list of your skills. All of them. Even the ones that seem insignificant. This has the potential to blow your circuits—in an extremely positive way—because you aren't one to take time to celebrate your accomplishments, much less blow your own horn. But acknowledging your capabilities is totally necessary if you are to do more than carry on. Your authentic self is asking you to move out of the self-imposed shadows and into the light.

Virgo | January

Overall Theme

At times, it feels like there is no relief in sight from the intensity pushing you to break out of old patterns so you can live a life free from unrealistic expectations while at the same time hanging on to the structures you built. The best thing you can do is focus on finding a way to reconcile what appears to be two different agendas. The key is to meld the two by recognizing that you don't have to cut yourself off from the past, but just release the stale and tired.

Relationships

Because you feel like you are walking a tightrope, you aren't really in the mood to navigate anyone else's world but your own. The underlying message is it's time to recognize that you don't always have to do the giving in relationships. It's okay to receive. So refrain from avoiding the people in your life. Instead, accept that you need support and ask for it.

Success and Money

This is not the month to test your security in either of these areas, simply because the shift taking place inside you makes it difficult to discern what is best for you. Maintain the status quo, even if that seems impossible. As much as you want to transform many aspects of your life, you need stability upon which to do that. And this part of your life supplies that.

Pitfalls and Potential Problems

It is extremely difficult for you not to engage in analysis paralysis. You know, where everything goes round and round in your head without relief and without any obvious solution. You need to be present with your life, which means staying in your body and not overtaxing your rational mind. That way, space is created, allowing you to see the real potential inherent in the upheaval you are experiencing.

Rewarding Days

4, 5, 17, 18

Challenging Days

2, 3, 22, 23

Virgo | February

Overall Theme

The pressure of last month disappears so quickly that you wonder what is real. Relax. You deserve to be calm and comfortable. Plus, you really have no energy to worry, which, of course, is unusual for you. Again, enjoy. You are processing in spaces and places in your consciousness that are immune to the logical mind.

Relationships

You are so, so mellow that you barely notice what other people are doing, never mind worrying about their choices, their attitudes, or their demands. This is likely to knock people sideways because they wonder what happened to you, especially since you seem uninterested in explaining yourself. After all, what is there to explain? You are in a metamorphosis.

Success and Money

Expect to experience unusual and out-of-the-box insights about your work, your career, and your purpose. They are definitely not ready for prime time, but they are inspiring and uplifting. It really is time to let yourself dream and create and visualize, even when what comes to you seems ridiculous and/or sublime. It's time to play with possibilities.

Pitfalls and Potential Problems

This month's energy may take you so far out of your comfort zone that at some point you are likely to panic. After all, going with the flow is not usually in your wheel house. How could it be? You are hardwired to always be making an effort. Well, you are. You are unwinding, lightening up, releasing an old way of life, and making space for being, not just doing.

Rewarding Days

9, 10, 23, 24

Challenging Days

16, 17, 25, 26

Virgo | March

Overall Theme

The crisis of rebirth is not over, in spite of your deepest hopes. It's time to recognize that the purpose of this ongoing, internal push to change is about one thing and one thing only: removing any obstacles to claiming and expressing your innate creativity in ways that work for you. It is not about proving you wrong or fixing any mistakes you think you made.

Relationships

You find yourself in a curious space, one minute detached and the next overwhelmed by all the unspoken emotional stuff you feel in others. Unclear what to do about living between two extremes, you try to make sense of them both, instead of recognizing that you are experiencing two different sides of yourself simultaneously. Be open to what this shows you about yourself rather than what it might say about others.

Success and Money

It's a good month to review your priorities, not in terms of what's been accomplished but in terms of whether they reflect what you value in your life right now. This leads to some startling revelations about how much you are moving outside the space you thought you were supposed to occupy. You truly want to explore what you can accomplish once you leave behind the need for comfort and predictability.

Pitfalls and Potential Problems

There's no doubt that you feel like you are living on top of a crumbling foundation. After all, life is pretty unsettling and you aren't certain you won't end up like Humpty Dumpty. Acknowledge your fear, but don't let it take up all the space in your life. You are going to emerge from this phase of your life renewed, regenerated, and full of hope. In the meantime, find something—a piece of art, a crystal, a symbol, a photo, or a quote, for example—to act as a sign of that shift.

Rewarding Days

12, 13, 21, 22

Challenging Days

10, 11, 24, 25

Virgo | April

Overall Theme

You experience a sudden release of burdens you didn't even know you had, and what's more, you decide not to try to identify them or analyze them. Which you find strange and yet liberating. Then it dawns on you how much you are changing, because the only thing that matters right now is that you feel light and bright and free. The gunk is gone. In its place is a space full of potential.

Relationships

You really want to have a party. To celebrate the new you and all the passion for life running around in every part of you. To thank those closest to you for their support. And to just have fun. It's been quite a while since you felt like having fun, and you don't want to let this moment pass. So do it. You'll find that everyone you know needs a party as much as you do.

Success and Money

It really is time to invest in yourself. The first step is taking seriously any thoughts, ideas, inspirations, or dreams that keep surfacing for your consideration. The second is to pay attention to anyone who talks openly about your talents and your potential. This is the month to begin planting seeds for a new and exciting future. You don't need to know the outcome. What you need is to trust your intuition.

Pitfalls and Potential Problems

Not only did you survive the most intense transformation of your life, but you emerged stronger and more aware of your authentic self. Of course, you think that you must immediately put all that to work, as if you didn't already put in a considerable amount of effort to birth this new you. Schedule a break or a vacation. You earned it.

Rewarding Days

8, 9, 23, 24

Challenging Days

13, 14, 27, 28

Virgo | May

Overall Theme

A new pathway for growth opens up early in the month, offering you the chance to take all your newfound confidence and creativity and put it to use carving out the next steps in your life. You feel inspired and ready to redefine your purpose so it reflects the hopes and dreams you found buried underneath your fears and your work ethic.

Relationships

Again, you feel like taking a break from the human race, but not because you are irritated or annoyed by people. Right now, you are so excited about what you want to do with your life that you are completely wrapped up in that. You know you aren't ignoring anyone, but do they know that? Be aware that you need to come up for air, take a time out, and reacquaint yourself with the rest of the world.

Success and Money

New avenues to create more abundance in both these areas begin opening up, so much so that you may find yourself overwhelmed. Some of these avenues come from others, and some come from inside you. Of course, you can't follow them all, and not all of them are suitable. Take a deep breath. Don't make any hasty decisions. Let things percolate and the appropriate steps will become obvious.

Pitfalls and Potential Problems

No sooner do you feel that things are about to settle down than the call to make more change presents itself. Part of you is convinced that you simply don't have the juice to engage in more change, while the rest of you welcomes it. Honor yourself and all your feelings and refrain from seeing one response as the only appropriate one.

Rewarding Days

2, 3, 22, 23

Challenging Days

4, 5, 25, 26

Virgo | June

Overall Theme

This is an eventful month full of optimism and enthusiasm. Immerse yourself in it, and refrain from looking over your shoulder to see if there's a price you have to pay for the *joie de vivre* streaming through your body and your consciousness. It's a sign that you tackled and transformed ingrained limitations and now you are tasting the joy of liberation. You earned it.

Relationships

You aren't really sure why you feel this part of your life is stagnant until you realize that you have fallen into some unhealthy habits in the way you connect to others. Your immediate response is to resist this awareness. Remove the need to blame yourself or anyone else. That way you can begin a process of reevaluating what you think a healthy relationship is and set out to do what it takes to implement the necessary changes.

Success and Money

Consider this a playground as you begin sorting and sifting through all the possibilities that bombarded you last month. After all, you know how much you like to think and analyze and think some more. The difference now is to do a little less analyzing and a lot more intuiting about potential outcomes. It's called following your instincts, something you tend to ignore in favor of endless circles of thinking.

Pitfalls and Potential Problems

You aren't always sure what to do when duty and obligation are replaced by freedom and openness, probably because it tends to short-circuit all those defense mechanisms you developed to protect you from doing anything wrong. Well, you freed yourself from that trap and the only consequence is the opportunity to be fully engaged in your own life instead of always hedging your bets, just in case.

Rewarding Days

16, 17, 26, 27

Challenging Days

4, 5, 11, 12

Virgo | July

Overall Theme

Maintain your equilibrium and don't drag yourself down. Otherwise, the return of some old fears and feelings of inadequacy threaten to knock you off balance because you thought they were gone forever. Therein lies the problem. Old habits and old perceptions are likely to rattle around inside you. It's your nature. The key is what you choose to do about them, not whether they still exist.

Relationships

You are likely to feel more than a bit anxious about relationships of all kinds. The inventory you started last month revealed a lot of the difficulties you experience with others as well as their sources. The one thing that stood out to you most strongly is how often you assume you are the one at fault when problems arise. And now you are unclear exactly what to do about that. Step one is to spend time with someone you trust and feel safe with. In other words, take care of yourself first.

Success and Money

Unfinished business shows up out of the blue, leaving you wondering what you are supposed to do. First, this isn't your problem, although someone wants you to believe it's your responsibility to take care of what needs to be done. Be clear. You don't need to do anything. You are not the one who failed to do their job. And make sure you let those in charge know what's happening.

Pitfalls and Potential Problems

It's not always easy for you to stand up for yourself because you often think it's easier to just take care of things than it is to say no, whether it's to others or to yourself. If you are to navigate some very choppy waters this month, you need to be able to do what works for you with a clear conscience and a clear set of boundaries. You are tired of everyone counting on you when you can't count on yourself.

Rewarding Days

13, 14, 23, 24

Challenging Days

4, 5, 25, 26

Virgo | August

Overall Theme

Patience is not your middle name. Nor is tolerance. Last month seems to have used up any reserves you still had of either one. So the best thing to do is to keep a low profile, take care of yourself, and be kind to yourself. Even the strongest, most resilient people find themselves up against a wall, with the feeling there is nowhere to go. When you get there—and you will—take a timeout. You deserve it. In fact, take a vacation.

Relationships

You continue on your path to creating more satisfying relationships by actually opening up about how challenging life has been for you lately. Much to your amazement, no one is surprised by your true confessions. This warms your heart and you realize you are not the only person on the planet who is willing to step up and help those around them. Your emotional battery begins to recharge.

Success and Money

A vague sense of dissatisfaction permeates much of your work life, which of course leads you to a round of What's Wrong with My Life? Nothing, really. What you are feeling is your imagination stirring up the need for you to leave behind old, outdated ideas of what is best for you. Unfulfilled goals are not a sign of failure. Rather, they are just things you didn't need to do.

Pitfalls and Potential Problems

When you are cranky, you immediately find fault with yourself. After all, that's coloring outside the lines of being perfect. The truth is no single human could achieve what you expect of yourself, and somewhere deep inside you know that. So when you are irritable, grouchy and just plain cantankerous this month, it's the wiser part of you letting you know you are tired of backing yourself into that particular corner.

Rewarding Days

10, 11, 23, 24

Challenging Days

7, 8, 27, 28

Virgo | September

Overall Theme

Internally it feels like somehow the universe opened up inside you and you can get on your own personal spaceship and head for parts unknown. This is both scary and invigorating. How do you harness all that energy in a practical, purposeful way? That will reveal itself. For now, you need to revel in how fantastic it is that all your hard work brought you to this space and place.

Relationships

As you spend more time celebrating yourself, the more hanging out with people feels like a joy and not a chore. And you discover that being present for yourself actually improves your connection with everyone in your world, which is definitely out of sync with your accepted model of good relationships whose focus is on making other people happy. However, you now know that being the master of your own happiness leads to true intimacy.

Success and Money

There's a huge focus on your financial resources this month, and it's triggered by an unexpected expense. Not that you don't have the resources to take care of it on a practical level. It's more the emotional reaction it elicits. You begin to hyperventilate and worry. Take a deep breath, review your financial affairs, and refrain from making any changes based on a knee-jerk response.

Pitfalls and Potential Problems

There's a growing sense that the future that awaits you promises a level of satisfaction that you long for but don't believe is possible. That's because you are convinced that you must hold something back, just in case disaster strikes. It's one thing to be prepared. It's another to get in your own way, to undermine yourself in the name of security, and to not trust yourself.

Rewarding Days

1, 2, 19, 20

Challenging Days

4, 5, 16, 17

Virgo | October

Overall Theme

There's one thing and one thing only at the top of your list of priorities: Straight answers. Complete answers. Meaningful answers. It's like you stepped into a world where no one speaks your language. Or they don't have a clue. Or they enjoy speaking in riddles. Or they are purposefully misleading you. None of these is acceptable to you. The only solution, as irritating as it is, is to keep asking for clarity. You will be happy you did.

Relationships

Expect some stunning revelations from those closest to you in the middle of some rather mundane conversations. Secrets of all shapes and sizes are revealed, leaving you a little speechless and unsure what you are supposed to do. The answer is simple: just listen. That's all that's required. No one is seeking anything from you. Not absolution, not approval, not input.

Success and Money

Your self-worth gets a huge boost when you are singled out and applauded for all that you contributed to the success of your company. In particular, a project you worked on heart and soul brings unexpected rewards. This is the beginning of a major shift in both your perception about the level of accomplishment you can achieve and in your boss's.

Pitfalls and Potential Problems

The only way to get through much of this month's communication dilemma is not to take it personally. What you are experiencing isn't really new. What is new is how much you are focused on being clearer about who you are and where you are coming from. This, in turn, makes you less willing to deal with obfuscation, obliviousness, and smokescreens. Just stay grounded and detached.

Rewarding Days

3, 4, 17, 18

Challenging Days

13, 14, 28, 29

Virgo | November

Overall Theme

Your attention is firmly fixed on moving forward with plans you made earlier this year. The only thing you need before you hit the launch button is a final review of the steps you outlined. You certainly don't want to overlook anything. Just don't get in a never-ending loop of oversight and miss a very potent opportunity toward the end of the month to get things off the ground.

Relationships

As you proceed with putting the above plan into motion, seek outside input from someone you trust. It's not that your plan is flawed in any way. What you are embarking on is outside your comfort zone and you need a little help settling down as you bounce back and forth between overwhelming excitement and profound dread. Sharing your dream and your process not only relieves all that but actually makes things more real and less like a fantasy.

Success and Money

It may be a challenge to stay focused on the more mundane aspects of your career right now because you are getting ready to initiate your new project. However, that's not the biggest concern. Stick to your intention to begin this endeavor solo. You need to put your stamp on it before you take anyone else on board, whether as a partner or as an investor.

Pitfalls and Potential Problems

The seeds you sow this month go deeper than the external accomplishments you are determined to make. They reflect the deep change you are making in how you see yourself in the world. So take time to celebrate the creative impulse within you that led to this. That's as important right now as the work you put into it. It's what will fuel you in the long term.

Rewarding Days

13, 14, 22, 23

Challenging Days

5, 6, 24, 25

Virgo | December

Overall Theme

Life is busy from sunup to sundown, and you are worried you are going to run out of gas. Your new project is taking off much faster than you anticipated, a new opportunity comes out of nowhere in your day job, and you are trying to find time to book a vacation. And then there's the regular day-to-day stuff. Just know that not only can you handle all this, but you will master anything that pops up.

Relationships

After a year in which your social life didn't see much action, you are suddenly on everybody's guest list. You are flattered but not sure this is the best use of your time right now. Well, you don't need to connect with anybody and everybody, but you do need to spend some time with the people who matter the most to you. Not because they feel neglected but because you are missing them.

Success and Money

The year ends with a level of confidence you didn't think possible when it began. You really do feel on top of the world, and it's about time. You might be working harder than ever, but it's exhilarating because you know you are the creative force behind it all. Get ready for what comes next. It will be fantastic.

Pitfalls and Potential Problems

The outcome of this year can be summed up in one sentence: You have inspired yourself. It's true. No longer do you need to look outside yourself to find your value, to acknowledge your strengths, or to know what path to choose. You took yourself to all sorts of uncomfortable spaces inside yourself and transmuted what you found there into a clearer, more defined, more positive picture of yourself. That is success. Just don't rain on your own parade, no matter how much you are tempted.

Rewarding Days

6, 7, 24, 25

Challenging Days

2, 3, 15, 16

Virgo Action Table

These dates reflect the best—but not the only—times for success and ease in these activities, according to your Sun sign.

	JAN	FEB	MAR	APR	MAY	JUN	JUL	AUG	SEP	OCT	NOV	DEC
Move						11, 12			1, 2			
New romance	13, 14						9, 10					
Seek coaching/counseling		10, 11						3, 4				
Ask for a raise					2, 3							
Vacation			12, 13								27, 28	7, 8
Get a loan				6, 7						12, 13		

Libra

The Scales
September 23 to October 22

Element: Air

Quality: Cardinal

Polarity: Yang/masculine

Planetary Ruler: Venus

Meditation: I balance
conflicting desires

Gemstone: Opal

Power Stones: Tourmaline,
kunzite, blue lace agate

Key Phrase: I balance

Glyph: Scales of justice,
setting sun

Anatomy: Kidneys, lower back,
appendix

Colors: Blue, pink

Animals: Brightly plumed birds

Myths/Legends: Venus,
Cinderella, Hera

House: Seventh

Opposite Sign: Aries

Flower: Rose

Keyword: Harmony

The Libra Personality

Strengths, Talents, and the Creative Spark

You simply cannot imagine a world in which people don't reach out for each other, don't care about each other, and don't feel that the most valuable thing you can do is create more peace and harmony. So yes, you are an idealist. One who believes the following: Everyone has something valuable to contribute. Everyone has a story worth telling. And everyone is essentially good and kind and ready to do what is best. All this adds up to a powerful gift for being open, welcoming, and inclusive. It just would never occur to you to shut anyone out. Not just because it's rude to ignore or snub people, but because you know that what other people have to share is life-affirming, inspiring, and/or enlightening. It's so obvious to you. Being open and present for others offers the kind of perspective you simply can't get when looking at life from only one point of view—your own. Somewhere in your DNA, you understand just how truly limiting that is. So out you go into the big, wide world, seeking connection and experience and truth. Sounds a little naïve and perhaps unrealistic to others, but it really is how you operate.

You simply can't and don't approach life or people from a place of doubt and distrust. That feels unfair and unkind to you. How can you build a better world if you don't give everyone a chance? You simply don't know to be anything but willing to welcome anyone and everyone into your life, because it's what lights the creative spark inside you. That's why you love meeting people. You just never know what will happen. And that really excites you because you know there's an indescribable alchemy that takes place, no matter how long that person is in your life. Deep down, you are aware that the change and growth you are likely to experience in your life is going to be initiated through your encounters with others. After all, you did not come to planet Earth to be a hermit. Where's the fun in that?

Blind Spots and Blockages

While you were busy relating to the known world, did you notice if you had a relationship with yourself? Yes, you are a person too. One worthy of time and attention, respect and love, consideration and appreciation, the very things you give others in abundance. Because, after all, you are the cheerleader of the zodiac—someone who is gifted not only at meeting others but at mirroring back to them all the wonderful things about them. However, you often forget to include yourself in the equation of your own life. Why? Because your attention is always focused outside yourself, partly because you are seeking to know yourself through other people and partly because you enjoy doing things to enhance the lives of others. This often leads you to work hard to take care of everyone else, assuming that they will return the favor one day. And when they don't, you are shocked. You immediately decide you must have overlooked some important detail or sentiment or cue, so you redouble your efforts, convinced this will do the trick and you will get the appreciation you seek. If that doesn't work—and quite often it doesn't—you get brittle and just a wee bit nasty, all the while acting as though everything is fine.

Time for a radical solution: get to know yourself. That means acknowledging yourself. You really don't need anyone else to tell you who are you. It's all there in the way you live your life. Turn your attention away from trying to please the entire world and toward pleasing yourself. You are the most important person in your life. No one else. After all, it's your life you are living.

Intimacy and Connection

There's no doubt that you have a powerful, innate gift for attracting people into your life. They instinctively feel your generosity of spirit, your willingness to accept them, and your genuine interest in who they are, all the right ingredients for initiating connection—provided by you. Unfortunately, you are not always paying attention to whether they are able to offer you the same things. Which leads to two things: you projecting your qualities onto them and you seeking their approval again and again when you don't get the same warm, kind, and caring response you give so freely. This definitely short-circuits any real intimacy, because that requires vulnerability on both sides, acceptance on both sides, and awareness on both sides.

The purpose of intimacy is not to define someone but to be open to them, to loving them as they are. Loving someone is not a project, or at least it shouldn't be. This is a trap you often find yourself in. No matter what you do, you can only give your 100 percent. It's up to the other person to give their 100 percent, and if they don't, nothing you say or do can change that. Just make sure you pat yourself on the back for giving all you could.

Values and Resources

You arrived on the planet with one singular purpose: to collaborate. In your heart of hearts, you know that growing and flourishing depends on how we relate to one another and ultimately how we build connections, partnerships, and community. To do that, we need to be willing to share thoughts and ideas so that a common vision and a sense of togetherness based on respect, not sameness, can emerge. Which is why your greatest joy is building bridges, building understanding, and building consensus. You truly believe that if everyone is prepared to really listen to each other, anything is possible. All that is required is an essential commitment to fairness, courtesy, and the ability to see another's point of view—all the things that come naturally to you and that you value highly.

Goals and Success

It's not always easy for you to define your goals, much less your idea of success, without seeking input from others. You really are a person who needs to talk things out. First, so you can actually get some perspective, and second, so you can test-drive it to see if what you intend to do is actually realistic. Too often, the people in your world believe that you are asking them to tell you what you should do, which is rarely your intention. However, if you run into any serious disapproval, you can choose to abandon your plans, thereby abandoning yourself. Just know that feedback from others is just that. The final decision is yours. When you honor your vision, everything you do feels more satisfying and, ultimately, successful, because you picked it.

Libra Keywords for 2020
Optimism, tenacity, self-esteem

The Year Ahead for Libra

There is so much going on right now that most of the time you find yourself unable to figure out exactly what course of action to take. One minute, you're grappling with deep, unresolved emotions that spring unexpectedly from some crevice in your consciousness where you stored them, and the next, you are clearly uncertain about what path to take. Or what matters to you most. Or who actually supports the authentic you. In short, you are dealing with issues of identity, meaning, relationships, and values, which is likely to make you feel like your entire life is under scrutiny—or is that under attack? The key here is to be gentle with yourself at the same time that you commit to standing firm and examining the truth of where you have been, what that means to you, and how you can use the insights you find to finish a powerful overhaul of your life from the inside out—something you began almost twelve years ago.

There is likely to be a power struggle between the urge to leave things as they are and the overwhelming desire to break free from any and all burdens, expectations, and obligations you sense are holding you down. Of course, there's a strong temptation to maintain the status quo, but you need to remember that you cannot turn back time. Trying to revert to old patterns because they feel safe and dependable is not an option if you are now aware that they are toxic. You must find a constructive way forward, using the wisdom you have accrued, to illuminate what is truly at your core and use that to build the kind of emotional structure that supports you rather than keeps you tied to empty, harmful, or discouraging beliefs and experiences. Here's where it can get a little dicey. You need to be mindful not to get caught up in an inner game of projection. It doesn't matter where this unsupportive, limiting material originated. You accepted it and believed it, which means you are the only one who can heal it and resolve it. Acknowledge the source at the same time that you put yourself in charge of changing the dynamic of how you see yourself and what your purpose in life is.

Part of this process finds you at odds with others throughout much of the year. This will not be comfortable, but it will push you to finally include yourself in your own life in healthier, more satisfying ways as well as give you the fuel to define clearer, less murky boundaries with the world at large. Resist any and all compulsions to feel guilty. It's true that others may not be happy about your transformation from doormat to fully present human. That's their problem, not yours. The truth is this shift is not going to change the authentic you. It's just going to bring it into the light.

Jupiter

Normally you find yourself in sync with Jupiter's energy. How could any self-respecting Libra not resonate with a planet whose message is one of optimism, hope, and enthusiasm? But this year poses a challenge for you. It seems that every time you turn around, Jupiter is luring you into a close-up with the less attractive parts of you, the parts that demand that you be in alignment with others at all costs. It's always a challenge for you to determine whether what you're doing reflects who you are and what you desire or whether you are responding to the need to keep others happy. The latter then leads to conformity and resentment, neither of which are high on your list of desirable responses, much less acceptable aspects of you. Aren't you always sunshine and light? No. Nor is anyone else, for that matter. Jupiter is asking you to acknowledge your current inner truth. You are between a rock and a hard place, trying to maintain your optimism in the face of an overwhelming amount of anger and frustration. The key is to know that you don't have to choose one over the other. Your optimism will not die just because you stop avoiding the length and breadth of all that you feel. In fact, there will be more space for your optimism, your heart, and your light once you free yourself from the prison of self-denial.

Saturn

You may not always like it, but Saturn is without question the voice of reality. His message is always clear: See things as they actually are, not the way you wish they were. He certainly doesn't believe in beating around the bush, painting the kind of pretty pictures that lead to disaster, or pretending that things are better than they are. So in 2020, the two of you are going to find your relationship to be a challenge. But before you decide that that equals a mess, take a deep breath and see that recognizing where you're at in your life is necessary if you are to use Saturn's gravitas in a way that helps you build an inner foundation based on what is real. So no turning away from the unpleasant or the difficult. That way, you will discover, much to your surprise, just how much energy it takes to always hide from reality if it doesn't come all wrapped up in something pretty. This is followed by another shocking revelation. Ignoring the parts of life that you don't like, that are painful, and that are diminishing robs you of being all that you can be and keeps you stuck in a picture of life that is often one-dimensional. Knowing and accepting what is real allows you to fly higher and further. So even though there are going to be many times in 2020 when you wish Saturn would find another galaxy to live in, you will take the dose of reality (because it will feel like you are being forced to do this) he serves up and liberate yourself in ways you didn't think possible. Because Saturn's gift and message are simple: Be accountable and you are free.

Uranus

As if you didn't already have enough to contend with, now you have Uranus knocking about in the deeper recesses of your consciousness, stirring up your psyche and taking you to depths you didn't know you had. The purpose of all this mucking about—because it definitely feels a little icky and a little weird—is to urge you to make use of the insight that comes from being open to exploring passion, intensity, darkness, death, and, most important, rebirth in all its forms—all the things that are normally considered taboo yet promise to lead you not just to a deeper connection to your life but to a deeper connection to others. Of course, this requires that you let go of your fear of what lies beneath the exterior of life and accept that life has many faces, some of which are ugly and frightening. The truth is that you will not turn to stone if you look beyond the obvious. Instead, you will find resources you didn't know you had: a strength, a determination, and a capacity for perseverance, all of which have always been there. Uranus is just jumping up and down in this part of your life so you can consciously make use of them. Step one is seeing what you are intuitively drawn to exploring as an avenue for making this transition. Whether it's art, gardening, oracle cards, stones and crystals, writing, creating an altar, or some other interest, something will certainly call to you. All you need to do is pay attention.

Neptune

The need for clarity is obviously paramount in 2020, with Jupiter, Saturn, and Pluto in Capricorn. However, Neptune is here to tell you that the clarity you seek must be based in a willingness to find a new vision for your life. The irony is that the harder you try to find that vision, the more elusive it is. That's because Neptune's energy is anything but structured. It is wispy, ethereal, airy, and often just out of reach. At least, until the time is right—sometime in 2020. Until then, you are haunted by the feeling that you really don't know what you are doing. Nothing seems to come to fruition in a way that even remotely resembles what you had in mind. This is not a sign that you are failing. Rather, it's a message from Neptune that you are seeking something beyond where you are right now. And the only way you can hear that message is to dissolve the predictable elements of your life that no longer work. Refrain from panic. Take stock of what is dissolving and ask yourself whether you are really sad to see those elements disappear. Surround yourself with images and symbols that are meaningful to you. Do a vision board. Pay attention to your dreams, daytime and nighttime. That way, you honor and nurture Neptune and yourself. And you will be ready to take the vision when it reveals itself and run with it.

Pluto

You are likely to feel that it's time to pay the piper, even if you aren't sure exactly what that really means. And you aren't wrong. It just doesn't need to be as ominous or overwhelming as it sounds. It's true that Pluto has been pushing you since 2008 to make what you now see as a life-altering transformation. However, when he first entered Capricorn, his energy felt more like a small whisper in your ear, largely because you really weren't ready to connect to the intensity he symbolizes. As the two of you got better acquainted, you were mesmerized by the invitation he offered to uncover what is the true source of who you are. But the more you opened yourself up and explored what his invitation really required, the more overwhelmed you became.

Pluto isn't warm or fuzzy, pleasant or polite. He's unrelenting and fierce, intense and purifying. And he's definitely committed to revealing anything ugly and rotting—not at all attractive in your world. However, his job is simple: to purge; to eliminate what may be threatening you from within. Definitely a sobering thought. So you began an interesting dance of "Do I or don't I?" Back and forth and back and forth. To transform or not to transform? Well, the answer will begin to reveal itself when Pluto and Saturn meet face to face on January 12 and set the tone for what you do to rebirth yourself going forward. As difficult as it is to embrace, pieces and parts of how you see yourself have outlived their purpose. Time to let them go so you have space to reveal who you are becoming.

How Will This Year's Eclipses Affect You?

Eclipses signal intense periods that highlight major growth opportunities for us in the process of creating our lives. They are linked to the lunar phases—specifically the New and the Full Moon—and involve the relationship between the Sun, the Moon, and the Earth. A Solar Eclipse is a magnified New Moon, while a Lunar Eclipse is a magnified Full Moon. Eclipses unfold in cycles involving all twelve signs of the zodiac, and they occur in pairs, usually about two weeks apart.

This year there are six eclipses: two Solar Eclipses (one in Cancer and one in Sagittarius) and four Lunar Eclipses (one in Cancer, one in Sagittarius, one in Capricorn, and one in Gemini). This mixed bag of energies signals a shift from last year's focus on redefining nurturing versus babysitting, obligation versus accountability, family versus career, time for self versus taking care of business, and feelings versus rational thought. Three of this year's eclipses (the Lunar Eclipse on January 10 and the Solar Eclipse on June 21, both in Cancer, as well as the Lunar Eclipse on July 5 in Capricorn) complete this cycle, while the new eclipse cycle calls on us to understand that there is no wisdom in living in an ivory tower, stuck in our belief that there is only one way to live life while cut off from that very life. Instead, we need to get down to the streets and actually experience our environment, talk to people, create a dialogue, and embrace diversity. Only then can we create a world that truly embodies freedom and opportunity. Three eclipses (the Lunar Eclipse on June 5 in Sagittarius, the Lunar Eclipse on November 30 in Gemini, and the Solar Eclipse on December 14 in Sagittarius) begin this process.

The first eclipse of 2020 takes place on January 10, and it's a Lunar Eclipse in Cancer, highlighting the ongoing desire you have to be sure that what you are doing with your life actually nurtures you and fulfills a deeper sense of purpose. No longer do you feel satisfied with just getting the job done, especially if the sole objective is to meet the expectations of others. So you push yourself to step outside your comfort zone, turning your innate people skills and your capacity to build consensus toward becoming a leader. Ironically, you discover that many already consider you a leader. Why? Because of who you are and how you act. Once that realization sets in and you see all that you have to offer, you are ready to hit the launch button. The remainder of the year's eclipses give you opportunity after opportunity to find a new avenue to both express and further develop your gift for leadership. The key is knowing that the very parts of you that make you an excellent team player are the same parts that can be used to guide and mentor and include others. After all, those are the qualities of a true leader.

Libra | January

Overall Theme

Running away is futile. Avoiding the internal reckoning burbling below the surface is futile. The time has come. Are you going to do more than pay lip service to letting go of what is toxic and unfulfilling in your life and actually let go? There's no doubt that you are overwhelmed, but you have the strength and the awareness to rebirth yourself. Just dust off your innate optimism. Face the fear that seems insurmountable (it's not), and the rewards will blow your mind.

Relationships

Well, as you dig in to overhaul the things in your life dragging you down or keeping you stuck, expect some pushback from people who depend on you to stay the same. How will they do it? By showing up in a flood of tears with a plethora of problems that only you can solve. Remember this: The problems are not yours, so you cannot solve them. You can listen and be supportive. But that's all.

Success and Money

It no doubt feels like you are never going to find the answer to the conundrum facing you in this part of your life: Do you stick with what you know or take a risk? Probably a bit of both. Build on the skills you have developed and use them to venture into new territory. It's time to trust yourself rather than the structures you are imbedded in. Security truly comes from within.

Pitfalls and Potential Problems

Accept that you are in a transitional phase where nothing is 100 percent clear. Nor is it 100 percent foggy. That applies to both your internal and your external reality, so don't try to force anything or give up anything or see yourself as a victim. This is life unfolding, not a test that you are going to fail. There are some powerful things emerging from deep within that promise to show you the length and breadth of your authentic self.

Rewarding Days

2, 3, 24, 25

Challenging Days

11, 12, 22, 23

Libra | February

Overall Theme

The desire to have fun and to play sparks a huge creative outpouring, one that shows you just how vibrant and alive your world, your life, and you can be. It's a powerful sign that all the effort you put into transforming old, rigid, and restrictive beliefs, patterns, habits, and perceptions is opening up a treasure trove of dreams you hid from yourself. Party on!

Relationships

You still like people. Yes, you do. Except for the following: whiners, drama kings or queens, and perpetual victims. Something truly has shifted inside you, allowing you to observe anyone who crosses your path with a never-before-experienced detachment. It's not that you have lost your compassion or tolerance. It's that now you are able to see people as they are without needing to save them, make them happy, or judge them. And you feel free.

Success and Money

Write down any and all ideas, no matter how far-fetched they seem, for further consideration. This is the best way to honor all that creativity flowing through you. And there's a lot of it. Enjoy the experience. There's plenty of time to figure out what comes next. Believe it or not, taking pleasure in what's unfolding inside you is the perfect foundation for the future.

Pitfalls and Potential Problems

Refrain from containing your joy and your excitement. It really is your time to emerge from the cocoon, to spread your wings, and to show the world your inner beauty. No more holding yourself back, waiting for approval, acceptance, or appreciation from the outside world. Right now, the only thing that matters is what you think, what you desire, and how you feel.

Rewarding Days

7, 8, 16, 17

Challenging Days

5, 6, 25, 26

Libra | March

Overall Theme

Work of all kinds rises to the top of your agenda, and that's okay, as long as you are in a position to set your own priorities. You really are ready to manifest your new future, and that means getting down to business. This is something you genuinely want to do, until you are inundated with demands to turn your attention to the needs of others. Time to practice saying no or turn the tables by asking them to assist you. That should clear the decks.

Relationships

The challenge is simple: not everyone knows how to respect you the way you respect them. This isn't a new awareness, but it is one that always knocks you off balance when it knocks on your door yet again, as it does this month. Rather ranting about how unfair this is, remember that the one thing you need right now is to respect yourself. You can't ask others to do what you have difficulty doing for yourself.

Success and Money

You are brimming over with plans and energy and excitement, so much so that you spend every waking minute engaged in creating a new model of success for yourself. One that is based on a burgeoning appreciation for your own capabilities. Just remember, this is a work in progress and you don't have to build the whole thing in one day, one week, one month, or even one year.

Pitfalls and Potential Problems

You find a lot of people want to weigh in on what you're doing. You don't have to listen. Really. Nor do you have to explain anything. This is a perfect time for you to let those people know that they don't have to like or approve of what you're doing, and that your choices reflect what matters to you, not what works for them. This is not confrontational. It's assertive.

Rewarding Days

12, 13, 26, 27

Challenging Days

10, 11, 24, 25

Libra | April

Overall Theme

No matter what you do, you're likely to feel like you are on the edge of a precipice. That's because the conflict between where you desire to go and where your fear thinks you should stay plays out in relationships of all kinds. Do not fold under the pressure of opposition, whether it comes from others or from inside you. You have a right to chart your own course in life. You just need to embrace that truth.

Relationships

This is your annual immersion in the ongoing question of your life: Who is more important—you or everyone else? Of course, you don't think it needs to be a case of either-or. And you are right. Except that not everyone else sees life as a collaborative experience rather than a competition. This year offers you the chance to let go of the need to get people to see the world through your eyes. Just be the role model for what you know.

Success and Money

You are fond of believing that no one sees you, much less listens to you or understands you. Well, you are about to have an experience in this area of your life that breaks down that perception and opens up the kind of opportunity you never envisioned coming your way. Once you get past the honor this shows you, take a good look at what is being offered. It may not fit what you really want.

Pitfalls and Potential Problems

You really don't like confrontation, which is why you find yourself with nothing to say or do if and when someone comes at you full force. Time to push back, firmly and strongly. It's not rude to say no. It's not unkind to put yourself first. You are tapping into such a powerful source of creativity, and it demands to be expressed. So honor yourself. Let others take care of themselves. It's not your job to make their lives palatable.

Rewarding Days

6, 7, 15, 16

Challenging Days

12, 13, 27, 28

Libra | May

Overall Theme

Expect life to move into the slow lane, so you can take time to catch your breath. Life really has been moving at breakneck speed both internally and externally, and a timeout is required to fully ground the shifts and changes of the last four months. Plus, it gives you a golden opportunity to take stock of where you're at, recharge your batteries, and create a strategy for the next steps you want to take.

Relationships

You are definitely uneasy about a number of less than satisfactory interactions you had last month. Not that you want to try to appease anyone or try to gloss over some very difficult conversations. You just don't like the way things were left. Well, you get the opportunity to address what happened when the people in question approach you to sort things out. Be truthful and things will work out.

Success and Money

Take time to review plans you have in place to grow the next phase of your career or your future purpose. Otherwise, unforeseen complications crop up. It's not that your plans are unsound. It's more a question of circumstances changing in ways you didn't anticipate. In the end, you are grateful you took time to recalibrate everything, because an added piece to the puzzle is revealed, making your dream even more satisfying.

Pitfalls and Potential Problems

There's no doubt you are gung ho, ready to rumble, and intent on pushing things forward as quickly as you can. It's because you are afraid that if you don't keep your foot on the gas pedal, you will lose your momentum and your nerve. Relax. You won't. The change you implemented is in no way superficial. How could it be? It comes from your authentic core.

Rewarding Days

3, 4, 22, 23

Challenging Days

12, 13, 29, 30

Libra | June

Overall Theme

The best one-word description for this month is "uncertainty." And that isn't the least bit acceptable to you. Everywhere you turn, the world is at a standstill. No one wants to do anything but take a tiny step forward and a huge one back. It's the way things are right now as a major shift in growth for the whole planet takes hold and everyone adapts. Just know this change offers you a formidable chance to succeed. Focus on that.

Relationships

Be forewarned. Your constant companion—at least it seems that way—is frustration. What's more, you appear to have run out of tolerance and acceptance. In short, you are cranky with people. Or is it yourself? Good question. One you need to answer before you spend any amount of time with anyone.

Success and Money

Take this time to review your finances, not because you are likely to uncover a problem but more because you are going to experience a sudden urge to go on a vacation or make a big purchase. Knowing how things stand ahead of time gives you the opportunity to treat yourself without worrying about the potential consequences. Plus, you are likely to give some thought to changing how you invest your money and how you invest in yourself.

Pitfalls and Potential Problems

Given your tendency to weigh everything more times than you can count before you finally make a decision, you are unprepared for the urgency you feel to go for it, no questions asked. You are both mesmerized by this feeling and terrified by it. Hence your irritability and your ambivalence, the first one reflecting your need to implement the changes you initiated and the other revealing your fear of doing just that.

Rewarding Days

23, 24, 28, 29

Challenging Days

4, 5, 18, 19

Libra | July

Overall Theme

Old patterns connected to duty and obligation knock you off balance, making you wonder if the changes you are pursuing really are in your best interest. Undoubtedly they are. Just know that when fear comes knocking, it's an opportunity to see how profoundly you are shifting in a new direction, and how much courage and strength it's taking to overhaul yourself from the inside out.

Relationships

For what may feel like the first time this year, you actually want to spend time with other people, although you do have some trepidation about whether you burned a bunch of bridges while you redefined what you desire from your relationships. Much to your surprise, you discover that the people who really do cherish you are okay with you showing up as a human being rather than a saint.

Success and Money

You face one last bout of hesitation about your path going forward, and for the first time, you see clearly how much you have let your need for other people's approval, as well as your own insecurities, interfere with doing the most important thing you can do: trust yourself. And that includes refraining from an all-out critique of your previous choices, no matter how tempting that is.

Pitfalls and Potential Problems

Choosing a new path in life is not the same as engaging in full-scale condemnation or dismissal of everything that preceded that decision. Life really is about taking your experiences and doing something constructive and affirming with them, which is exactly what you are doing. So don't rain on your own parade. Instead, find a way to celebrate the person you are becoming.

Rewarding Days

16, 17, 29, 30

Challenging Days

4, 5, 18, 19

Libra | August

Overall Theme

There are a couple of conflicting desires this month. One is to take a vacation. After all, shifting your whole life requires more effort than you could have ever imagined. The second is to just dig in, push forward, and keep your eyes firmly focused on your future goals. Just know you don't have to choose one over the other. There's room to do both, because each is important in its own way to your overall well-being.

Relationships

You just can't believe how much more fun and nurturing your relationships are turning out to be now that you've decided to include yourself in them. This amps up your optimism and enthusiasm, because you now know people actually appreciate you. You were so busy looking at them that you didn't realize they were looking at you. What a life-affirming revelation!

Success and Money

Be ready to cross paths with someone who has the potential to be a significant part of this part of your life going forward. What you need to recognize is that it is meant to be a business relationship—at least to begin with. So you need to look at this person through that lens first. You are not auditioning for a new best friend. Rather, you are attracting a true supporter.

Pitfalls and Potential Problems

You are still grappling with the notion that not only is it okay to take care of yourself, it's necessary. So again you come face to face with the truth that you are as responsible for limiting yourself as sometimes you thought others were. The gift in that is knowing that the power to change your life resides in you, not in pleasing, appeasing, or bowing down to anyone.

Rewarding Days

2, 3, 10, 11

Challenging Days

7, 8, 17, 18

Libra | September

Overall Theme

Take time out daily to do something to nurture yourself. Otherwise, there's the possibility that you could hit a huge wall as you try to make sense of all the weird energy ricocheting through your life. It's just leftover residue from your purging process colliding with the mixed messages you keep bumping into everywhere you go. Everyone and everything is confused or confusing.

Relationships

As long as your only desire is to play, have fun, and keep things joyful, this area of your life is a safe place to hang out while it looks like the whole world is going crazy. Be careful of anyone who wants to dump their problems in your lap, not because you can't be supportive but because you simply have no interest in jumping in to fix anything right now. And that's a healthy way to be. Listen, but offer no solutions.

Success and Money

It definitely feels like no one has a clue what they're doing. Well, that's not exactly accurate. What is true is that one minute, everything is clear, and the next, the fog rolls in, leaving uncertainty and frustration in its wake. Accept that this isn't the month to take any risks or make any hasty decisions. There are just too many moving parts in play to make sense of what to do next. Stick to the tried and true.

Pitfalls and Potential Problems

You're worried that you're losing your compassion and your tolerance, because you really have no space for taking care of anyone else. The truth is that they aren't lost. They're just in short supply. This is a temporary state of affairs as you dissolve the last bits of toxicity from your life. So direct your kindness and generosity toward yourself. You deserve it.

Rewarding Days

8, 9, 26, 27

Challenging Days

11, 12, 24, 25

Libra | October

Overall Theme

This is the time of year when you are in your comfort zone. And what a relief it is to be there. That is, until the intensity you have been navigating off and on throughout 2020 ramps up once again. No need to panic or be scared. It's time to harness that energy in a productive way, embracing the passion for life you uncovered while shedding all the emotional garbage you accumulated.

Relationships

You are often quite self-conscious about revealing your own hopes and dreams as well as your inner fears and insecurities. That's quite a lot to keep to yourself. The reason? You are afraid of criticism or scorn or people simply not understanding what you want. Well, that all seems to change in a heartbeat as you find yourself opening up quite unexpectedly. This is a sign that you are present for yourself in a new and healthier way.

Success and Money

No taking the back seat or minimizing yourself this month. You are front and center, in the spotlight, and loving every minute of it. What's more, you speak with authority and find to your delight that you aren't intimidated when someone disagrees with you. It's the official unveiling—in a professional sense—of the more authoritative you. Congratulations!

Pitfalls and Potential Problems

The number-one thing to avoid right now is second-guessing yourself. Think of yourself as a baby taking their first steps. Everything isn't going to go smoothly. You are likely to be a little wobbly and unsure, but you know you can get where you're going. And if you fall down and go boom, you can trust yourself to get back up and carry on, with renewed confidence and trust in yourself.

Rewarding Days

3, 4, 17, 18

Challenging Days

1, 2, 15, 16

Libra | November

Overall Theme

You are likely to feel a little under siege right now, as you search to find a sense of equilibrium in the middle of a series of unexpected challenges. Individually, they are not a big deal, just small problems with straightforward solutions. It's the number of them and the timing of them. Take solace in knowing you can handle them, no matter how unsettled you feel. And when all is said and done, you emerge victorious and proud of yourself.

Relationships

The key to harmony in this part of your life is straight-talking. It's the only way to avoid the creation of a potentially difficult triangle involving two people you love. Do not take sides. Do not get in the middle and try to mediate a solution. Be clear with both of them that you care and you trust that they can work through it. Your honesty and frankness will inspire them to do just that.

Success and Money

During your deep dive into your own psyche, you haven't allocated a lot of time or attention to your financial well-being. Until now. You are suddenly compelled to take a look at your spending habits, convinced you dropped the ball. You didn't. Your need to do a once-over is more about evaluating whether the way you are allocating your resources reflects what you truly value.

Pitfalls and Potential Problems

You can't make the kind of profound change you did this year without being tempted to take a microscope and examine everything you ever did. That's healthy, as long as you do it to understand the whys and wherefores, with the view of using what you find to create a better life. It's unhealthy if it becomes an exercise in figuring out what's wrong with you. So stop any negative self-talk before it really gets started.

Rewarding Days

7, 8, 15, 16

Challenging Days

17, 18, 24, 25

Libra | December

Overall Theme

As 2020 comes to a close, you feel like you climbed Mount Everest—in high heels. It really has been that kind of year. One where you felt stretched beyond your ability to adapt. One where you wondered if the foundation of your life might shatter, dissolve, or disappear. But here you are, full of enthusiasm, optimism, and hope, ready to not just cope with life but flourish and prevail. The gift of this year turns out to be finding what you're truly made of: courage, strength, and love.

Relationships

It gives you so much joy to be among those you love and who love you just as much. Gone is the belief that people don't value you, don't care about your well-being, and don't hear you or see you. And the person who turned this around was, in fact, you. Because you decided to respect and honor yourself. Awesome!

Success and Money

Now that you stopped having a panic attack about how successful you can be or whether you are financially stable, celebrate by patting yourself on the back, by getting yourself a Christmas present, and by throwing a party for yourself. No need to worry about 2021. Everything is on track to make that a big year for you.

Pitfalls and Potential Problems

It's true that you are the biggest optimist in the world when you're in a group of people. But when you are alone, not so much. All the what-ifs pop up in the back of your mind and block out all your natural buoyancy. The solution? Take fifteen minutes to let them say what they must. Then close the door. You proved to yourself this year that you can deal with anything.

Rewarding Days

6, 7, 17, 18

Challenging Days

2, 3, 15, 16

Libra Action Table

These dates reflect the best–but not the only–times for success and ease in these activities, according to your Sun sign.

	JAN	FEB	MAR	APR	MAY	JUN	JUL	AUG	SEP	OCT	NOV	DEC
Move						2, 3				26, 27		
New romance				15, 16				3, 4				
Seek coaching/counseling	13, 14								1, 2			
Ask for a raise							14, 15					
Vacation					12, 13							17, 18
Get a loan		1, 2	26, 27								27, 28	

Scorpio

The Scorpion
October 23 to November 21

♏

Element: Water

Quality: Fixed

Polarity: Yin/feminine

Planetary Ruler: Pluto (Mars)

Meditation: I let go of the need to control

Gemstone: Topaz

Power Stones: Obsidian, garnet

Key Phrase: I create

Glyph: Scorpion's tail

Anatomy: Reproductive system

Colors: Burgundy, black

Animals: Reptiles, scorpions, birds of prey

Myths/Legends: The Phoenix, Hades and Persephone, Shiva

House: Eighth

Opposite Sign: Taurus

Flower: Chrysanthemum

Keyword: Intensity

The Scorpio Personality

Strengths, Talents, and the Creative Spark

Your strength arises from one simple truth: Nothing escapes your notice, even if it doesn't look like you are paying attention. You are stealth personified. Not that you consciously intend that to be the case. It just is. So much so that you are often unaware of it yourself, or at least how it comes to be that you just know how someone is feeling, whether someone is hiding something, whether someone has an agenda, or whether there is a plot afoot. Step into a room and you can read the prevailing tides with ease, all the little nuances and messages floating around in the ethers, looking for a place to land. For you, this is where the truth lies. It's not in the social niceties or the outer façade you know everyone has. It's beneath the surface, and you sense all those undercurrents because for you, they hold the key to everything that is vital and truly revealing.

After all, you just have to know what is really going on. For you, knowing is power, not because you intend to use what you know for any nefarious reason but because it gives you that extra edge in protecting yourself. After all, you are deeply and profoundly aware of all the facets of human nature, and this awareness creates an automatic suspicion and skepticism about what the people around you intend. Hence that well-developed radar that probes anything and everything around you, and that innate talent for digging deep—whether it's into the motivations of others, into finding a solution to complex problems, or even into yourself. You are a researcher of life: how it works, what it means, how it affects you, etc. It's this proclivity that provides the impetus for your creative spark. Because in digging into all that is, you discover unexplored ideas and paths that take you out of the known qualities and quantities of your life to a world of possibilities just waiting to be mined and alchemized into something truly insightful and transformative, whether it's a piece of music, a spiritual truth, a new way of being yourself, a technique for healing, or a scientific breakthrough. It's always all there just waiting for you to find it. And find it you will.

Blind Spots and Blockages

As long as you don't need anything or anyone, you think you are safe. But what you neglect to take into consideration is desire. It's what runs your nature. And if you don't acknowledge that and use your passion constructively, it runs amuck in your life and makes you wonder why things aren't as black and white as you expect or prefer. After all, you tend to see yourself as black and white, yes or no, good or bad. Which is ironic, because not only do you see the complexity in the lives of others but you also understand that life is a challenge, full of the unexpected and the surprising. But when it comes to your life, well, that's a different story.

Life is supposed to be simple and straightforward, with no hidden agendas. After all, you do everything to make sure all your bases are covered. No one is more vigilant than you or has the deep insight and acumen that you do, right? Well, all that is mush in the face of desire. You forget that at your core, you run on pure emotion, not intellect or rationality. And all anything or anybody has to do is speak to that desire, which is always lurking under the surface, and you are a goner. You are hooked, no matter how you dress it up. Then all your carefully observed insights are left in the wake of an overwhelming and intense desire for whatever has awakened that deep-seated longing. Accept your true nature and stop dragging yourself through the eye of a needle. You can't control the volcano of passion that is always just a heartbeat away. Let yourself embrace life.

Intimacy and Connection

Ah, intimacy. It's perhaps one of your least favorite words in the English language. Not because you don't crave it at a deep level. After all, you have a deep longing to merge with someone. It's because you must first confront your fear of being vulnerable, of being completely open, of showing all of who you are without any filters. Which, quite frankly, terrifies you. Whether you are willing to admit it or not—and most times you are not—you are profoundly sensitive and easily wounded. That makes it difficult for you to put yourself at the mercy of someone else's response to your innermost being, with all its idiosyncrasies, foibles, secrets, and, well, warts. You definitely don't want to feel the rejection or the loss of connection that taking that risk might create. So you stay hidden and wonder why you can't find the depth of connection you seek. And yet you attract an ongoing number of people who, within five minutes of meeting you, are telling you all about their deep, dark secrets, their crises, or their pain. They see and know how gifted you are at accepting and supporting them. Paradoxical, isn't it? Apparently you believe that no one can offer you what you are so clearly able to give others. Perhaps the key to finding the intimacy you desire—because, after all, superficial connections really don't work for you—is to accept all that you are without reservation or judgment. Being vulnerable to knowing yourself is the very thing that can create the space for the kinds of meaningful relationships you desire.

Values and Resources

You are in a constant search for what is truly meaningful to you for a variety of reasons, not the least of which is it forms the foundation of what you value, which, in turn, determines the path you take in life. This makes it almost impossible for you to place any importance on something that either doesn't make sense to you, doesn't have any merit, or simply doesn't resonate with you at your core. This can be a rather complex and lifelong pursuit because you are rarely satisfied with a cursory examination of anything that holds the potential to transform your life, which it must initially promise or you won't bother. After all, what would be the point of pursuing it otherwise? So whether you are aware of it or not, your core value is always going to be the willingness to transform, and your core resource is your capacity to do so.

Goals and Success

You are profoundly driven to succeed and on your own terms. However, what you define as success is often quite different from the norm, because it's not necessarily about how it measures up to the expectations of others as much as whether it meets your deep need for personal satisfaction. In other words, you need a calling first and a career second. It's difficult for you to imagine spending a lot of time on anything that doesn't elicit enthusiasm, passion, or even interest. Your goal is not to spend your life mired in boredom or disinterest. That truly is the next best thing to a death sentence. Does this mean that you will not do less-than-exciting things to achieve your goals? Of course not. As long as they are steps on the path and not the destination.

Scorpio Keywords for 2020
Passion, purging, purifying

The Year Ahead for Scorpio

Your motto for this year might well be "The Force is with me," because it certainly feels that way. The question is how will you use your power: wisely or as a weapon? Because with that power comes the reality that you are destined to get in touch with a lot of thoughts and ideas and experiences you suppressed in the past because you thought it unwise to share them, either with yourself or with others. As usual, all this buried stuff rises up from the depths of your being without warning and without much to soften the impact. And you know what happens when you tap into anything in your life that carries that much weight, that much influence over you. You want to get it up and out. Purge yourself. Purify yourself. That is the Scorpio way. You don't always know why you need to do this. You just know you must.

The truth is you have a built-in security alert that lets you know when the time has come to release what is toxic. However, it's not always clear exactly what you are likely to do in response to this profound push from within. If it feels particularly uncomfortable, you try to shove it back where it came from. This doesn't work—at least not in the long run—because it's only a matter of time before the internal pressure builds up again to the point where you can't ignore the underlying demand to transform the garbage into something useful and supportive. This is particularly true of 2020, as Saturn meets Pluto, making you feel claustrophobic and trapped. It's important to recognize that although you may feel this is somehow connected to outside forces in your life, you need to know that you and you alone have the power to release yourself from the grip of all this emotional junk. Because make no mistake, it is emotional. Anything you have submerged that deeply always is. Ignore where or how you took it on. The only thing that matters is why. That holds the key to the alchemy you are being asked to perform, and illuminates how you will use all that powerful energy surging through your physical, emotional, intellectual, and spiritual bodies.

The choice is yours. Will you recognize that the impetus for change comes from within and embrace this opportunity to lighten the load and clear space to express the passion for life that exists at the very core of who you are? Or will you, in your discomfort and fear of what lies within, look for ways to project what is surfacing onto any available human within range of where you stand? The former promises a rebirth of all that you are and wish to be. The second almost guarantees that you find yourself stuck in a never-ending cycle of bitterness and cynicism and potentially confrontation. Sounds a little harsh, but that is what happens when you avoid harnessing all that you are, light or dark, so you can express the whole of who you are. So accept the challenge, stare down anything unpleasant, and 2020 will mark the kind of turning point in your life that you never forget.

Jupiter

You aren't always sure just exactly what you are supposed to do with Jupiter and his Pied Piper energy. After all, you are suspicious of anything or anyone who tells you that things would be easy if only you would get with the program. Well, Jupiter's message is never quite as simple as that, and he's certainly going to demonstrate that to you in 2020. His invitation or demand is to get you to talk. Not just about anything, mind you, but about what you are really feeling and experiencing. Now, before you shove that notion away, know that this is one way for you to alleviate all the internal pressure building in your consciousness. The irony is you feel compelled to speak, but you are finding it difficult to break through your innate inclination to keep the most important aspects of who you are to yourself. A part of you knows it's time to let go of the notion that this is the only and best way to protect yourself, yet you feel trapped by that belief. Well, Jupiter is here to help you open up, not so you can put yourself in any danger but so you can understand that vulnerability offers you the chance to be stronger. Time to stop hiding from yourself and be yourself.

Saturn

The reality is that Saturn is going to demand that you make some important decisions throughout 2020. It's not that you aren't interested in doing that or that you don't sense that this year represents a profound shift in your life. You just don't like being pushed to do anything. You may be fluid in the deeper terrain of who you are, but on the surface you are unyielding if you sense any attempt to invade your space and compel you to do something against your will. In fact, you are so hypervigilant about that happening that it creates a level of suspicion and mistrust that, in turn, creates unnecessary stumbling blocks in the path of your life. Well, Saturn is here to challenge that particular modus operandi and urge you to assess the reality of how you go about making your life happen, all for the purpose of creating a powerful and very workable foundation for your life going forward. It may feel like he just wants to make trouble for you, but there are times when you need to be willing to see the truth of where you're at, what you've done, and how you get in your own way. Saturn's job, at the purest level, is always to illuminate consequences. This is not something that always appeals to you, because like much of the human race, you are convinced that this is a secret indictment of your life. That is not Saturn's ultimate intention. Rather, he knows that in the process of being accountable for you and your life lies a golden opportunity to take whatever you experience and put it to use. In other words, it's not what happens to you that is as important as what you choose to do with it. Therein lies character.

Uranus

It's been almost a year since Uranus started shaking up the last few things in your life that you believed you could count on, the things you thought could never be changed or altered. Whether it was your values, relationships, beliefs, creativity, purpose, or desires, he continually poked and prodded you by turning things upside down, leaving you unsure what to make of a chaos that not only rattles you but shocks you. Uranus's gift—and there is one, if you can see past your initial resistance to the discomfort he creates by insisting that nothing, but nothing, is immune to change—is to break apart anything that stands in the way of the depth and breadth of the transformation being initiated by Saturn and Pluto. You simply cannot nail anything down. You must be fluid and willing and vulnerable. It's the only way to truly grow, which is all Uranus is interested in.

Neptune

This year is guaranteed to symbolize one thing: making choices. Like most of the rest of the planetary family, Neptune comes with his own set of possibilities, ephemeral though they may be. And just because they are not substantial in a physical sense does not lessen their potential impact. This is a key awareness if you are to navigate what Neptune signifies in 2020. Will he be a welcome sanctuary for you or an invitation to escape reality? And how will you be able to differentiate one from the other? The truth is that at times you won't be sure whether you are hanging out in a space that relaxes you and relieves a lot of the stress you feel or whether you are just running away from what seems intolerable by shutting out the world completely. First, recognize that there's a very thin line between them, one that is easily blurred and easily crossed. Second, the actual choice is what you do with all this wispy, floaty, dreamy energy. If you use it as an inspiration, a vision of what comes next in your life, then it doesn't really matter whether you are meditating or escaping. However, if you disappear into this energy and use it as a smoke screen to disconnect from participating in your life, then you are abdicating your responsibility to yourself. There's no doubt this is an intense year and you will need to take a break. Just remember to invite yourself to dream, imagine, and create rather than freeze your feelings, numb yourself out, or dull your senses. The first is a sanctuary, the second escapism.

Pluto

No more time for pondering, analyzing, purging, or purifying old ways of being. The day or maybe the year of reckoning is here. You will have to decide just how far you are willing to go in answering the call to take the necessary actions to transform your life. Because when push comes to shove, it's not enough to get rid of the detritus in your life; you must replace what is decayed with something that is vibrant. That means translating all those inner sparks, all that inner intensity, into a living, breathing symbol of not just who you are but how you intend to conduct your life. It's true that's a tall order, but if anyone has the natural capacity to do this, it's you. Just take a deep breath and realize all the things you've done since 2008 (when Pluto first entered Capricorn) to prepare for this very time. There's no doubt you are going to feel like you are wearing your insides on the outside, because you are. It's required if you are to rebirth yourself. In doing so, you take all that power you have within and use it to express your essence, your passion, and your intensity in ways that no longer bottle you up but instead liberate you and honor you.

How Will This Year's Eclipses Affect You?

Eclipses signal intense periods that highlight major growth opportunities for us in the process of creating our lives. They are linked to the lunar phases—specifically the New and the Full Moon—and involve the relationship between the Sun, the Moon, and the Earth. A Solar Eclipse is a magnified New Moon, while a Lunar Eclipse is a magnified Full Moon. Eclipses unfold in cycles involving all twelve signs of the zodiac, and they occur in pairs, usually about two weeks apart.

This year there are six eclipses: two Solar Eclipses (one in Cancer and one in Sagittarius) and four Lunar Eclipses (one in Cancer, one in Sagittarius, one in Capricorn, and one in Gemini). This mixed bag of energies signals a shift from last year's focus on redefining nurturing versus babysitting, obligation versus accountability, family versus career, time for self versus taking care of business, and feelings versus rational thought. Three of this year's eclipses (the Lunar Eclipse on January 10 and the Solar Eclipse on June 21, both in Cancer, as well as the Lunar Eclipse on July 5 in Capricorn) complete this cycle, while the new eclipse cycle calls on us to understand that there is no wisdom in living in an ivory tower, stuck in our belief that there is only one way to live life while cut off from that very life. Instead, we need to get down to the streets and actually experience our environment, talk to people, create a dialogue, and embrace diversity. Only then can we create a world that truly embodies freedom and opportunity. Three eclipses (the Lunar Eclipse on June 5 in Sagittarius, the Lunar Eclipse on November 30 in Gemini, and the Solar Eclipse on December 14 in Sagittarius) begin this process.

The first eclipse of 2020 takes place on January 10, and it's a Lunar Eclipse in Cancer, highlighting the need for you to finish cleaning out your internal, emotional dungeon. You may believe you have purged yourself of any and all unhealthy emotions and thoughts, but there are bound to be a few you overlooked, lurking in the nooks and crannies. The good thing is that they are easily released. The bigger question is what will you replace them with? This eclipse encourages you to define a new set of guiding principles, one that honors and respects the things that define you: your powerful feeling nature, your capacity to dig deep into life and all its highways and byways, your passion and intensity, and your built-in understanding and awareness of the light and dark of human nature. No more denying who you are in order to conform to outside expectations. With this process complete, you are ready to apply your new sense of self to the next phase of your growth, which is exploring just what you value and why—another opportunity for you to use your deep powers of understanding to heal yourself.

Scorpio | January

Overall Theme

You begin the year feeling like you are at the end of your rope. It's just one cycle coming to a close and a new one about to begin, on a number of levels. Remember this experience, because it's one you will encounter many times in 2020 as you sort and sift through a bunch of leftover emotions in preparation for your initiation into a fresh life perspective and a renewed sense of your own worth.

Relationships

You really aren't sure exactly what is up with the people in your life. They all seem to have gone soft. Well, that's only because you are feeling pretty squishy yourself and you can't seem to hide it, which means you are likely projecting your own reality outward. So before you decide to get all prickly, take a moment to ask yourself if you want to deal with the consequences of that particular choice.

Success and Money

More than a little tired with the status quo, you begin a search for the key to what to do next. Refrain from looking at your outer circumstances for the sense of direction you seek. You need to look inward to define just what your issue is with your current circumstances. Much to your surprise, you may find that the financial rewards you are getting are not enough to inspire you to stay where you are.

Pitfalls and Potential Problems

It always comes as a bit of a shock to you when you outgrow where you're at in your life, a state of affairs that has had you in knots for more than a couple of years. Though you undoubtedly find it frustrating, there's a reason for this slow and steady transformation. You need the foundation that you lay to be one upon which you can build lasting results.

Rewarding Days

5, 6, 17, 18

Challenging Days

10, 11, 12, 29, 30

Scorpio | February

Overall Theme

Rarely are you overwhelmed by life being floaty and ill-defined. In fact, you often welcome it as a break from the intensity that normally drives you. However, you are not at all enamored with the lack of focus that plagues you as February begins. You want to get something—anything—accomplished, but everything seems to vaporize without warning. Relief is on its way if you can hang on until mid-month, when you can put all your preparation to good use.

Relationships

You really want people to stay out of your way, and you don't really know why. You just seem to be going through one of your periodic phases of leave-me-alone. Be clear about your need for a timeout, rather than being bored or disinterested or, worse, rejecting. Not everyone is as attuned to your moods as you expect them to be.

Success and Money

Several possibilities present themselves as a viable solution to your need for a new beginning. Just don't act hastily. In fact, stay where you are, because a project you worked long and hard on is about to create some unexpected success and abundance, the kind that offers support for the future and a feather in your cap.

Pitfalls and Potential Problems

You are not a happy camper when you feel your will is being thwarted. So take a good look at what your expectations are right now so you don't end up shooting yourself in the foot because you want what you want, when you want it. It certainly feels like you have been patient for a trillion years, but what's required right now is not patience but trust in yourself and what you invested your passion and belief in.

Rewarding Days

1, 2, 23, 24

Challenging Days

5, 6, 25, 26

Scorpio | March

Overall Theme

The more the month goes on, the more you become a human dynamo. Or is that superhero? There are days when you are likely to feel you can conquer anything. Your energy is off the charts and your capacity for completing things in record time has everyone looking at you with a new appreciation. Enjoy! This is your reward for staying the course and not letting your frustration get the best of you.

Relationships

Expect some surprising revelations from all corners of your life, from your partner to the new person at work. It seems everyone needs you to hear them out, because you are perhaps the best listener they know and the most discreet as well. The truth is they have a lot on their plate— some of it painful, some of it heartbreaking, some of it scary. Be open-minded, and do not offer solutions unless asked.

Success and Money

You are so energized by the success of your hard work and the goodwill you created that you wonder if you really do need a new path in life. Try not to back yourself into a case of either-or, and recognize that your current triumphs are part and parcel of what comes next, even if you can't see exactly what that looks like. It's better to move on at the top of your game rather than when you feel depleted and disinterested. Success breeds success.

Pitfalls and Potential Problems

Use your energy wisely this month. You can get everything accomplished that you envision without running at maximum speed every minute of every day. It's better to strategize how you want to expend your energy than to let your intensity and excitement run you in circles. That way, you emerge with everything complete and your physical and emotional well-being intact.

Rewarding Days

12, 13, 26, 27

Challenging Days

4, 5, 24, 25

Scorpio | April

Overall Theme

Your desire for freedom from the known quantities and qualities of your life suddenly makes everything seem dull and dusty and without merit, and that may very well be true. However, use this desire as fuel to find ways to change what needs to be changed, while preserving anything that is truly supportive of you and where you want to go. This is a much better response than just blowing everything up.

Relationships

You definitely feel compelled to speak your mind to anyone who will listen, even though you aren't really sure why or what you want to say. The challenge you face is being prudent about what comes out of your mouth, because if you meet with any kind of judgment or resistance or ignorance, you will be tempted to engage in verbal diarrhea—letting fly just to relieve all that pressure you feel inside. Remember that you can say what you need to say and still be kind.

Success and Money

The bloom seems to have come off the rose. All the wonderful accolades you received last month and the satisfaction you felt at a job well done recede, and you are left with the awareness that you aren't quite as content with your current position as you wanted to believe. Time to accept that the decision you made to create a new purpose for yourself is right.

Pitfalls and Potential Problems

The pressure from within is definitely putting you to the test, and you aren't sure you like it. Why can't things just stay the same? That is always your question when you are on the verge of a major life transition. What you always forget is that you are the one pushing for this and that it's not a whim, it's an imperative.

Rewarding Days
8, 9, 22, 23

Challenging Days
2, 3, 27, 28

Scorpio | May

Overall Theme

A deep sense of relief engulfs you as the inner pressure to make big, sweeping changes in how you live your life abates and you begin to see the outline of where you are going. It has not been an easy transition from old to new. It's not that you expected it to be, but it's always a joy to find yourself out in the light again. And you know without a doubt that you have once again pulled yourself out of the swamp.

Relationships

Gone is the feeling that you are on the verge of kicking some of the people in your life to the curb and walking away. Not that some of them are going to get a full reprieve. You are still watching those people out of the corner of your eye. However, you realize you need to take time to be certain of your motives before doing anything rash. You'd really hate to kill any relationship just because you are recovering from frustration and irritation.

Success and Money

Your head is full of so many ideas and possibilities that you are having difficulty shutting off the flow. Rather than try to make any plans based on what is burbling to the surface or even any sense of what some of them symbolize, tune in to your innate radar, identify the ones that appeal to you, and find a way to keep track of them. The rest is just flotsam and jetsam that is meant to entertain you.

Pitfalls and Potential Problems

It's exciting to feel all that space inside you liberated by your determination to process, heal, and purge the detritus that once occupied parts of your consciousness. Just don't be in any hurry to fill it up. Enjoy the feeling of airiness and light. You earned it. Plus, you really need to give yourself time to rejuvenate and recharge.

Rewarding Days

6, 7, 15, 16

Challenging Days

10, 11, 17, 18

Scorpio | June

Overall Theme

Life is more than a little confusing, because you feel like are moving in slow motion and hyper speed simultaneously. Strange but true. Your body is intent on taking it easy, while your mind and spirit are zipping around, full of anticipation and enthusiasm. No sense in trying to choose one over the other. You need both. So, honor what each is asking of you.

Relationships

You continue to mull over what you are seeking from others. Most of the time, you insist you don't need anything from anyone. Which is in many ways healthy, except when you use it as a barrier to intimacy. Recognize that what you are pondering is not what you need from others, but what you really desire from connection. This, of course, means you need to learn to be available to yourself first.

Success and Money

Take some time to review just how you manage your finances and whether what you do with your money is actually a healthy reflection of your self-worth. This promises to be an eye-opening experience. No matter what conclusions you come to, be cautious in taking action. You may not have as clear a path forward as you think.

Pitfalls and Potential Problems

You really don't like it when things feel all wobbly. It unnerves you. Which is why you are challenged to maintain your equilibrium as you feel pulled from extreme to extreme. First of all, what you are going through isn't as extreme as you perceive. You are just hypersensitive to any unexpected irritations after months of living on the edge. You are in the middle of a huge recalibration so all your systems are a little out of whack.

Rewarding Days

2, 3, 16, 17

Challenging Days

4, 5, 21, 22

Scorpio | July

Overall Theme

Old fears and habits come back to haunt you, freezing you in your tracks. It's momentary and not a sign of imminent disaster. No matter how much work you do to purge and transform yourself, there are always going to be experiences that trigger thoughts and emotions you thought you had sent to the dumpster, never to return, to start whispering in your ear again. What's important is how you respond. They don't have power unless you give it to them.

Relationships

You feel ready to embark on a new way of relating to people, especially those closest to you. All the effort you put into sorting out a number of the confusing beliefs and attitudes about relationship has led you to one important conclusion: you can trust yourself to be open and vulnerable, knowing that it isn't any more harmful to you than being perpetually suspicious. Time to get rid of your barriers.

Success and Money

In your infinite wisdom, you decide to torture yourself about anything and everything connected to both of these aspects of your life. Raining on your own parade not only stops you in your tracks but also erases all the momentum you built to change your path. This is the epitome of self-defeating behavior. Time to use your intensity to do something that benefits you, not tears you down.

Pitfalls and Potential Problems

Refrain from engaging in full-scale pessimism. This is dangerous to your emotional and physical well-being, and you are likely to miss the opportunity to shift back into a positive gear. You are deeply aware that life is not always sunshine and lollipops, but you resent it and take it personally when bumps show up in the road. Stop expecting life to be smooth sailing. A bump is just a bump, not a mountain.

Rewarding Days

13, 14, 27, 28

Challenging Days

4, 5, 25, 26

Scorpio | August

Overall Theme

With your equilibrium restored, you turn back to your life with determination in your eyes and fire in your belly. You are so ready to take on any challenge that crops up. After all, it can't be any more intense than facing the self-imposed demons you dredged up last month. Now that you have proven to yourself for the umpteenth time that it's draining to do this to yourself again and again, you are determined to turn over a new leaf. And so you do.

Relationships

You feel mellow and completely open to connecting to others without any walls up and without any preconceived ideas about what is supposed to happen. This is both a delight and a surprise. Normally, you are ready to put on your armor at any sign of insensitivity or manipulation. Now you are able to see that who people are and what they do is about them, and you trust yourself to know what to do.

Success and Money

This is a great month to network. What's more, you don't really need to seek out opportunities to meet the right people to support you and your new vision. They are destined to cross your path. All you need to do is make yourself visible by going places and connecting with people you already know.

Pitfalls and Potential Problems

There's no doubt that you are a brand-new you and are firing on all cylinders. Which means, of course, that you are impatient. After all, you have only two speeds—zero and 180—and you feel you've been stuck at zero for most of this year. Just take it easy or you will burn out, and that won't help you create the future you desire. Take a vacation. You deserve to reward yourself.

Rewarding Days

9, 10, 23, 24

Challenging Days

7, 8, 17, 18

Scorpio | September

Overall Theme

You are definitely in overdrive, so much so that you are exhausting yourself by running in circles. At the heart of this is an obsession with getting something–anything–done. You are like a horse that's been in the barn all winter. You just want to gallop. And that's understandable. However, choosing to be pushy as a way to get the job done isn't going to accomplish anything. Take all that energy, find a focus for it, and end the month satisfied and happy with what you achieve.

Relationships

You are in love with love, which leads you to be so warm and fuzzy that it makes everyone wonder if you have lost your mind or are playing some elaborate game. The truth is that you are finally expressing the softer side of who you are, the part you generally keep hidden because you are convinced it makes you look weak. Not anymore. Now you feel whole.

Success and Money

This is a good month to ask for a raise or a promotion or to seek a partner to help you launch a new business idea you have, or all of the above. Although you are on track to make a change, there is still much to be done to make that a reality. Plus, your current circumstances offer some unforeseen advantages that play out over the next few months.

Pitfalls and Potential Problems

You are not always willing to give things time to develop naturally because you are afraid that if you don't act immediately, you will squander the opportunity. This often creates the opposite of what you intend. Remember, the seed planted today doesn't flower tomorrow. It needs time to grow and develop. As do your plans.

Rewarding Days

6, 7, 19, 20

Challenging Days

3, 4, 24, 25

Scorpio | October

Overall Theme

This month, not everything seems to work out quite the way you planned, and you find yourself in a constant state of adjustment. Things are rattling around in your unconscious, work is a test of your patience, and no one seems to have any clear plans or answers. The best thing to do? Take the pressure off yourself and do what you can. This too shall pass.

Relationships

It comes as a surprise when you realize everyone is as frustrated as you are. And no, it's not something in the water. This is just Mars in retrograde motion, turning his energy inward—the opposite of his natural state of being. So it feels like everything is either going backward or is stagnant. It's not. Take some time to recalibrate what you want to accomplish in this area of your life and everything will settle down.

Success and Money

Be prepared for an unexpected piece of information to throw a monkey wrench into the timeline you created for your new venture. Use this as an opportunity to take a look at your entire plan. There may be something you overlooked, which makes this experience more of a blessing and less of an inconvenience.

Pitfalls and Potential Problems

Turn away from the mess you think the rest of the world is in, and focus on your hopes and dreams instead. Allow them to expand and inspire you. It's the only antidote to all the stop signs you keep encountering. That way, you stay connected to your determination and will be ready to move when things get back to normal.

Rewarding Days

3, 4, 17, 18

Challenging Days

1, 2, 15, 16

Scorpio | November

Overall Theme

There is nothing worse than being all dressed up with no place to go, which is the perfect description for you as you sit and wait for the tide to turn in the middle of the month so you can finally run free. And maybe a little wild. In private. Just know that the various steps you took to prepare yourself for this moment are all in place, and now it's go time.

Relationships

You might feel a little uncertain about one of your closest relationships. It's because you sense the person in question is in some sort of trouble, and all you want to do is help. Wait for them to come to you. It's true that they need your help, but they are likely to clam up if you broach the subject first. Not because they don't trust you but because they are overwhelmed and a little scared about how you might react.

Success and Money

Don't be alarmed about any rumors you hear in your workplace. Someone is just trying to muddy the waters, either to protect themselves or to create the kind of uncertainty that always undermines morale and trust. Steer clear of responding to what is being said. When everything comes to a head—which it will—you will be beyond reproach. Ultimately, it's a tempest in a teapot.

Pitfalls and Potential Problems

It's going to be a challenge not to get caught up in the traumas and dramas all around you. Just remember that you have the skills and the awareness to deal with the energies and situations that are knocking everyone else off balance. Jumping in to save people from themselves will only create unnecessary complications for you. After all, misery does love company.

Rewarding Days

13, 14, 22, 23

Challenging Days

4, 5, 29, 30

Scorpio | December

Overall Theme

All systems are definitely go, and you couldn't be happier. Time to launch yourself into the future with a clear head, an inspiring vision, and enough passion and drive to create everything you desire. And it's all because you dug deep inside yourself and found the strength and the tenacity to do what you believed unthinkable. Free yourself from any obligation to conform to anything inherently damaging to you. Bravo!

Relationships

As you look around at your life, you are truly grateful for the love and support you received this year as you navigated what you now see as a major crisis in your life. The interesting thing is you aren't really sure how to acknowledge it, largely because you are embarrassed that you took it for granted. In fact, there were times when you were so engrossed in your process that you didn't even see the gift this was. Well, to begin with, take a deep breath and say thanks.

Success and Money

The total Solar Eclipse on December 14 puts a tremendous focus on your financial reality. Look past that and see that it's time to examine how you value yourself. This is necessary to create the success you are planning. You are more than just the person who always gets the job done. You are creative and passionate, determined and strong—all things needed to succeed in initiating the life you want to live.

Pitfalls and Potential Problems

Accept that there is always going to be something else for you to trans-form. This year you turned yourself inside out to rid yourself of a lot of toxicity and to find a new appreciation for who you are. What's next is to put all that into practice, which means confronting any limitations you have about how much success you deserve. For now, enjoy the rest of 2020. The impetus for the next change will arrive before you know it.

Rewarding Days

10, 11, 24, 25

Challenging Days

13, 14, 27, 28

Scorpio Action Table

These dates reflect the best—but not the only—times for success and ease in these activities, according to your Sun sign.

	JAN	FEB	MAR	APR	MAY	JUN	JUL	AUG	SEP	OCT	NOV	DEC
Move		1, 2									26, 27	
New romance			12, 13			11, 12						
Seek coaching/ counseling				6, 7						3, 4		
Ask for a raise					2, 3				20, 21			
Vacation	17, 18						9, 10					
Get a loan								10, 11				7, 8

Sagittarius

The Archer
November 22 to December 21

Element: Fire

Quality: Mutable

Polarity: Yang/masculine

Planetary Ruler: Jupiter

Meditation: I can take time to explore my soul

Gemstone: Turquoise

Power Stones: Lapis lazuli, azurite, sodalite

Key Phrase: I understand

Glyph: Archer's arrow

Anatomy: Hips, thighs, sciatic nerve

Colors: Royal blue, purple

Animals: Fleet-footed animals

Myths/Legends: Athena, Chiron

House: Ninth

Opposite Sign: Gemini

Flower: Narcissus

Keyword: Optimism

The Sagittarius Personality

Strengths, Talents, and the Creative Spark

You are a seeker: of truth, of experience, of expansion. This leads to you wanting to know and be and do everything you fancy, whether it's climbing Mount Everest, traveling the world, getting your PhD, volunteering to teach overseas, starting a nonprofit to save the oceans, living in an ashram for a year, and the list goes on. You were born to search for meaning. The only way for you to do that is to always be ready, willing, and able to drop what you're doing and follow the call to experience something new. How else can you possibly be sure that what you already know is enough? Does it tell the whole story? Is it actually true? What else is out there that might expand your consciousness? This is your never-ending reality. One that you cannot and, quite frankly, do not want to ignore.

Of course, your search can take many forms. The key is you are free to pursue your quest, whether it's on a physical, intellectual, emotional, or spiritual basis. When the demand to expand your horizons rises up from within, you feel you have no choice but to heed the call. It is, in your mind, part of your DNA. And you are right. This, of course, requires a freedom that others see as risky, unnecessary, and even silly. Why can't you just be satisfied with the status quo? Why do you have to ask so many questions? Your reply is simple. How can I not? It's as intrinsic as breathing. You are, after all, in search of more than just information or even knowledge. You seek wisdom. And to do that requires a willingness to initiate, to take risks, to question, and to sign up for any adventure you see fit. This is you expressing your creativity in the simplest yet most profound way. It's what feeds and nurtures your soul. Taking life and meeting it head-on, with the sole intention of becoming more than the sum total of your parts.

Blind Spots and Blockages

Get ready for the shock of your life. There is no freedom without accountability, aka responsibility. The latter is perhaps your least favorite word in any language because you believe it's code for limitation and interference. The irony is that this fear of being boxed in actually drives you to run from anything that ultimately might be meaningful and purposeful. But isn't that what you're looking for? Leaves you in a bit of conundrum, wouldn't you say?

You have to stop thinking that there is a secret plot designed to tie you down and keep you from experiencing all that life has to offer. Your blind spot is not accepting that life does require a certain amount of structure, a certain amount of focus. Without that, things can actually become meaningless because there's no context, no framework, no perspective. Running around for the sake of running around is not likely to give you what you are seeking: answers. To everything, including the meaning of life. Of course, you need the freedom to pursue any and all threads and experiences that offer you the chance to expand your understanding and your awareness, but you need a foundation from which to do that. And that foundation is based on you finding something you believe in and acting in accordance with whatever ideals or principles reflect who you are. You have to know where you are before you can figure out where you are going. This isn't limiting. It's actually wise. The truth is that running away can be just as limiting as being hogtied. Except, in this instance, you are doing it to yourself. The solution? Stop trying to escape life and actually live it, with all its warts and complexities. Know that no matter where you are and what you are doing, there is something enlightening and illuminating for you to discover.

Intimacy and Connection

You are always curious about how everyone else lives. This is your first point of connection, but if, upon further inspection, you find that you are not met with a similar openness or inquisitiveness, you quickly turn your attention somewhere else. You simply cannot build intimacy where there is what you consider inflexibility, intolerance, judgment, or even disinterest. All these add up to choosing to live in a bubble, completely disconnected from the very diversity of culture, thoughts, experiences, and adventures that living on planet Earth offers up. That's definitely not how you want to live. This, of course, often limits the number of people you feel truly sympatico with. Which, quite frankly, isn't an issue for you. Because you need freedom above all, it's impossible for you to see yourself in a relationship with anyone who doesn't share your need to make choices free from obligation, to follow your call to adventure whether you are exploring places or ideas, and to feel unfettered by rules and regulations that simply don't appeal to you. These are basic requirements, not whims. Without them, a relationship is likely to be a prison for you.

What others think of as security, you see as being tied down and unable to be, much less breathe—not at all the recipe for a deep, intimate relationship. So you resist with every fiber of your being the traditionally accepted picture of intimacy, where two become one. It just doesn't make any sense to you. In fact, you see it as a restriction, not an expansion. And what is life if not the opportunity to grow in any possible way you can? This is more than an ideal to you. So much so that you are quite capable of walking away from anyone who is willing to try to control you. After all, that's not loving. Or respectful. Or generous. All the things you truly desire to be in a relationship.

Values and Resources

You definitely see these two things as interchangeable, probably because you feel that the values you base your life on are your most important resource, the very things you choose to build your life on. The one requirement? Your values must truly reflect who you are at your core, which is a challenge because finding that out is a lifelong journey. This leads to a number of shifts and changes in what you find worthy and what you decide is significant, not because you are inconsistent or fickle but because as you experience life, you unveil more and more of who you are. What was valuable to you at age twenty may or may not be what you find important at age forty. What remains constant is your generosity of spirit, your enthusiasm, and your openness, keeping you from the biggest danger of all: becoming self-righteous.

Goals and Success

You desire success, but on your own terms, which makes it imperative for you to define exactly what that means to you. This can lead to you wandering off the beaten path in order to explore any possibility that strikes your fancy before you can actually do that. From there, you have no difficulty setting goals and deciding what course of action you want to take. The key is always going to be committing to something that has the potential to do more than fill your bank account. You want abundance in all its forms. So whatever path you pick must offer food for the soul, the intellect, and the heart.

Sagittarius Keywords for 2020

Accountability, hope, stability

The Year Ahead for Sagittarius

How to best describe in simple, clear terms a year that promises complexity, discomfort, and, just for good measure, a dollop of confusion? Normally, you are completely okay with things being open-ended. It gives you the feeling that anything is possible at any given moment. For you, this is an invitation to possibility, rather than something that strikes fear into your very being. Well, not so much this year. Because the potential of 2020 has more to do with exploring your insides at a depth and intensity that isn't always your first choice. Certainly, you are always up for engaging in exploration and discovery. Just not on an emotional level. Your motto is "Some things are best left alone," kind of a case of been there, done that, time to move on. So when life gets complicated—as it will this year, with the mix of energies knocking on your door—you aren't sure this is a journey you want to undertake.

As a fire sign, you like things to be direct, easily tackled, and easily mastered. That isn't what's on the agenda this year. Things are kind of twisty, messy, thorny, and convoluted—an average trip into the recesses of your deeper consciousness, where you hide all of your difficult, painful, and disappointing experiences; things that underlie, in powerful ways, your sense of self-worth and hence your whole value system. Granted, this process began in 2008, when Pluto entered Capricorn, but now the heat is turned up to high as your planetary avatar, Jupiter, joins both Saturn and Pluto in Capricorn, amplifying the need for you to face all that discomfort. There's little doubt you are going to feel trapped, with nowhere to go but inside. And you won't like it. However, that is of little or no consequence if you want to emerge from this cauldron cleansed, purified, and more at ease with yourself.

You may be an intrepid adventurer, except when it comes to emotions. Which is paradoxical because exploring that part of life promises you more freedom than ever before. However, that isn't how you see it, largely because you are convinced that emotions inhibit you and trip you up, with all their unnecessary complications. Well, this year offers you the chance to transform that belief—which truthfully is more of a fear—and discover that the opposite is true. Being emotionally connected actually helps you create the life you want by linking you more closely to your essence. So instead of running all that you sense through your brain and trying to make sense of it that way, you can now run it through your heart. This, in turn, makes you freer in all parts of your being. Knowing and accepting this is the key to delving deep into your emotional reservoir and finding the wisdom to release anything that undermines your trust and faith in yourself. The end result is exhilarating, liberating, and energizing.

Jupiter

There are times in 2020 when you are likely to believe that all the lights have gone out, because it's difficult to find the well of optimism and enthusiasm usually at your beck and call. In fact, you feel downright depleted of all the things that usually define you. Just think of it as a course correction. You are definitely not going to spend the rest of your life down in what you think are the dumps. Rather, it's a case of getting down to business, which is one of the signatures of Jupiter in Capricorn, especially if he's hanging out in that sign with Saturn. After all, Capricorn is Saturn's territory, and Jupiter must defer to him. This is the reason why you are feeling a little heavier and more serious than usual. In order to maintain your equilibrium, ask yourself what you can do with this energy. Not all experiences that truly expand your life come with a feeling of euphoria or excitement. Some of them come with a steadiness of purpose that inspires and uplifts you from a place of having your feet firmly planted on the ground. After all, your innate nature is about exploring every possible avenue to find meaning. So this year, your adventure is to be open to the gifts of accountability, stillness, prudence, and perseverance. This prepares you for a major change at the end of 2020, one that promises to break apart anything that stands in the way of building a future that you can't quite see yet.

Saturn

Saturn's message is clear. There is no time to waste in 2020. Use every moment purposefully and with the intent to redefine whether you are actually living in a way that reflects what you find meaningful. It's one thing to say you believe something, but it's another to put it into practice, to demonstrate it clearly by your actions. Words without action are just that—words. At some point, you need to get past endless seeking, pondering, preaching, and debating. You must do something. Build something. See something through to the end. So says Saturn. Which brings you face to face with the ongoing disconnect between you and Saturn. There's no doubt that Saturn often considers Sagittarius to be flighty and unreliable, but that's because he defines everything in terms of what's concrete. That's where the value is. Of course, that insults your very being, because you believe the value of what you make lies in its meaningfulness. Otherwise, why would you create something that doesn't matter? Well, in 2020, you must bridge this apparent divide, one that quite frankly is a symbol of your need to be in the right. Time to see that it isn't a case of either-or. This truly is a year when you need to build something both meaningful and concrete, because there is a part of you that needs something to show for all your efforts to find meaning in living, and because you feel the need to show up and be counted. No doubt you will resist this, but in the end, you will answer this very powerful invitation because you know deep within that this is the next step in a new kind of adventure. And you just can't turn that down.

Uranus

With all the noise Saturn is making, you may not notice Uranus busily knocking things over and generally making a mess. At least that's what it feels like when you actually take time to acknowledge the ongoing frustration and irritation plaguing you. Nothing seems to be unfolding easily or in a straightforward manner, leading to a constant need to adapt again and again. Once you get past how annoying this is, you can see Uranus is doing what you need him to do: breaking down old habit patterns and shattering deeply entrenched ideas, and basically anything threatening to hinder or stop the much-needed transformation you are going through. The one that finds you erasing any misconceptions about what you truly value and, in particular, any that affect your self-worth. The reality is you really want to be taken seriously, but that cannot and will not happen if you stick stubbornly to your belief that you need freedom at all costs. This does not expand your life in any meaningful fashion. It actually keeps you stuck in a perpetual cycle of immaturity, which is neither meaningful nor wise. Time to reframe what it is to truly grow. To do that, you need Uranus's help in ridding yourself of the outworn and the toxic. He is definitely going to force you out of the weeds of your past and push you into the future. A future with the kind of freedom that is built on an authentic understanding of yourself.

Neptune

You are profoundly in need of a respite from all the rumblings, upheavals, and internal dissonance created by Saturn, Uranus, Pluto, and even your friend Jupiter. So Neptune's apparent invitation to leave the scene, to disappear, or to close your eyes and hope that everything goes away looks extremely attractive and maybe even necessary. Rather than listening to that siren call, know that this is not the solution. Of course, you need to nurture yourself by creating quiet moments, by seeking inspiration from within, and by doing things that energize your natural optimism and enthusiasm. These are the positive sides of Neptune, the things likely to buoy your spirits and give you a vision of what comes next—much more life-affirming than any form of escapism. Make no mistake. Dropping out of your life or pretending everything is just fine, or both, promises the kind of outcome you don't want to live with. Granted, it's not always easy to tell whether you are taking a break or escaping, except that the first comes from a place of hope, while the second is birthed by fear. Keep that in mind and it will be much easier to use Neptune's energy constructively in 2020.

Pluto

The push-pull going on in your psyche makes you wonder if you shouldn't just surrender and get it over with, even though you aren't really sure what that means. It's more of a compulsion than an actual plan. Know this. That feeling, as overwhelming and overpowering as it feels, is a sign that you are in a transitional stage, moving from an old sense of who you are to a complete rebirth. It's not unlike being in the birth canal, just before you were born. And, similarly, one of its major characteristics is you have no choice but to let go. This is not something particularly appealing, because for you it means giving up. The reality is that you aren't capitulating. Far from it. True, there are forces beyond your control pushing you forward, and you are likely to be a little scared. But you have been preparing for this since 2008, and this step, the next step, is to trust yourself, just as you always do when you are ready to embark on a new adventure.

How Will This Year's Eclipses Affect You?

Eclipses signal intense periods that highlight major growth opportunities for us in the process of creating our lives. They are linked to the lunar phases—specifically the New and the Full Moon—and involve the relationship between the Sun, the Moon, and the Earth. A Solar Eclipse is a magnified New Moon, while a Lunar Eclipse is a magnified Full Moon. Eclipses unfold in cycles involving all twelve signs of the zodiac, and they occur in pairs, usually about two weeks apart.

This year there are six eclipses: two Solar Eclipses (one in Cancer and one in Sagittarius) and four Lunar Eclipses (one in Cancer, one in Sagittarius, one in Capricorn, and one in Gemini). This mixed bag of energies signals a shift from last year's focus on redefining nurturing versus babysitting, obligation versus accountability, family versus career, time for self versus taking care of business, and feelings versus rational thought. Three of this year's eclipses (the Lunar Eclipse on January 10 and the Solar Eclipse on June 21, both in Cancer, as well as the Lunar Eclipse on July 5 in Capricorn) complete this cycle, while the new eclipse cycle calls on us to understand that there is no wisdom in living in an ivory tower, stuck in our belief that there is only one way to live life while cut off from that very life. Instead, we need to get down to the streets and actually experience our environment, talk to people, create a dialogue, and embrace diversity. Only then can we create a world that truly embodies freedom and opportunity. Three eclipses (the Lunar Eclipse on June 5 in Sagittarius, the Lunar Eclipse on November 30 in Gemini, and the Solar Eclipse on December 14 in Sagittarius) begin this process.

The first eclipse of 2020 takes place on January 10, and it's a Lunar Eclipse in Cancer, highlighting your continuing efforts to nurture the feeling, emotional side of who you are. This hasn't been an easy process for you, because being vulnerable or sensitive doesn't come easily to you. It's not that you don't have a generous spirit or a caring nature. You do. They just aren't the dominant features of your personality. The crucial facet of this evolution—because you have grown—has been a willingness to build intimacy with yourself, rather than putting all your focus on the solar side of your nature. Consequently, you feel more integrated, because there is a dialogue between your insides and your outsides. This continues throughout the rest of the year, no matter the sign the eclipses are in. However, there is a shift in how this growth expresses itself beginning in May. In the eighteen months that follow, you find yourself developing new pathways in being yourself. Along the way, you are likely to confront a number of old patterns you created in how you show up in the world and how you deal with the people in your life. This is a natural expansion of what you are already doing, not a major bump in the road. One that promises to revitalize you.

Sagittarius | January

Overall Theme

There's no question that the year begins with you feeling off: not quite yourself, not quite sure exactly what's going on. In fact, it seems like you're standing on ground that is continually shifting. And you're right. Take solace in knowing that this is happening to everyone and that you, with your talent for adapting to ever-changing circumstances, can and will ride this out. It's just going to be a bit jarring.

Relationships

It's not so much that you feel allergic to people right now. You simply don't have the capacity to engage, not even from a place of basic curiosity. It's like all the words coming at you hit a wall and you don't even comprehend what's being said, leaving you a little astounded but unable to take down whatever barrier is in the way. The bottom line is you really need a timeout right now, and your deeper consciousness is creating enough space for you to do that.

Success and Money

You aren't at all sure exactly where you are going in this area of your life. It's been an interesting year of reevaluating what is meaningful to you. Do you need to change your attitude and approach to what success is and where it fits in your life? And what about your financial resources? Are you locked into a pattern of behavior that doesn't serve you?

Pitfalls and Potential Problems

There's no doubt that you thrive on adventure. Except the kind that backs you into an emotional corner, because it not only is the one area of your life that comes with too many duties and obligations but is the one you feel unable to master. Time to realize it's about engaging and taking part, something you do with such ease in the rest of your life, rather than overcoming or conquering. The latter is just a sign of your discomfort.

Rewarding Days
4, 5, 29, 30

Challenging Days
10, 11, 12, 22, 23

Sagittarius | February

Overall Theme
You breathe a huge sigh of relief as your confidence returns. It's always a challenge for you when you lose sight of that inner compass, the one that always seems to know how and when to take action. Last month, you felt like you were sitting on a rocket, with so much energy to burn yet no faith or sense of direction. Get ready. All that power is unleashed now. Just make sure you have a plan.

Relationships
You are more than a little confused by everyone's reluctance to even talk to you. Well, they didn't really understand your need for space last month. In fact, it looked a lot like a lethal combination of grouchiness, ingratitude, and withdrawal. Refrain from defending yourself. Just tell the truth about where you were at, then invite them to have fun. No one can resist a combination of honesty and play.

Success and Money
One of the most concrete things that emerges from all your internal questioning is the awareness that not only you do you need to revamp much of how you see both money and success, but you are driven to do it. You feel you have no choice. After all, you have difficulty living life in a way that holds no meaning for you.

Pitfalls and Potential Problems
There continue to be deep rumblings in your psyche. Don't be alarmed or annoyed. You are engaged in a deep healing process designed to purge unhealthy and painful beliefs about who you are. The truth is that your only purpose has always been to follow your own instincts and find whatever nourishes you and your soul, not to make sure you live a life designed by the status quo. The key here is to recognize that although you do your best to ignore what others say, their opinions and judgments do affect you. Time to let that go.

Rewarding Days
16, 17, 25, 26

Challenging Days
3, 4, 18, 19

Sagittarius | March

Overall Theme

Ordinarily, you love the rush of life going up and down and around. Repetitiveness and monotony leads to boredom and a very unhappy Sagittarius. Well, you find you'd like a little bit of predictability, as one minute you are ready to conquer the world and the next you are looking for anywhere you can hide. Welcome to the rollercoaster. The healthiest and the most effective thing you can do is stay focused on projects and plans, and you emerge stronger and more determined.

Relationships

Please find someone you can confide in about the turmoil you are experiencing. It's one way to maintain your sanity as well as realize you are not alone in confronting a whole host of fears and insecurities that seem to spring fully formed out of thin air. Sharing allows you to release some of that inner pressure and helps you understand the source of all this detritus. Which, of course, is your own psyche.

Success and Money

Be cautious about spending. Make sure you aren't trying to buy your way out of your anxiety, because that won't work. It may offer temporary relief, but you may regret it later. Especially if you go on a spree. Of course, this doesn't mean don't spend any money. Just don't overdo it. A little retail therapy never hurt anyone.

Pitfalls and Potential Problems

It's true that you feel like you are trapped in a cage with a lion, the lion being a deep sense of dissatisfaction with life. On a deeper level, this symbolizes how discouraged you are. If there's anything that can knock you completely off balance, it's feeling that there's no light in the world, that all the hope and optimism you can muster doesn't always make everything right. That's true, but you will rise up again. After all, who else is going to be the eternal optimist?

Rewarding Days

8, 9, 26, 27

Challenging Days

4, 5, 16, 17

Sagittarius | April

Overall Theme

Expect a huge emotional release that chases all the clouds out of your life, leaving you with a new infusion of enthusiasm and zest for life. Strangely, it leads you to dig down and get serious about purpose and intention. You find yourself wanting to make your mark in the world in solid and practical terms. Not only do you know it's the next step in creating a longer-lasting sense of satisfaction, but now it's part of a new definition of the kind of legacy you want to leave.

Relationships

As serious as you find yourself in other parts of your life, this is where you can play. And you definitely need that. So be as social as you like. Travel, if you want, but not alone. You may feel you owe a bunch of people an apology. You don't. You can, however, in the middle of having a good time, acknowledge the support you received and how grateful you are.

Success and Money

Revitalized, your attention turns to what steps you can take to change the facets of your career or work life that aren't working for you. Don't be surprised if nothing concrete shows up at first. Rather, you may be bombarded with a bunch of weird and wacky but fascinating ideas that don't come with a complete outline of what to do. Play with all of them. See which one sparks the most interest in you. Go from there.

Pitfalls and Potential Problems

It's wonderful that you want to get down to business, but remember that the pathway to accomplishment is always going to go through your imagination and your desire to take a risk. It's true that you can use tried-and-true methods to achieve what you want, but you always need to give your creativity free rein first. It truly is not a waste of time. Plus, you cannot achieve what you desire by using all that energy on anything you already decided is tired and outworn.

Rewarding Days

10, 11, 20, 21

Challenging Days

2, 3, 28, 29

Sagittarius | May

Overall Theme

A major energetic shift brings a return to feeling comfortable in your own skin. This comes as a relief, because in spite of the optimism you experienced in April, you were uncertain about that ever being true again. Well, now you know you can't keep a spirit like yours down for very long. You always find a way back home to yourself.

Relationships

An opportunity to redress an imbalance you created in how you relate to people suddenly presents itself. But before you make any attempt to talk to anyone about the revelations surfacing, you need to do some real internal digging into the root cause. This is necessary if you want to avoid further complications, especially since this is not something that can be resolved by seeking absolution from others.

Success and Money

Because everything feels like it's going in reverse rather than forward (as you'd hoped or even planned), it's best to turn your attention to anything that needs review, recalibration, or restarting. Upon closer inspection, you find a plan or project that showed a lot of promise months ago but got lost in the shuffle, or perhaps it needed time to mature. Either way, carry on.

Pitfalls and Potential Problems

The only fly in the ointment this month is you chafing at what you perceive as life slowing down to a dead crawl. The purpose of this is to give you the opportunity to put in place the proper foundation for a new phase in your life. This month, take stock of much you have accomplished and celebrate where you are, not where you are going.

Rewarding Days

2, 3, 17, 18

Challenging Days

10, 11, 26

Sagittarius | June

Overall Theme

You are busy, busy, busy as opportunities crop up every time you turn around, which lights you up and frustrates you simultaneously. Why? Because there's a lot of talk and not much action. Relax. This month is about gathering contacts and connections for future endeavors. Besides, there's more than enough things on your plate that need completing.

Relationships

Resist the temptation to take a me-versus-them approach to your relationships. No one, but no one, has been trying to trap you, keep you down, or control your life. That's just what you believe. And even if that is true at times, you are so hypersensitive to not finding yourself in that position that you always find a way to free yourself. The next seventeen months are all about you creating a healthy way to be connected, one that respects you and the other person.

Success and Money

You are truly excited about what is in store for you. The challenge continues to be the glacial pace at which life is unfolding. You have so many ideas and so much energy that you really don't know what to do with yourself. Create a list of priorities. Apply yourself to creating a plan. This will ground you. One word of caution: Be circumspect about who you share things with. A certain degree of keeping your cards close to your chest is needed right now.

Pitfalls and Potential Problems

It's difficult for you to restrain your enthusiasm. After all, it's so innate. Well, you don't have to, but you do need to keep the reasons for it under wraps. You have the kind of idea that promises to change your life profoundly, and it needs time to fully blossom before you put it out into the world. Plus, it really is nourishing you at a deeper level, and sharing it will dissipate both your energy and the potential of the idea.

Rewarding Days

11, 12, 25, 26

Challenging Days

4, 5, 21, 22

Sagittarius | July

Overall Theme

All the wind goes out of your sails. Life feels heavy and uncompromising and rigid. Try to see it as the final sprint to the finish line of a marathon. Everything hurts and you are having trouble breathing, but getting across that finish line is going to change your life forever. Not only will you have a deeper appreciation for yourself and for what you are made of, but you will know yourself at a depth you didn't know existed. You are steadfast and unwavering when it really counts.

Relationships

You find, much to your surprise and maybe dismay, that not everyone knows what to do with the new and improved you. However, their resistance creates a resistance in you, one that expresses itself quietly and determinedly. No one is going to be able to interfere with who or what you choose to be. Especially when you are committed to a clearer, healthier version of you.

Success and Money

Take time to review whether you are up to date in taking care of the financial side of your life. Something may have fallen through the cracks. After all, life has been pretty intense. It's a problem easily resolved, so don't let it get in your head and muck about. There's a lot going on right now that requires you step into a new role, and you can't afford to waste valuable energy on a minor matter.

Pitfalls and Potential Problems

There's no getting around the fact that this year has been a mixed bag of conflicting energies that took all your willpower and adaptability to master. And this month is no different, although you are sure it's worse than ever. Not so. Unless you make it so. Refrain from amplifying your irritation and anxiety. Do something life-affirming.

Rewarding Days

8, 9, 23, 24

Challenging Days

4, 5, 18, 19

Sagittarius | August

Overall Theme

No need to move any mountains of any kind, nor is there any heavy lifting to be done. Life is bright and sunny, yet you are more than a little reluctant to get on board with that. Not that you aren't relieved. It's just that part of you is certain someone is playing a practical joke on you. Well, you really can relax. And book yourself a vacation—pronto. You need a change of scenery to truly enjoy this shift as well as recharge those batteries.

Relationships

Normally you don't describe yourself as a romantic, but right now you are imagining how you can create a little more of that kind of energy in your life. It's not that you ever thought it was silly. You just didn't understand it. The key here is to ask your partner to share what they think that is and then define it for yourself. On a deeper level, you are looking for new ways to nurture intimacy.

Success and Money

You are pretty content with this aspect of your life. Projects are humming along, the work environment is supportive, and you are bubbling over with enthusiasm about your future. What's more, there's the potential for a promotion or a change in your role. Keep that in mind when an unforeseen drama is created. And stay out of it.

Pitfalls and Potential Problems

It's been so long since it hasn't felt like you were two steps away from some kind of disaster. Well, you can trust that you navigated all the pushing and pulling that defined your life and did more than survive. You emerged with newfound inner power and a new understanding of what is truly important in your life. So take yourself off the hot seat.

Rewarding Days
9, 10, 25, 26

Challenging Days
15, 16, 27, 28

Sagittarius | September

Overall Theme

The constant refrain in your head is "get the job done, get the job done, get the job done," which turns out not to be a problem. No matter what is required, you are more than ready, willing, and able to do it. This reflects a commitment you aren't necessarily aware you made: to make life work in ways that honor all that you are. Sure, you love freedom, but you now know you need more than that to be content.

Relationships

This area of your life isn't exempt from a compelling need to make sure everything is working properly. Just try not to push people to tell you every itty-bitty thing you may have done to irritate, disappoint, or hurt them. It's kinder to yourself and to them to ask them what being loved looks like to them. This is more likely to create what you are seeking.

Success and Money

A more complete picture about what you wish to create emerges from an unexpected conversation with someone you trust completely. What shifts your world is a comment about your strengths and abilities and how they actually inhibit you. This seems counterintuitive until you realize you need to grow beyond them and develop other aspects of yourself.

Pitfalls and Potential Problems

There's always a point where you shift your life in ways that appear to be contrary to what you always believed and you wonder if you are being true to yourself. This springs from the notion that what was once important to you must always be so, and that in letting go, you are going to lose some vital part of yourself. Actually, the opposite is true. Hanging on to what is no longer valuable is shutting off the opportunity to grow and expand.

Rewarding Days
13, 14, 21, 22

Challenging Days
11, 12, 24, 25

Sagittarius | October

Overall Theme

The focus turns completely to long-term hopes and wishes as your creative drive soars. This could be a truly inspiring month, provided you keep your impatience in check. Otherwise, you run the risk of shutting down all the sparkly, imaginative stuff that is such an antidote for all the trials and tribulations you slogged through. The purpose of all this playtime in your brain is to give you a sense of direction for the future.

Relationships

A clearer understanding of how you intend to change your relationships arises from the very honest conversations you had in September. You now see things from a number of completely different perspectives. At first, it surprised you to know that not everyone is looking for the same thing. It actually set you off on an exploration to find out what you desire, outside of your intrinsic demand for freedom, which now allows you to initiate a fresh approach.

Success and Money

Now is the time to circle back on a number of contacts you made earlier this year, particularly in June. It promises to open up the kind of opportunity you might never have considered before. But upon further examination, you realize that what you bring to the table isn't really summed up by your current job description. Your skill set is much broader than that.

Pitfalls and Potential Problems

Not much is likely to upset your equilibrium as long as you keep your attention fixed on your goals and intentions. This is a month when you are and will be in the driver's seat. And if anyone or anything shows up to challenge that reality, the best thing to do is ignore it.

Rewarding Days

3, 4, 25, 26

Challenging Days

6, 7, 28, 29

Sagittarius | November

Overall Theme

This may not be the most comfortable time of the year for you. The biggest reason? There's still difficult, painful stuff buried inside you. Stuff that threatens the new paths you carved out for yourself. Obviously you feel you spent ample time shining a light into the darkest corners of who you are. So do you really need more time in the dark? Apparently, the answer is yes. Just know that bringing all those ghosts out of the darkness liberates you.

Relationships

You start November pleased with the progress you are making in improving your relationships. But then you get some feedback that's not very reassuring. Don't let what you hear affect you or deter you from fulfilling your intention. Remember, you chose to transform this part of your life to honor what you now know is meaningful to you, not to meet someone else's expectations.

Success and Money

There's so much to think about, and yet there are days when you seem unable to focus. Take note of those things that make your mind go blank. It's a sign that you have no real connection to the invitation, project, or idea being presented to you. Weed through them so that when the light turns to green mid-month, you are clutter-free and ready to give your all to what you value.

Pitfalls and Potential Problems

All that stuff lurking in the back of your consciousness needs to be released. It's taken up enough time and space. Plus, it can't hurt you and haunt you any more than it already has. So invite it to come out of the shadows. Acknowledge it (which isn't the same as feeling it). Recognize what it was meant to show you about yourself. Then let it go.

Rewarding Days

13, 14, 26, 27

Challenging Days

4, 5, 16, 17

Sagittarius | December

Overall Theme
Plan a party, a very special party. Call it "I Made It Through 2020 and I Got Out Alive!" or some variation on that theme. After all, you deserve to celebrate what you accomplished in facing a plethora of challenges to your identity, your values, and, well, everything that makes your life meaningful. And you uncovered the depth and breadth of what really makes you tick.

Relationships
You feel good about everything and everyone. So there ain't no one able to rain on your parade this month. Nor should they. You are definitely in the mood to be generous, both with time and with all your other resources, which include your charm and your immeasurable capacity for fun and laughter. And laugh you will, most especially at yourself, which is a sign that you are back on the light side of life.

Success and Money
There isn't anything you aren't ready to tackle as this year comes to an end. Plus, you sense a big change in the direction of your life just around the corner. You can't put any words or any form to it. You just know it's coming. Oh, you are curious about where it will take you and what you might leave behind, but essentially your message is "bring it on!"

Pitfalls and Potential Problems
Everything dark and painful is no longer even on your radar, and you want to shout hallelujah. So do it. You are stronger, more vibrant, and definitely more grounded than you were at the beginning of 2020. Embrace that rather than leaning on it, and 2021 will be a further expansion of the best parts of who you are.

Rewarding Days
4, 5, 22, 23

Challenging Days
15, 16, 29, 30

Sagittarius Action Table

These dates reflect the best—but not the only—times for success and ease in these activities, according to your Sun sign.

	JAN	FEB	MAR	APR	MAY	JUN	JUL	AUG	SEP	OCT	NOV	DEC
Move			21, 22						1, 2			
New romance						14, 15		3, 4				
Seek coaching/ counseling					6, 7						13, 14	
Ask for a raise	13, 14						23, 24					
Vacation				15, 16								17, 18
Get a loan		28, 29								3, 4		

Capricorn

The Goat
December 22 to January 19

♑

Element: Earth

Quality: Cardinal

Polarity: Yin/feminine

Planetary Ruler: Saturn

Meditation: I know the
strength of my soul

Gemstone: Garnet

Power Stones: Peridot, onyx
diamond, quartz, black obsidian

Key Phrase: I use

Glyph: Head of goat

Anatomy: Skeleton, knees, skin

Colors: Black, forest green

Animals: Goats, thick-shelled
animals

Myths/Legends: Chronos,
Vesta, Pan

House: Tenth

Opposite Sign: Cancer

Flower: Carnation

Keyword: Ambitious

The Capricorn Personality

Strengths, Talents, and the Creative Spark

Your strengths are many. Drive, focus, and ambition top the list, along with an innate integrity that pushes you to do your best. You are definitely not content or satisfied unless you say with complete confidence that you did everything humanly possible to achieve whatever objective is set out. Now, of course, it is imperative that you define your own parameters, because you know instinctively this is the key to your personal well-being. For you, success is achieving the goal you set for yourself. Ultimately, it is as important to you to make your favorite dessert well as it is to organize a huge event that earns you accolades. There must be the potential for success in everything you do. Otherwise, what's the point?

Success is not about the magnitude of what you do, but about the sense of accomplishment it gives you. It's about the content, not the context. This is a defining principle for the way you live your life, one that encompasses another powerful aspect of who you are. You are purposeful and pragmatic. You are the realist of the zodiac, which manifests in your ability to plan, organize, and problem-solve. It gives you great pleasure to take all the moving parts in any endeavor and mold them into a positive outcome. You know that life doesn't work without some kind of structure. Otherwise, everything is just floating around in a vacuum, without any form, which just doesn't make any sense to you. Life without form? Not possible. Or preferable. So your creative spark ignites when you are asked to give form to life's potentials and possibilities. Taking a nascent idea or concept or inspiration and shaping it into something solid and useful is the greatest act of creativity you can imagine. This is what keeps you seeking new and different ways to practice the mastery that is so important to you. For you, life is meaningless and empty without the promise of new mountains to climb, new vistas to see, and new visions to make real.

Blind Spots and Blockages

The first thing you need to do is take a timeout. The world isn't going to pass you by in the time it takes to read this. Have you considered that everything in life isn't supposed to be a struggle? Now, before you bluster and bristle and mutter under your breath about hard work, consider

224 Llewellyn's 2020 Sun Sign Book

this. Hard work and struggle are *not* the same thing. Sure, you thrive on challenge, on achieving things, on creating something concrete. But too often, your lack of flexibility creates struggle where none exists, which leads directly to your blind spot: not seeing the value of sitting back and letting things run their course once you have set them in motion. You really don't have to manage everything, oversee everything, run everything. In fact, trying to do so just leaves you with a mountain of frustration that you always have to climb over in order to get back to any sense of equilibrium. Because, of course, you can't admit you simply can't control everything. This would require you take a step back and accept the reality—yes, I said reality—that control is an illusion. Instead, you beat your head against the nearest brick wall over and over again, expecting a different result. Because what could possibly be wrong with your plan? Probably nothing. But stuff happens.

At the root of this ongoing conflict is a basic lack of trust. This makes it hard to enjoy anything, especially when your mantra is fear. Combine the two and you find that somehow you are always the one elected to carry everything. Being indispensable because, well, somebody has to be. Who said? Actually, no one but you. This is a classic Capricorn rationalization, one that is always going to inhibit you, limit you, and leave you holding the bag. Because again, somebody has to. But, why you? The danger here is not realizing that life actually happens from the inside out, and that all those external demands you just have to take care of do not add depth and dimension to your life. They just take up space. Better to take charge of your own life, instead of trying to get everything in the world to line up to your specifications.

Intimacy and Connection

You have as much need for warmth and affection as anyone. It's just that your natural inclination is to hold back and/or present yourself as impervious to emotions. Part of that is connected to your susceptibility to guilt, part of it to your wariness of the motives of others, and part of it to your need to prove yourself by being responsible for, well, everything. All of which you believe puts you at the mercy of others, aka vulnerable. And you are absolutely, positively afraid of vulnerability. All this makes it hard for anyone to get to know the real you, much less create any kind of intimacy. After all, intimacy is built on openness, not protecting yourself behind a wall so thick that even you have difficulty getting through to yourself. The irony is, if you are shielding yourself from others, you are also disconnecting from yourself, because your subconscious doesn't discriminate between you and others. The first step to building intimacy is to begin a dialogue with yourself. Listen to your feelings. Let your emotions surface. Make sure that with each step you take, you feel strong and grounded. See it as a process where you are building muscles, in this case, feeling and emotional muscles. Once you get comfortable with being in your feeling body and you embrace that gift, you can move on to opening the door to those closest to you.

Values and Resources

You are a results-oriented person, and you see no reason to apologize for that. After all, the proof is in the pudding. You just don't see any sense in hitting the start button if you haven't considered the potential outcome of your plan, or if you haven't bothered to develop whatever is necessary to carry things to fruition. This boils down to one simple thing: discipline. Something you value more than you can put into words. All the talent, all the best ideas, or all the drive and ambition in the world don't add up to anything if you don't do the work, if you don't mold, shape, or master what you have at your fingertips. Intention is just the beginning, not the whole enchilada. This you know in the deepest parts of your soul. It's truly what guides you instinctively to make the choices you do.

Goals and Success

These two aspects of your life are so entwined in your consciousness that to think about one is to automatically conjure up the other. So every time you set a goal, you are choosing success. And, of course, you are rarely without a goal of some kind, day in and day out. Because goals are a basic tool that you use every day, not a New Year's resolution or something on your yearly performance evaluation at work. Goals truly are intrinsic to the way you get things done. They are present all the time. They help build success in bits and pieces. They are the signs that bolster your confidence. They are the steps along the path, not the end result. You simply cannot imagine how your life could function without them. Not only do they make your life work, but they lead very naturally to success.

Capricorn Keywords for 2020

Imagine, release, restructure

The Year Ahead for Capricorn

There may be times in 2020 when you are convinced you are going to implode. Or is that explode? Or both? You barely take a breath as the new year dawns and you already feel an internal pressure so deep and so all-encompassing that you cannot get your mind, your heart, or even your body around it. Normally, you are willing to stand and face any and all challenges. But this one makes you wonder if you shouldn't choose from a menu of possible ways to avoid dealing with it all. Know this. That won't work. Not even for a little bit. No matter where you run, no matter how you numb yourself out, no matter where you try to hide, you cannot escape the demand being made. Oh, you may very well believe this is about people and problems outside yourself—work, relationships, and family, to name a few—but this is an inside job. Which is likely to frighten you, since you often shy away from what's inside you.

That fear will fade away as soon you realize how liberating it is to know that because this is about you and only you, you are the one in charge of responding to this crisis. One you have been preparing for since 2008, by transforming the way you are in the world, by taking your rightful place as the most important person in your life, and by embracing a passion for life you didn't always allow yourself to claim, much less own. This is the last step and, quite frankly, the most important one. You've already done most of the heavy lifting, pushing yourself outside your carefully constructed reality to find pieces and parts of yourself that created a more integrated awareness of who you are. Now it's time to birth that new picture in a concrete, stable, and grounded way, which translates to no more hiding in the work you do or the responsibilities you bear. Time to stand in your power and be your own superhero. Tear down anything and everything that weighs you down. Return any responsibility you carry for the lives of others, especially if they are more than capable of taking care of themselves. Resign from the I'm Indispensable Club. Then craft a whole new path for yourself, one that allows you to use all your gifts to create a vibrant life that nourishes you.

Jupiter

Jupiter is the lantern that will see you through the darkness this year, but only if you cast aside your innate skepticism about what he brings to the table. You are always wary of his approach to life because you believe it to be unrealistic and irresponsible, so says the realist to the optimist. After all, you resist calling yourself a pessimist, much less seeing yourself as one. The way you see it, you are perfectly willing to embrace the upside of life as long as you've earned it, but you are really not sure about the practicality of optimism and hope when it looks like the odds are stacked against you. This year provides the perfect test for you, as you are pushed to the limit of your capacity for transformation and you need some confidence and faith to see you through. Call on Jupiter. Find a picture of him. Get a crystal or stone associated with him or the qualities he represents. Buy yourself a piece of clothing that features a color associated with Jupiter. Research symbols connected to Jupiter and put it someplace where you can see it. Because you are an earth sign, bringing Jupiter's energy into your world physically is quite necessary. Be clear of your intent though. If you just plunk these things into your world without declaring what your objective is, Jupiter can amplify the challenges you are facing rather than easing the tension and showing you the light at the end of the tunnel, something you not only need to support you this year, but something that helps shift worn-out and toxic ways of looking at the world. All this gives you a deeper appreciation of what he offers and how vital he is to your life moving forward. After all, how can you grow your life if you resist his invitation to expand?

Saturn

Be aware. And most of all, be prepared, at least mentally and physically, as Saturn approaches Pluto for the summit to end all summits. Of course, because Saturn is the boss of Capricorn, he assumes natural authority over all things in this sign, including Pluto. Who, to say the least, is reluctant to bow down or be subservient in any way. The upshot of this is that you are likely to feel a war going on inside you that you can't quite put into words as these two planets try, at some points unsuccessfully, to negotiate an agreement. The key here is to remember that Saturn always prefers the status quo unless you can show him compelling reasons to change. And even then, he is likely to balk until he gets past his belief that something or someone is trying to control him. This is you in a nutshell, because you are Saturn personified.

Meanwhile, Pluto has been enticing you, then inviting you, and finally pushing you to transform negative aspects of your life since 2008, and he views Saturn's arrival as interference in his mission. This leads, not unsurprisingly, to a standoff. One taking place inside you, bringing up all manner of fear, anger, and a whole host of other mixed feelings. So you are liable to feel like a dinghy sitting on top of a tsunami until you find a way to process the complexity of what is going on without creating the kinds of complications that only make things worse. But how? First, you need to understand that you cannot undo all the changes inspired by Pluto. You cannot put all those deep feelings, all those profound insights, and all those significant things you discovered about yourself back in a box on a shelf. It will create long-term damage, not just to your core but to everything you do moving forward. Once you accept that, turn your attention to how you can use this internal rebirth in practical (Saturn) and passionate (Pluto) ways to build a life that honors the very best parts of you.

Uranus

In the middle of all the disconcerting things being thrown at you by Saturn and Pluto, you are loathe to acknowledge anything that might add more instability to your life. While it's true that Uranus's reputation certainly suggests he is likely to do that, you may find his poking around in your life a welcome distraction. After all, he isn't interested in disturbing your emotional equilibrium as much as he is encouraging you to use your creativity to alleviate the intensity with which you experience everything right now. Of course, this isn't without its challenges. You may find it hard to concentrate or produce anything concrete, which may make you wonder what the point is in doing it. Uranus's reply? To take you outside the box you are in and find new inspiration and new direction. To play and have fun. To simplify your life by removing anything no longer necessary to how your life functions on a daily basis. In other words, to get you to examine any habits so deeply embedded in you that you don't know the last time you actually questioned whether they worked for you anymore.

Neptune

Your brain is mush. At least, it feels that way. Every time you try to analyze, organize, or communicate anything that requires sequential thinking, you find yourself in a bit of a fog. Instead, you want to daydream or sit and wait for inspiration. This seems strange to you, especially as you tackle the demands of Saturn to get with the program. Except you aren't sure what that is, because your mind is busy following the wispy little tendrils of the unknown constantly dancing around inside your head.

And the very thing you pride yourself on—the ability to focus on putting one foot in front of the other—seems a thing of the past. This is actually a blessing, even though it's outside your comfort zone. The truth is that Neptune is encouraging you to use his energy to create new pathways of thinking by calling on imagination, not rational thinking. This is a perfect solution to dealing with your ongoing struggle to integrate the demands of Saturn and Pluto.

Pluto

Pluto's message to you is candid and blunt: Stick with your transformation. The only reason it suddenly feels oppressive or questionable is because, as you near the end of this process, your fear of losing yourself and everything you've built is going to take one more shot at derailing you. Old habits and patterns quite often have a life of their own and are reluctant to die or be healed. At one time, they were effective coping strategies, especially when you were too young to take care of yourself. But now they stand in the way of you reaching your full potential. No matter what Saturn whispers in your ear about keeping the tried and the true, Pluto is inviting you to a new reality, unencumbered by anything toxic. This doesn't mean a full-scale abandonment of anything you truly treasure, just an opportunity to rebirth yourself from the center of your authentic core. It's certainly true that Pluto's energy has the potential to be destructive, but that only happens if you choose to ignore the chance it offers, a chance that has its source deep inside you. So as you grapple with Pluto and Saturn, remember that. It's all you.

How Will This Year's Eclipses Affect You?

Eclipses signal intense periods that highlight major growth opportunities for us in the process of creating our lives. They are linked to the lunar phases—specifically the New and the Full Moon—and involve the relationship between the Sun, the Moon, and the Earth. A Solar Eclipse is a magnified New Moon, while a Lunar Eclipse is a magnified Full Moon. Eclipses unfold in cycles involving all twelve signs of the zodiac, and they occur in pairs, usually about two weeks apart.

This year there are six eclipses: two Solar Eclipses (one in Cancer and one in Sagittarius) and four Lunar Eclipses (one in Cancer, one in Sagittarius, one in Capricorn, and one in Gemini). This mixed bag of energies signals a shift from last year's focus on redefining nurturing versus babysitting, obligation versus accountability, family versus career, time for self versus taking care of business, and feelings versus rational thought. Three of this year's eclipses (the Lunar Eclipse on January 10 and the Solar Eclipse on June 21, both in Cancer, as well as the Lunar Eclipse on July 5 in Capricorn) complete this cycle, while the new eclipse cycle calls on us to understand that there is no wisdom in living in an ivory tower, stuck in our belief that there is only one way to live life while cut off from that very life. Instead, we need to get down to the streets and actually experience our environment, talk to people, create a dialogue, and embrace diversity. Only then can we create a world that truly embodies freedom and opportunity. Three eclipses (the Lunar Eclipse on June 5 in Sagittarius, the Lunar Eclipse on November 30 in Gemini, and the Solar Eclipse on December 14 in Sagittarius) begin this process.

The first eclipse of 2020 takes place on January 10, and it's a Lunar Eclipse in Cancer, offering you the opportunity to continue creating a healthier and more nourishing emotional foundation, first for yourself and then for the relationships in your life. This process began in November of 2018 and ends this year. Too often you are likely to suppress or repress the feeling side of your nature, because you aren't always sure what its value is, especially in a world that sees feelings and emotions as inconvenient at best. This is a point of view you have adopted, not because you really believe that but because it seems easier to get through life without giving space to something that often leaves you feeling inadequate. After all, you are not a touchy-feely kind of person, one who seems to personify being sensitive, caring, and compassionate. You demonstrate how you feel by what you accomplish. Isn't that what's most important? Yes and no, as you have discovered. You now realize how hard you have to work to keep the feeling part of yourself under wraps and how much that diminishes you at a fundamental level. It disconnects you from essential aspects of yourself and isolates you from deeper relationships with others. And last but not least, it interferes with you and your imagination, something you begin to explore as the eclipse pattern changes throughout the year.

Capricorn | January

Overall Theme

Even though it feels like your life is about to come to an end, it isn't. However, be aware that the pressure to make up your mind about where you want to go and what you truly want to do shows no sign of abating. It's actually amplifying. And no, you don't have to crawl out of your skin to alleviate what you are feeling. Just know you are on the verge of a rebirth. To accomplish that requires that you let go of anything rigid or limiting.

Relationships

Much to your astonishment, being around people brings tears to your eyes. Try not to recoil or look for a place to hide. Those tears are a sign that you are seeking deeper connection with the people you love, that you know how much you isolate yourself, even though you don't mean to do so. Honor yourself and welcome your desire to be more present for what you feel, not just what you think or do.

Success and Money

It's going to be difficult to figure out exactly what to do next in this part of your life, in spite of an unrelenting demand from within to sort everything out and get on with it. Except what does that really mean to you? At one time you knew the answer to that, but now you aren't so sure you want to continue on the same old same old path. The problem is you aren't sure you have a clear alternative.

Pitfalls and Potential Problems

No matter how hard you try to answer all the questions demanding your attention, it's simply not going to happen. Not because you lack the capacity to do so, but because it isn't time to find the concrete solutions you so desperately desire. The shift you are going through is about honoring the new vision of your life that is emerging. Answers and solutions will come later.

Rewarding Days

17, 18, 27, 28

Challenging Days

9, 10, 11, 12

Capricorn | February

Overall Theme

You aren't really sure exactly where to focus your attention, provided you can even get your mind to line up with your intentions. One minute you are happily concentrating and making plans, and the next everything seems to vaporize. It's like entering a space-time continuum that you just can't get your head around. Accept that this is about expanding your ability to think imaginatively, not rationally, and some very interesting possibilities emerge.

Relationships

Your mission, if you choose to accept it, is to forge new ground in how you connect with others. Of course, this promises to push a lot of buttons inside you, because this is uncertain territory for you. Opening yourself up and being sensitive, never mind vulnerable, is something that scares you, probably because you need someone to tell you what the rules are first. Otherwise, how do you know what to do? The answer? Be yourself.

Success and Money

An idea you threw out into the ethers of your workplace a number of months ago suddenly comes back around for serious consideration. This surprises you, most likely because you didn't see the potential in it yourself when you suggested it. Well, this is a sign of the shift going on in your brain and the considerable potential for the future this represents.

Pitfalls and Potential Problems

You know that the changes you are going through are necessary. After all, who is better at determining what is truly essential? No one but you. But still, you want to rebel, you want to resist, and you are downright angry. This is a response to all the times in your life when you did what you were obligated to do. Just remember, it's not duty driving you. It's choice coupled with desire.

Rewarding Days

1, 2, 23, 24

Challenging Days

5, 6, 25, 26

Capricorn | March

Overall Theme

For the first time in a long while, you know you are on solid ground—on the inside. Which you now realize is the source of true security. So when you once again feel that unrelenting pressure to choose the right path going forward, you are no longer overwhelmed. You meet the challenge with strength and confidence.

Relationships

Time for some fun, some laughter, some hanging out. The stuff you often consider a waste of time because you aren't clear what its purpose is. Not everything in life has to be serious or work. A lot actually gets accomplished by building strong relationships and acknowledging just how much these things create better mental, emotional, physical, and spiritual health.

Success and Money

Work takes a back seat to a certain extent as you find better ways to manage your time and commitment. You now know that keeping your nose to the grindstone doesn't always produce the results you seek. This signifies a shift in your definition of success. What you wish to create is equal parts creativity and hard work.

Pitfalls and Potential Problems

Give yourself permission to acknowledge how hard this transformation has been. Of course, you are profoundly aware that life isn't always easy. However, it really is okay to celebrate your fortitude and your determination rather than quietly falling limp in a corner. This not only lifts your spirits but actually puts you in first place in your own life.

Rewarding Days

8, 9, 26, 27

Challenging Days

6, 7, 21, 22

Capricorn | April

Overall Theme

As you embrace the major shift in your whole approach to life, you find, much to your dismay, that old fears resurface about whether change is a good thing or not. That's because part of you still wants to manage or control how that change is going to manifest. Don't be discouraged. Just trust yourself to make the choices and take the actions that offer you growth.

Relationships

You now find yourself capable of hearing what others share with you without responding in one of two ways, either by seeking to help them or by interpreting what they are saying as a judgment of you. Neither of these is healthy or wise, or necessary or true. Sharing is really about offering perspective and building intimacy, both of which you desire.

Success and Money

Expect a little rough water in your work life. Someone feels threatened by you, and they are inclined to try to undermine your reputation. Don't take the bait. You don't need to defend yourself to anyone, least of all this person. Stay focused on your goals. A new opportunity is in the offing.

Pitfalls and Potential Problems

You definitely need to take time out for yourself, if only because you are truly tired. Well, maybe exhausted is a better word. It makes you susceptible to any negative energy bouncing around in your life. Be clear. This is not yours, so don't take it on. The best protection is to give yourself permission to do something nourishing and positive every day.

Rewarding Days
8, 9, 22, 23

Challenging Days
2, 3, 28, 29

Capricorn | May

Overall Theme

It's a month of mixed blessings, which, of course, translates to riding a rollercoaster and hoping you're still in one piece at the end. One minute you are exhilarated, the next scared out of your wits. The strange thing is there are gifts in both states of being, which surprises you. Yet you now view life more fluidly, making it possible for you to use all your experiences in pursuit of your goals, rather than judging them as either a success or a failure.

Relationships

It's one thing for someone to sit down and clarify what their desires and needs are in a relationship. It's quite another to use that as camouflage for dumping all their dissatisfaction in your lap, expecting you to atone for what they believe are your past transgressions. You cannot change the past, and intimacy is not built on finding fault or blaming. Make that clear and then ask how the two of you can create a healthier relationship.

Success and Money

Things don't move as quickly as you intended. In fact, you are convinced they aren't moving at all or are going backward. See this as a time for redefining your goals and boundaries. For too long, you have been picking up the slack in an area that is not your responsibility. It's commendable to help out, but you need to stop before this becomes a permanent part of your job description. Draw the line now.

Pitfalls and Potential Problems

This month was not sent to plague you or test you. It's just life. One word of caution: Don't expect everything in your world to change overnight. You are still in transition from the old to the new at the same time that you are implementing your fresh, new approach. It's likely to be a little confusing and imperfect. Be kind to yourself.

Rewarding Days
2, 3, 15, 16

Challenging Days
10, 11, 25, 26

Capricorn | June

Overall Theme

New challenges—as if you needed them—make their presence known in surprise fashion. It's like someone tapped into all your hopes and wishes and then pulled the rug out from under your feet. Take a deep breath. That gives you enough time to realize that not only is this an inside job, but it's time to take a look at some self-defeating behaviors you've hidden from yourself.

Relationships

You are still trying to sort out the difference between barriers and boundaries. This allows you to begin looking at how easy it is for someone to trigger guilt in you. And that is the key to understanding why you build the walls you do. You are already inclined to take on too much responsibility for everything, and having those walls is intended to protect you from taking on more. Except they don't really do that. Rather, they keep you trapped inside yourself.

Success and Money

Work doesn't hold the same fascination for you as it usually does. Instead, you find yourself exploring a number of innovative ideas that simply won't be ignored. The more you try to concentrate on what's expected of you, the less content you are. This is just another sign that how you see yourself in the world is transforming. Enjoy. You'll still get your job done.

Pitfalls and Potential Problems

There's one fear that continues to rear its ugly little head. You aren't sure you are going to like who you are becoming. The real problem here is that you don't know if you can give up looking at the world from a good/bad, right/wrong, success/failure paradigm. You can and you will, as long as you recognize how unhealthy it is for you and how many problems it has created.

Rewarding Days

11, 12, 25, 26

Challenging Days

4, 5, 21, 22

Capricorn | July

Overall Theme

Call this a time of last hurrahs. Time to say goodbye to a number of beliefs and habits that keep you stuck in a never-ending cycle of questioning yourself, with the sole purpose of finding out what's wrong with you. You now realize that doing so doesn't meet the litmus test of what is helpful, useful, and productive. It only keeps you trapped.

Relationships

Gone is the belief that you need to take on more responsibility in order to prove yourself. Gone is the fear that you can never come close to meeting the expectations of others. Your only responsibility is to yourself first—of course, in a healthy, life-affirming way. It's one thing to be unwavering and single-minded in the face of what life dishes up and another to use your strength and dedication to prop up other people's worlds.

Success and Money

There's no doubt that the rebirth you are going through has shifted a number of things in your career/work. And this month you get to see how true that really is, as you find the clarity and strength to challenge a situation that always leaves you holding the bag. You are no longer willing to clean up messes you didn't make.

Pitfalls and Potential Problems

It's been a long, long journey to redefining self-care, self-nurturing, and self-love. You always thought the path to that ran directly through the satisfaction of taking responsibility for whatever was put on your plate, until you realized that often leaves you drained and exhausted and not always able to do your best. Now you know that taking care of yourself isn't selfish. It's actually necessary if you are to fulfill your commitments.

Rewarding Days

13, 14, 23, 24

Challenging Days

4, 5, 25, 26

Capricorn | August

Overall Theme

There's a part of you that is truly tired of always being careful, wary, and circumspect. You'd just like to throw caution to the wind, even for a little while. So do it. But only in areas of your life that require a dose of spontaneity. Otherwise, be content with the slow and steady progress you are making in the overall trajectory of the changes you're determined to make.

Relationships

You are truly inclined to step in and support anyone struggling with the challenges of life. After all, you do know what it feels like to be overwhelmed by trials and tribulations. The change here is that you openly address how this feels, rather than just offering solutions. This reflects a newfound wisdom. The process of life requires honoring both the practical and the feeling realms.

Success and Money

Be sure that you don't decide to play fast and loose with your financial resources. This could lead to making an investment or creating a partnership that isn't on solid ground. Take time to gather and analyze all the information you can get your hands on. Otherwise, it's fine now to treat yourself to a purchase or a vacation that recharges your batteries. Even you need pampering.

Pitfalls and Potential Problems

Because you have a natural inclination to regret things, this is not a month to push anything beyond your comfort zone, including the healing and purging process you are on the verge of completing. Not because you are likely to create any long-term problems but because you don't really have the energy. No matter how impulsive you feel.

Rewarding Days

9, 10, 27, 28

Challenging Days

7, 8, 15, 16

Capricorn | September

Overall Theme

It's not that you feel contentious or argumentative. You just want to be heard. You want people to take seriously the changes you are making. And you want acknowledgment. Not the kind that's empty and without meaning but the kind that actually shows you that are seen and appreciated for who you are, not what you do. This marks a major change in how you view your place in the world.

Relationships

Your inner strength and knowledge of yourself has grown so much that you feel safer in your own skin. It has not always been easy for you to trust yourself or others in relationships, because this requires an openness and a sensitivity that you find questionable, if not dangerous. However, that is fading and your intention to be candid and vulnerable takes you and others by surprise.

Success and Money

Don't be surprised if you feel you aren't on solid ground at work or in your career, even though everything is fine. This is just your fear talking. You took a moment or two to review the actions you took to change anything that wasn't working for you or fair to you, and now you are having a mini-meltdown. Acknowledge your panic. Then let it go.

Pitfalls and Potential Problems

Remember that no matter what you choose or do, you are always going to institute a review of all decisions and actions you take. The reason? You need to see how the consequences align with your original plan. This is both wise and necessary. The challenge this month is to see things clearly and not through the filter of worry.

Rewarding Days

2, 3, 17, 18

Challenging Days

12, 13, 24, 25

Capricorn | October

Overall Theme

Grateful for a pause in the action, you find time to catch up to yourself. You suddenly see with great clarity just how much you challenged, pushed, and transformed yourself with an intensity you didn't know you could conjure up, never mind apply. Once you recover from the shock, pat yourself on the back. And find a meaningful way to celebrate yourself, whether or not it feels comfortable.

Relationships

This area of your life is likely to feel like a ping-pong game as you fluctuate between striking a note for freedom from outside influences and the desire to meet people halfway. The key is to know that asserting yourself is not equal to condemning your relationships and that building a bridge with others is about creating consensus, not finding a 50-50 solution.

Success and Money

Even though the time may not be right to push ahead with an idea, a plan, or a project that you are deeply invested in, take time to make sure there aren't any loose ends or parts that are not completely thought through. Not only is this useful, but it leads to an interesting potential you didn't see in your initial strategy.

Pitfalls and Potential Problems

Home and family matters surface, leaving you wondering if you overlooked or ignored important things happening right under your nose. It's true that some of this has been percolating for a while, but if you set aside the guilt trip you seem intent on taking, you realize that although this is something serious, it is easily rectified now that you are giving it your full attention.

Rewarding Days

3, 4, 26, 27

Challenging Days

15, 16, 29, 30

Capricorn | November

Overall Theme

Long-term hopes and wishes end up on a collision course with immediate demands and complications you didn't see coming. Take a moment to realize this isn't a sign that you need to abandon the vision you have for the future, nor is it a message that you overlooked anything. Stuff happens. And in this case, it's connected to someone else dropping the ball. Refrain from rescuing anyone. Carry on with your dreams.

Relationships

You decide that it's time you expanded your social network to reflect the changes you are going through. It comes as a shock to you to discover that some of your tried-and-true friendships no longer uplift you. You just don't have a lot in common with them anymore. What's more, you didn't see it coming. Well, you can add people to your life without subtracting anyone.

Success and Money

The latter half of the month promises a major step forward in your future, and it's not even connected to anything you have in the planning stages. It comes out of the blue. At least it looks that way, until you remember a conversation you had a few months ago. This is definitely a turning point. One full of so much promise and potential that you are almost speechless. Don't overthink this or question its possibilities. It's real.

Pitfalls and Potential Problems

Of course, you prefer the straightforward and the predictable. Well, that isn't what you are going to get this month. Yet you are going to love what is offered to you, so much so that it may lead you to wonder why you are the one in line for such good fortune. Just remember how hard you have worked to give yourself permission to be the best that you can be.

Rewarding Days

17, 18, 27, 28

Challenging Days

5, 6, 29, 30

Capricorn | December

Overall Theme

It feels like there's a crowd stomping around in your unconscious mind, stirring up a bunch of unwanted and difficult feelings, ones you can't really connect to anything concrete. Just know that this is part of your new growth process, one that asks you to have faith in where you are going and also invites you to be inspired by yourself and your imagination.

Relationships

Your sensitivity to everything in your life overwhelms you, and you think the best solution is to be a hermit until it passes. Not so. Out in the big, wide world is someone who promises to help you make peace with the tender, hopeful part of yourself. So get out there. Meet people. Just avoid large groups or parties with too much alcohol. That you definitely can't handle.

Success and Money

There's every possibility that you will face a major conflict about expenditures this month. Recognize that this isn't so much about money as it is about energy. You want to be generous at the same time that you feel miserly. The best way to resolve it is to be generous to yourself by honoring you in any given moment, rather than playing the either-or game with yourself.

Pitfalls and Potential Problems

This year ends with the sense that you are on the verge of more change. And you aren't really sure how you feel about that. The healthiest thing you can do for yourself is remain fluid. That way, you will see immediately that this shift is about stepping outside the known to create what you truly desire, not a secret plan to pull the rug out from under your feet.

Rewarding Days

7, 8, 25, 26

Challenging Days

13, 14, 29, 30

Capricorn Action Table

These dates reflect the best—but not the only—times for success and ease in these activities, according to your Sun sign.

	JAN	FEB	MAR	APR	MAY	JUN	JUL	AUG	SEP	OCT	NOV	DEC
Move				15, 16						3, 4		
New romance			12, 13						1, 2			
Seek coaching/counseling						2, 3						18, 19
Ask for a raise		14, 15						3, 4				
Vacation	13, 14						14, 15					
Get a loan					15, 16						17, 18	

Aquarius

The Water Bearer
January 20 to February 19

Element: Air

Quality: Fixed

Polarity: Yang/masculine

Planetary Ruler: Uranus

Meditation: I am a
wellspring of creativity

Gemstone: Amethyst

Power Stones: Aquamarine,
black pearl, chrysocolla

Key Phrase: I know

Glyph: Currents of energy

Anatomy: Ankles, circulatory
system

Colors: Iridescent blues, violet

Animals: Exotic birds

Myths/Legends: Ninhursag,
John the Baptist, Deucalion

House: Eleventh

Opposite Sign: Leo

Flower: Orchid

Keyword: Unconventional

The Aquarius Personality

Strengths, Talents, and the Creative Spark

Your mind is your everything: your sanctuary, your guide, your source of entertainment, your first line of defense, your interpreter, your playmate, and the list goes on. It's inconceivable to you that people don't hang out in their mind and don't use its gifts, whether it's to solve problems or have fun. After all, is there possibly any better way to navigate life than through a flexible and open mind? Not for you. A strong mind equals a strong will. This alone sets you apart from others, not just because you are intelligent but because your mind and your consciousness like to wander past the boundaries of what is known. That is perfectly natural to you, and it leads you to ask questions and seek answers that no one else seems interested in, which you simply can't comprehend.

For you, life needs to offer limitless opportunities to see beyond the construct of physical reality to a space that looks empty but that you know is full of knowledge waiting to be discovered. The promise of change and growth and diversity is more than just exciting to you. It's the cornerstone of life. Otherwise, things become static and begin to die. You feel that at your very core, and it's completely antithetical to who you are and your reason and purpose for living—which, in its essence, is to chart your own course rather than adhere to the status quo just because. If that makes you a rebel and a nonconformist, so be it. You simply cannot grasp limiting yourself or anyone else either. You need to be free to make a choice, any choice, and to pursue your creative spark—curiosity—and where it might take you. You are always open and capable of standing back and observing your experience as an opportunity to grow and change rather than a demonstration of ineptitude, failure, or stupidity. After all, experience is what shows you not only truth but also potential, which is something you are always seeking. Of course, this constant reaching for the unknown makes you an idealist. And that is perfectly okay with you. It's better than being stuck.

Blind Spots and Blockages

While you are busy rebelling, have you noticed how many times you shoot yourself in the foot? At some point, the pain has to register. There's a difference between standing up for your ideals and willfully refusing to accept that anyone else has a brain capable of intelligent insight. You resist and resist and resist until there's nothing left to resist. Then maybe you capitulate—begrudgingly. Of course, this is your built-in defense mechanism. The one you use consistently to be sure that you are, in fact, doing what works for you, rather than following someone else's directions.

Your need to be in total charge of your own life, combined with a deep fear of being judged in any way, shape, or form, results in this hair-trigger resistance and often outright rejection of the most basic input from others. What if nobody really was telling you what to do? What if they had a really insightful observation or a practical piece of knowledge that expanded your life and made it work more effectively? What if they really are being supportive? Well, then, you might have to take a step back and acknowledge your blind spot. Sometimes you are so busy looking outside the box that you forget that what's inside the box—the tried and true, the predictable—is often helpful, most likely because it has stood the test of time. Not everything needs to be rejected outright and reexamined over and over again before you embrace it and give it your stamp of approval. The truth is that this need to resist and rebel creates the very limitations you are always afraid will impede you. Take a step back and see that being rebellious doesn't need to be an occupation. Or the sole thing that identifies you. Or that chip on your shoulder. Because that actually keeps you from doing anything with the all the talent, ability, and creativity that lives and breathes inside of you.

Intimacy and Connection

You love people—unless. That might well be your motto, for at least three reasons. One, you simply cannot create any kind of connection with anyone if there is no intellectual sympatico. That translates to people who are actively engaged in using their mind as more than a way station for the mundane parts of life. You must be met by curiosity and true interest. Second, you cannot handle anything less than authenticity. This is most probably because you are not very good at faking anything, so it follows that there is no path to intimacy with anyone who isn't going to show up as they truly are. You just don't understand the necessity of playing games. It makes no sense to you. Third, you will disappear at any sign of judgment. Again, you see no reason to expend your energy building a relationship with anyone who has already decided you are unworthy, especially if they don't know you. You are always in awe of the human capacity to judge someone as inadequate based solely on some characteristic they cannot change. All of this often leads people to believe that you are aloof and cold, which then pushes you deeper into yourself and makes you wonder whether what others call intimacy is really just a set of tests and rules that keep people from knowing each other. Sure, you are detached. The better to observe life. And people. Not for the purpose of judging it, but for the purpose of gaining awareness, both of yourself and of humanity. People truly fascinate you. You just wish people knew how much you celebrate and respect who they really are.

Values and Resources

It can often feel, both to you and to others, that what you value is always shifting and changing. And on the surface, that is often the case. You are not one to dismiss a thought, idea, or belief out of hand without considering it. So you ask questions and delve further, not because you have lost sight of what's important to you but because you are open to seeing things from different perspectives. How else can you grow if you insist on closing your mind to anything outside your own experience? After all, you might miss something truly extraordinary that transcends your whole life. That possibility, that potential, is the fuel that keeps you open and expectant, which you truly believe to be the best and only way to live your life.

Goals and Success

How you define this part of your life rests on one simple requirement: You choose the goals, you define what success is to you, and you follow the path that makes sense to you, even if it looks off-kilter or totally illogical. This often means equal helpings of experimentation and confusion, until it really becomes clear what your calling is. Because that is what you are searching for. Not a job, not even a career—although it can be both of those things. You need to feel a depth of passion and commitment to whatever you choose to spend your life doing, and finding that can often take time as you get to know yourself and what actually makes you tick. But when you finally home in on the path that lights up your life, you can and will create the kind of success that not only makes you proud of yourself but also makes the world a better place.

Aquarius Keywords for 2020
Courage, laughter, optimism

The Year Ahead for Aquarius

Normally, you are not bothered by what feels like a number of energies running amok in your life. After all, it can often be the best kind of entertainment at the very least, or stimulation at best. No matter what, it always gives you something to observe and use as potential points of growth. However, this year you are going to chafe at the steady diet of unpredictability, because even you need peace and quiet some of the time. Well, there's not going to be a lot of tranquility, whether it's in your outer world or your inner world. Things are so noisy on all frequencies, but especially spiritually and emotionally, that you are ready to jump out of your skin. You feel so unsettled. It's like your whole life is being rearranged, yet you can't really see how or why. You simply intuit it. Well, it might help to know that you are right. And that all you can really do is take the myriad threads, which don't seem to have much connection to each other, and follow the ones that offer a promise of the future and release the ones that symbolize past fears and difficulties. This sounds easy, but it won't be. You will need to call on your angels or your spiritual support network to give you a much-needed dose of optimism. It's not that you don't have the fortitude to move through this. You do. The challenge here is creating space in your consciousness to actually get the job done.

Jupiter

You might be tempted to put Jupiter on your blacklist this year. After all, you are certain he's causing a lot of trouble by stirring up things you'd rather keep hidden from yourself, like your fears, insecurities, and painful experiences. You are fond of having everyone believe that you are not affected by all the mundane aspects of life that keep other people tied in knots, that your capacity for detachment not only shields you but also allows you to see things so clearly that you don't fall into those particular black holes. This, of course, is simply not true. Why? Because the intellect is notoriously inept at dealing with the emotional content of life, because it simply doesn't speak that language. Yes, the intellect can make sense of the pieces and parts of how things feel, but it doesn't feel them. Which is why you like to observe how you feel without actually engaging in it. It's kind of like standing at the edge of a pool of water, insisting you know what it's like to get wet. Well, Jupiter is asking you to liberate yourself from all those pent-up emotions as well as the propensity to disconnect from them. Certainly, it's a big task, one that Pluto has been working on for quite some time. Jupiter can and will amplify this process. So you can either resist or put your whole body in the water. The former promises more difficulties, while the latter offers the kind of release you deeply crave.

Saturn

Saturn is the realist, the pragmatist, the planet whose main focus is making sure that the form and structure of life reflects what is useful and essential. Of course, he thinks he has all the right answers and isn't sure how he feels about sharing his space (Capricorn) with interlopers like Jupiter and Pluto. After all, they are being pushy and disrespectful, first, by not listening to him, and second, by trying to take over a process he believes he needs to take charge of. Because in the end, Saturn is the one who will help you actually make the changes in the outer world that Jupiter and Pluto are insisting on. It's not that Saturn doesn't see that your inner life needs a transformation. He's already been hard at work, helping you decide which facets of your world are worth keeping. However, right now he's worried that the pressure intensifying deep inside you may result in the destruction of parts of you that are healthy. Not all of you needs to be purged, so he's definitely going to put on the brakes if he feels you are heading for the edge of a cliff. Your challenge is to know when to move cautiously so you are prepared to deal with the consequences of what you are shifting and when to follow your gut instinct, your knowing, to a space and place inside you that is free of toxic waste—a place where you can truly begin to initiate a life that is not haunted by the judgments you've experienced in the past.

Uranus

So while you are trying to figure out how to traverse the drama going on in your inner life, Uranus is disrupting and challenging what you value and why. Strangely, this is somewhat easier for you to manage, partly because it's out there in the open and partly because this is an area of your life that you constantly examine to see if it reflects the growth you are undertaking. The major area of discomfort here is that Uranus is not particularly happy in the sign of Taurus. He feels weighed down and heavy there, contained and hampered by all manner of earthy things he doesn't really resonate with. And because he is your planetary avatar, you feel the same. It's not that you don't understand the need for stability, security, and something solid to stand on. You do. What you can't fathom is why or how this translates to being stuck. What value is there in hanging on or holding on to anything that has outlived its usefulness? Ironically, that is the question Uranus is asking you. So take an inventory of anything in your life that you place value on. Even yourself. This is the first step in clarifying exactly where you're at and how you may have settled into patterns and habits that don't reflect where you're at, much less where you're going. The truth is that you often move into new states of being and forget to clean out your energetic closet because you are much more enamored with what's fresh and exciting than what's stale and boring. Uranus is inviting you to finally get around to getting the job done. That way, you are ready for the next stage of the Uranus-in-Taurus journey: finding your true value to yourself.

Neptune

Fizzy and fuzzy. That describes how you feel when you tune in to Neptune. Because, like Uranus, Neptune is connected to things outside the known, you feel a certain affinity with him. Except when you can't make heads or tails of what he's showing you. It feels like everything and nothing all at the same time, which is often precisely the point when Neptune is involved. His message is always the same: Let it all go, let it pass, let it be. This is something even you tend to view as the end. But the end of what? Nothing or everything? Welcome to Neptune's world, where the kind of clarity called for in the physical world just doesn't exist. This turns your brain to mush, and your frustration level hits the earthquake zone, especially this year. With all the upheaval you're feeling as Jupiter, Saturn, Uranus, and Pluto stir the pot, you are ill equipped to take yet another jab in your psyche, disturbing what is left of your equilibrium. You already wonder if anything in your life is the least bit solid, so Neptune's invitation to more of the same is the icing on a very unattractive cake. Maybe, just maybe, if you could quiet the chattering, logical, fearful part of your brain, you could embrace the magic and the vision that is the true gift Neptune has to offer. This actually promises to give you a pathway to cope with the endless uncertainty in your life.

Pluto

It's not unfair to say that you're tired of Pluto's insistence that you engage in emotional archaeology for yet another year. Enough really is enough. Well, not yet. As much as you wish you could turn this process off, you can't. It's going to continue whether you participate or not, so opting out will only create more stress, not less. Especially since the purpose of all the digging is to ferret out any and all deep-seated anxiety that plays in the background of your consciousness, questioning how effectively and authentically you're living your life. As much as you insist on going your own way, you harbor secret fears that this is not okay, that somehow you should just follow the well-worn path. Well, Pluto has definitely forced you to look at that whole internal dialogue and stop taking an either-or approach to it. Being true to yourself doesn't mean choosing one over the other or creating a hard-and-fast set of rules. Instead, it is trusting yourself to know how to honor yourself and do what's best for you, whether it's stepping outside the box or keeping to the road, or a blending of both. This is essentially what you have been grappling with since 2008. It's just that this year feels harder and more difficult. Well, it's because you now have to take all the work you've done and are doing and actually translate it into your everyday life. You always insist that you want to live your life free of obligation, duty, limitation, fear, and rigidity. Time to do it.

How Will This Year's Eclipses Affect You?

Eclipses signal intense periods that highlight major growth opportunities for us in the process of creating our lives. They are linked to the lunar phases—specifically the New and the Full Moon—and involve the relationship between the Sun, the Moon, and the Earth. A Solar Eclipse is a magnified New Moon, while a Lunar Eclipse is a magnified Full Moon. Eclipses unfold in cycles involving all twelve signs of the zodiac, and they occur in pairs, usually about two weeks apart.

This year there are six eclipses: two Solar Eclipses (one in Cancer and one in Sagittarius) and four Lunar Eclipses (one in Cancer, one in Sagittarius, one in Capricorn, and one in Gemini). This mixed bag of energies signals a shift from last year's focus on redefining nurturing versus babysitting, obligation versus accountability, family versus career, time for self versus taking care of business, and feelings versus rational thought. Three of this year's eclipses (the Lunar Eclipse on January 10 and the Solar Eclipse on June 21, both in Cancer, as well as the Lunar Eclipse on July 5 in Capricorn) complete this cycle, while the new eclipse cycle calls on us to understand that there is no wisdom in living in an ivory tower, stuck in our belief that there is only one way to live life while cut off from that very life. Instead, we need to get down to the streets and actually experience our environment, talk to people, create a dialogue, and embrace diversity. Only then can we create a world that truly embodies freedom and opportunity. Three eclipses (the Lunar Eclipse on June 5 in Sagittarius, the Lunar Eclipse on November 30 in Gemini, and the Solar Eclipse on December 14 in Sagittarius) begin this process.

The first eclipse of 2020 takes place on January 10, and it's a Lunar Eclipse in Cancer, highlighting the intense examination of all things in your life related to how you feel about, well, everything. For you, that's a big job, and one not easily undertaken, since you have a tendency to confuse feeling with emotion. You get a lot of feelings, aka insights—your famous light-bulb moments. However, you think they arise out of your rational mind. They don't. They come from that part of your brain connected to sensing, feeling, and, yes, emotion, which is why you get confused. Feeling and emotion are deeply connected, but they are not the same, This is something you are definitely working to understand, even though you aren't sure why. Well, there is a deep evolutionary push to clarify this mix-up so you are able to create space for more insights, more brilliant perceptions, and just more inner joy. The stumbling block is that you really don't trust emotions. They make you uncomfortable, so you ignore them, repress them, or supress them, because you view them as unnecessary and perhaps even obsolete. This, quite frankly, inhibits all your innate wisdom, intelligence, and cleverness. Emotions are how you express your feeling nature. So if you shut them off, you close off much of the access to the sensing and feeling part of yourself, the part of you where all the brilliance resides. This year provides several more opportunities through the ongoing eclipse cycles to fully honor and appreciate how fundamental opening up to this potential is. The bottom line is that you end up being profoundly more connected to your own authenticity. How can you truly be yourself if you are expressing only one aspect of who you are?

Aquarius | January

Overall Theme

Who turned out the lights? Seriously, who did it? You are pretty sure it wasn't you. After all, why would you make yourself fumble around in the dark? Well, the who isn't as important as the why. You really need to take stock of what is going on deep within you, so a number of uncomfortable situations crop up that leave you totally clueless about what to do. Don't panic. Embrace the experience, and the answers rise up from unexpected places.

Relationships

Right now, you're feeling so sensitive and so emotional that you simply can't grasp what's happening, leaving you speechless. How can you share this experience when you can't put it into words, never mind a complete sentence? Maybe you could just be present with yourself. Listen to yourself. This actually paves the way for a number of satisfying connections with others.

Success and Money

You begin the year with some very clear goals in mind and enough energy to fuel a trip to the moon. But things don't pan out quite the way you intended as you get easily sidetracked by a number of other possibilities. Rather than being frustrated with yourself, recognize the gift in playing with the future. The time for your goals to manifest isn't that far away.

Pitfalls and Potential Problems

The temptation to resist dealing with the stuff piled high on your plate is irresistible. In fact, you are on the verge of a temper tantrum. So much for your clear thinking, capacity to adapt, and love of change. Do they only show up if you initiated the change in direction? Take a deep breath. You know things go sideways, and you can't control that. Figure out how you want to deal with the unforeseen and carry on.

Rewarding Days

5, 6, 17, 18

Challenging Days

10, 11, 12, 23

Aquarius | February

Overall Theme

The ups and downs of last month pass and you feel like your usual self again, only better. Of course, you are aware that this is a temporary respite. After all, your antennae are always attuned to the future. Refrain from trying to anticipate what's around the corner. Instead, enjoy the interesting mixture that life presents to you. One minute you're ready for anything, and the next you're in need of a nap.

Relationships

You are busy minding your own business when a number of people suddenly require your immediate attention, which isn't the issue. The real problem is the somewhat mundane challenges they insist they need help with, things you know they can easily handle on their own. Of course, this irritates you. Remember, you can say no. Or you can listen to their tales of woe and then tell them quietly how much you trust them to fix it themselves.

Success and Money

The number of delays and unforeseen complications pile up. The irony of this is that your part of the work equation is fine. You are ready to get the show on the road, but it feels like no one else has a clue. While they are busy sorting out the glitches at their end of the world, start work on a new idea or ideas currently keeping you awake at night. That way, you can get some sleep and be productive.

Pitfalls and Potential Problems

You are definitely not fond of stop and go, especially when it's mostly stop. Consider this an opportunity to prepare for the intensity and stress that life promises in the next couple of months. It's nothing you can't handle. You just need to clear your circuits so you meet everything with grace and confidence rather than impatience and grumpiness.

Rewarding Days

11, 12, 26, 27

Challenging Days

6, 7, 21, 22

Aquarius | March

Overall Theme

There are not enough adjectives to describe just how life unfolds this month. Quite simply, it's all over the place, with very little consistency and an endless number of questions, none of which seem to get answered. Don't worry. Turn your attention inward. It's time to do a major purging of thoughts, emotions, and past experiences in readiness for a powerful change in your circumstances.

Relationships

You are somewhat befuddled by how you feel about people. One moment you are attentive and supportive, and the next you can't focus. And it's not because you are bored. You are fluctuating back and forth between the desire to connect and an inner push to spend a significant amount of time alone. Accept this and act accordingly. That way, you get the time you need and you don't create needless problems with others.

Success and Money

You get some really good news about your future, but you are asked to keep it quiet. That doesn't bother you. What does is not getting actual details and a firm commitment. Relax. Everything is going to work out. You just don't like not having a complete picture, especially since this change is something you've wanted for a long time.

Pitfalls and Potential Problems

Ah, change. Something you love if it happens according to your plan. The problem with part of last year and the start of this year is that what's going on doesn't seem to bear any resemblance to what you had in mind. Remind yourself what this change represents to your growth instead of focusing on the details. You'll be more content and hopeful and less impatient and anxious.

Rewarding Days
8, 9, 26, 27

Challenging Days
4, 5, 16, 17

Aquarius | April

Overall Theme

Your optimism and hope return in a big way, following an intense beginning to the month, signified by a fear that you are unable to free yourself from a number of things haunting you. Just when you think you are trapped, something shifts deep inside you. Not only are you relieved, you are joyful. This sets the table for a remarkable new beginning.

Relationships

It's going to feel like you literally flipped a switch. Gone is the need for *any* alone time. You need people. Right now. And for one specific purpose: To have fun. Lots and lots of fun. Possibly a short trip or a vacation. Who knows? You are open to suggestions as long as it involves good conversation, laughter, and entertainment. Or maybe a little romance?

Success and Money

Find someone who can give you some solid guidance and direction. You've been sitting on an idea for quite a while, one that you play with and then push away over and over again. It just won't go away. So you really need an outside opinion—but only from someone who really knows their stuff and won't think you are crazy. After all, you wonder if you aren't.

Pitfalls and Potential Problems

Things calm down considerably and space opens up to move forward. And you don't trust it. Well, you can trust yourself. That's the key. If you are waiting for everything to line up perfectly, you'll be waiting for a long time. The truth is that you are anxious and uptight, afraid to take any step. This will pass as soon as do something that expands your world.

Rewarding Days

6, 7, 25, 26

Challenging Days

13, 14, 27, 28

Aquarius | May

Overall Theme

Life continues on the upswing. In fact, things couldn't be better. Your confidence returns and you realize how vital a part your lack of willingness to give up plays in not just handling what comes your way but actually making use of your experiences to grow your life. For the first time in months, you are sincerely satisfied with who you are.

Relationships

A curious thing happens. All your interactions last month bring up a whole host of questions about who is in your life and why. It's not the precursor to a full-scale purging of people from your life, but more an examination of what you value in your relationships. This leads to some interesting revelations about how much you are shifting and going in a fresh direction.

Success and Money

Be cautious in managing this area of your life. After months of feeling like you were pushing a rock up a hill, only to have it slide down again, you want to treat yourself. Just don't be extravagant, not because you shouldn't spend money but rather because you may regret what you purchased. As for work and/or career, expect a pleasant surprise.

Pitfalls and Potential Problems

You definitely feel you've been held down for far too long and it's time to break free and do what you want. Indeed. Just make sure you take a good look before you take any big risks. Optimism is one thing, but foolhardiness is another. Otherwise, you could undermine all the progress you made. And you know how much you hate repeating things or going backward. So find a creative way to declare independence from the pile of detritus you sent off to the garbage dump.

Rewarding Days

4, 5, 22, 23

Challenging Days

10, 11, 25, 26

Aquarius | June

Overall Theme

For the second month in a row, you are all sunshine and lollipops. And yet the world feels very stale and worn-out. Well, it's not the first and it certainly won't be the last time you find yourself at odds with your environment. So do what you do best. Be the rebel. Be the person who signals that life is changing and it's something to be celebrated, not feared. Things will get a lot brighter.

Relationships

It's not in your nature to be disrespectful. You just ask a lot of difficult and challenging questions, which others often interpret as impolite and even insensitive. This always short-circuits your brain, because your questions come from curiosity, not judgment. Well, you get a chance to address this ongoing dilemma this month. Be open to how others feel. Hear them out. This leads to a deeper understanding of how to connect without crossing lines.

Success and Money

A creative project that's gathered dust for several months finds its way back to the front of the line. And you are delighted. The truth is you forgot all about it in the midst of all the angst bubbling up from your emotional underground. It's such a welcome breath of fresh air that you want to toss aside all the predictable stuff and immerse yourself in a creative thinking binge. Just know there's space for both.

Pitfalls and Potential Problems

Once again you find yourself in conflict with your expectation that everyone ought to see the world the way you do. The irony is that you don't always see how intolerant that is. The key here is to recognize that your expectation is linked directly to the desire to find like-minded people, to find community, to find authenticity in others. Once you make that distinction, you feel a weight lift off your shoulders.

Rewarding Days

2, 3, 16, 17

Challenging Days

6, 7, 21, 22, 23

Aquarius | July

Overall Theme

It feels like that underground river in your unconscious, the one you keep trying to navigate, is about to flood once again. Yet you are not overwhelmed. You know you are about to master this wild, intense, and unpredictable life passage—finally. So you are exhilarated, not afraid. Now, this doesn't mean you expect a smooth transition. Far from it. You just trust yourself implicitly—a welcome and hard-fought accomplishment.

Relationships

Your grace under pressure attracts many of those around you to seek support, insight, and, well, a good shoulder to cry on. And because you now understand how deep a crisis almost everyone is and has been confronting, you are more than happy to oblige. If there's one thing you love, it's sharing knowledge and creating wisdom.

Success and Money

Even though neither of these two areas is first and foremost on your radar, it's imperative that you not ignore them. There are decisions you are asked to make right now that have the potential to affect both, not immediately but further down the road. So pay close attention and don't rush into anything. Use both your intellect and your intuition to guide you.

Pitfalls and Potential Problems

The deep emotional purging and healing process is almost complete, and you can feel a tremendous surge of creative energy just behind it. However, you cannot bypass the last step in clearing out all the crap you stored deep within where you couldn't see it, much less deal with it. All that's required is releasing the past, not reliving it. Energize that daily and you will be fine.

Rewarding Days

10, 11, 25, 26

Challenging Days

4, 5, 19, 20

Aquarius | August

Overall Theme

Things feel far too uncomplicated, at least compared to the last several months. Even when you felt on top of the world, you were still more than a little cautious. And now that the pressure is finally off—at least from an internal perspective—you are a little discombobulated. Enjoy the space. Use all that energy coursing through your body to make things happen. After all, there's quite a number of goals you set for yourself that you can now fulfill.

Relationships

A lot of unexpected love and appreciation comes at you from all directions. It seems you are on everybody's list of favorite people. It dawns on you that the more of your authentic self you share with others, the more they acknowledge you. This is surprising. After all, you thought conformity was the key to intimacy. Now you know it's sincerity, something you truly value and something that comes easy to you.

Success and Money

You feel like a kid in a candy store. There are so many choices to make, and all of them full of potential and promise, that you just don't know where to start. It doesn't matter. Pick one, knowing full well you can shift gears back and forth. Just be ready to put one of them on the fast track to success, both professionally and financially. Time to strut your stuff. You will be rewarded.

Pitfalls and Potential Problems

You are past the point where you need significant mentoring in any area of your life. This isn't arrogance. It's not superiority. It's not overconfidence. It's truth. You pushed yourself to eliminate whatever stood in the way of you claiming your own gifts. It's not egalitarianism to constantly diminish yourself in favor of others. It's unfair and unnecessary as well as unkind. You've gained a lot of wisdom. Celebrate it.

Rewarding Days

3, 4, 24, 25

Challenging Days

16, 17, 28, 29

Aquarius | September

Overall Theme

You really just want to get down to business, to get all that stuff piled up in your life either dealt with or organized. That way, you can dig deeper into all the exciting new ideas and opportunities that keep presenting themselves on a daily basis. You need to be able to determine which of them are dreams that can come true and which are wishful thinking. Either way, you are in for a fun ride.

Relationships

You are so excited by how you feel about life that you want to share your enthusiasm with everyone. At this point, it's wiser to talk only with a select few people you really trust. Not everyone knows how to celebrate or accept the new trajectory you are on. Plus, you are still in the midst of this very important shift and quite susceptible to input from others. It's okay to be over the moon without telling everyone why.

Success and Money

The basic things you value in yourself haven't changed, nor will they. What is changing is your ability to see yourself clearly so you truly understand what you have to offer. This definitely comes into play throughout the month as you put yourself forward for a new project and go in search of a way to bring one of your dreams to fruition. Both actions birth a new perception of yourself as a leader.

Pitfalls and Potential Problems

You are on the verge of an unprecedented rebranding of yourself, first within yourself and then with others. The biggest challenge is to recognize that this won't turn you into someone you can't stand. You are not in search of applause. You are in search of the best way to express and build on your potential, to simply feel the joy of being authentic rather than always minimizing yourself and feeling the discomfort of doing that.

Rewarding Days

1, 2, 27 28

Challenging Days

12, 13, 24, 25

Aquarius | October

Overall Theme

The word "vacation" has not been in your vocabulary for quite some time. You know, the kind where you leave everything behind, clear the clutter from your brain, and just hang out in the moment. Well, it's time to take one. You need a break so you will be ready to take charge when you are blessed with a surprising offer toward the end of the year—one that signifies a major turning point in your life and one you definitely won't see coming.

Relationships

You find yourself longing for something deeper and more meaningful in your relationships, except you aren't sure you can clearly define that. This is very directly connected to how much better you know yourself and how much more you value who you are. Because this is still a work in progress, it may take some time to know how to achieve more intimacy with others. You are still creating it with yourself.

Success and Money

Your contributions in your career/work environment are noticed and appreciated, partly because you definitely outdid yourself and partly because you are no longer content to be in the background. This makes it a great time to seek a better salary to reflect what you accomplished. After all, you solved a serious problem and saved a lot of money.

Pitfalls and Potential Problems

Everything is just fine, thank you very much. So why do you feel on edge and dissatisfied? Well, it isn't really about the current state of your life. It's more about the leftover fatigue from all the hard work you did mentally, emotionally, physically, and spiritually to grow yourself at the same time that you met all your other responsibilities in life. Pat yourself on the back. Oh, and don't forget that holiday.

Rewarding Days

5, 6, 18, 19

Challenging Days

11, 12, 29, 30

Aquarius | November

Overall Theme

Your outer world is humming along, yet you feel you can't relax. There's something in the offing, but you can't quite put your finger on it. Well, that's because there's a final cleanup going on deeper in your consciousness. It's not something you can quantify, so don't try. Let it flow without interruption, as uncomfortable as you might feel, and by mid-month you'll feel liberated and clear as a bell.

Relationships

Not everything in life can be described in words. Some of it really is like riding a wave, which describes your whole approach to relationships this month. You want to hang out, share, laugh, and enjoy much more than intellectualize the whys and wherefores of your connections. You just don't seem to have much interest in dissecting, processing, or redefining what makes you or anyone else tick.

Success and Money

The light turns green on a number of the irons you have in the fire, leaving you trying to make a choice about which one to focus on. When you realize you are uncertain about how much energy you want to put into your work environment versus directing it all into a project that has the potential to set you up as an entrepreneur, it gets a whole lot clearer. You don't need to make it either-or. Right now, you need to integrate both into your current plan.

Pitfalls and Potential Problems

As much as you claim to like change, what you don't realize is that you aren't always in love with the growing pains that go along with it. This month offers you the opportunity to build the capacity to go with the flow without working so hard to nitpick the whole process or anticipate exactly where it will take you. Just know this is necessary and you will appreciate what it creates in the end.

Rewarding Days

8, 9, 10, 22, 23

Challenging Days

5, 6, 29, 30

Aquarius | December

Overall Theme

A sense of anticipation infuses your life. You just know that all the pieces that make it up are about to coalesce in a manner you simply cannot quantify. And you are right. You are on the verge of the kind of shift that happens once in a lifetime. Contained in it is the opportunity to take complete charge of everything with a strength and a belief in yourself that may shock you—in a completely life-affirming way.

Relationships

You continue to bask in the pleasure of just being around others and being open to what that brings. This is especially helpful in your work life. However, be aware that at least one person is going to show up with an agenda that pushes all your buttons. Stay calm. Just because they want to play a game of Whose Fault Is It? (with the implied answer being that it's yours) doesn't necessitate you joining in. Listen. Don't comment. And everything will work itself out.

Success and Money

It's a good month to begin building a stronger support system for the goals you are already pursuing. You realize that one of your dreams has huge potential, and you aren't sure you can do it all by yourself. First, be clear about what is going to work for you so that when you identify the best people to join you in this glorious adventure, you know what role they are to play. And yes, you are the leader.

Pitfalls and Potential Problems

So what does it mean to be a leader? This is a question that is going to crop up for the next year or more. Too often, you believe being a leader is prescribing the course of everyone else's life. No, that's being a boss. For you, being a leader is about building a sense of community, and by not just talking the talk but also walking the walk. Use those values—in other words, be true to yourself—and you will create success.

Rewarding Days

17, 18, 24, 25

Challenging Days

15, 16, 29, 30, 31

Aquarius Action Table

These dates reflect the best—but not the only—times for success and ease in these activities, according to your Sun sign.

	JAN	FEB	MAR	APR	MAY	JUN	JUL	AUG	SEP	OCT	NOV	DEC
Move												
New romance					6, 7	9, 10		10, 11				17, 18
Seek coaching/ counseling	13, 14						15, 16					
Ask for a raise		14, 15		15, 16								
Vacation										13, 14	22, 23	
Get a loan			21, 22						1, 2			

Pisces

The Fish
February 20 to March 20

♓

Element: Water

Glyph: Two fish swimming in opposite directions

Quality: Mutable

Anatomy: Feet, lymphatic system

Polarity: Yin/feminine

Colors: Sea green, violet

Planetary Ruler: Neptune

Animals: Fish, sea mammals

Meditation: I successfully navigate my emotions

Myths/Legends: Aphrodite, Buddha, Jesus of Nazareth

Gemstone: Aquamarine

House: Twelfth

Power Stones: Amethyst, bloodstone, tourmaline

Opposite Sign: Virgo

Flower: Water lily

Key Phrase: I believe

Keyword: Transcendence

The Pisces Personality

Strengths, Talents, and the Creative Spark

At the core of your being are the two things you rely on most to create and interpret your life experience: imagination and intuition. These characteristics are not easily quantifiable or explained, not that that's a problem for you. You see them both as necessary to a vital and vibrant life. The very thought that everything can be defined or measured by the five senses is both disturbing and impossible to you. It leaves so much of what it is to be human out of the equation, such as the aware-ness of potential and possibility, the expression of hope and joy, and the space for creativity and compassion—all the things you hold in place by virtue of just being you.

On a truly deep level, you wish to exemplify by your words and actions all the most uplifting and inspiring aspects of the human experience: Show always what it is to love unconditionally. Show how to suspend incredulity to invite the unknown and unexplained into life. Show how to dream big and beautiful. Show how to find the beauty within. Show how to be connected to your inner reality as the true source of what hap-pens in life. All this so you don't lose sight of the divine, so you infuse your everyday life with the spirituality that you believe is your natural birthright. This is an enormous commitment, both to yourself and to the world, and one that is fueled by the creative spark imbedded in your sensitivity. You must feel and sense everything in order to navigate life, in order to be fully present in every moment with your heart wide open. Of course, this is risky. And often difficult. The world isn't always a reflection of all that is grace and light. Yet you persevere, often quietly and lovingly. After all, where would the world be if you abandoned faith and optimism?

Blind Spots and Blockages

Toss the rose-colored glasses. The pink shade of reality can be just as limiting as never having a dream. The challenge of living in the third dimension—yes, it really does exist—is grounding those dreams in reality, not living in an alternate reality that is wispy and insubstantial, choos-ing it every minute of every day and avoiding anything that calls on you to participate in the physical here-and-now. Sure, you are positive it's safer. Maybe, maybe not. What's true is that life can be painful for you, because you are tuned into it in a very different way than the rest of the world. You arrive on the planet with the capacity to connect to absolutely everything, and you, quite frankly, don't understand the concept of separation or duality. You innately seek oneness and never stop trying to achieve it, leading to experience after experience that makes the physical world duller and duller, less and less attractive.

So you create a special refuge inside you, one where all that is possible is alive and vibrant and life-affirming, where everything is beautiful and wonderful. But living there and not bringing your faith and optimism and creativity to light every day can leave you feeling just as hopeless as abandoning the part of you that births all those possibilities. Your blind spot is not seeing that you need to live your dreams instead of just having them. Otherwise, you are adrift, with no particular direction and no particular destination, leaving you feeling empty and disappointed. The solution is not to refuse to engage but to get out there on the front lines of life and show the world who you are and what you bring to the table. Being yourself is actually the point, not having a series of dreams disconnected from life.

Intimacy and Connection

Your challenge is not establishing contact with others but rather knowing where they end and you begin. You so easily find yourself in the energy and space of those around you because you are quite simply a natural empath. It's almost as if you were designed to tune into the reality of the whole planet and everything on it. This kind of ability ought to make it easy to build intimacy with others, but not necessarily, because that requires that you are as present for yourself as you are for the other person. That isn't easy, because once you merge with them, you aren't sure exactly how to find your way back to your own space, if you are even aware that you are separate. In fact, you can quite unconsciously come to be like the other person. This makes you a human chameleon, one who is quite talented at adapting to your surroundings by becoming a mirror. In the process, you may lose yourself for long periods of time until something startles you into an awareness of yourself, usually something that belittles the very things you hold most dear. Then you are forced to acknowledge that your relationship is neither the model of perfection you desire nor one that is particularly transcendent. This can take you in one of two directions: repeating the same pattern or taking steps to create a healthier relationship—one that is based, first and foremost, on you taking part as your authentic self. No need to abandon your vision of what you desire, although it might need a bit of tweaking. Just make sure you include yourself.

Values and Resources

It's truly easy for you to describe your resources, and they all lie within your heart, your mind, and your soul: faith, sensitivity, compassion, intuition, imagination, and the ability to love unconditionally. They are also the core of what you value and hence the core of who you are. To live a life devoid of the capacity to express any or all of them is the greatest fear you have. Your challenge is accepting that you do not have to express them all the time, that you can actually discern whom to share these gifts with, and that sometimes the person who requires them most is you.

Goals and Success

The biggest challenge for you is finding a way to quantify what either of these things mean, much less what they are. It's definitely difficult to discover within yourself the hard, finite answers that everyone else seems to be able to delineate so easily. Well, of course that approach doesn't work for you. It's partly because you know that your life is so much more than what is contained in the experience of the five senses, so it's often a challenge to zero in on how you can demonstrate them in a concrete, measurable way. And it's partly because life itself is so fluid that what you chose as a goal or a path to success last week may already be replaced by something else. This is what fuels your creativity and passion: the innate knowledge that you can and will let go of anything that does not strike the appropriate chord within or does not ignite or initiate a deeper expression of your imagination.

Pisces Keywords for 2020
Enthusiasm, substance, success

The Year Ahead for Pisces

The year begins with an overwhelming sense of heaviness, but that's a good thing for you. Of course, what you describe as heavy is really being grounded, with both feet touching the earth simultaneously, metaphorically and energetically speaking. This is not always your forte, but now you welcome it with open arms. Why? Because you just want to get focused and get down to business. You long for something solid and concrete. In fact, you are compelled to find a way to express the wealth of inspiration and imagination that is your constant companion in practical, physical terms. Enough of all this dreaming, visioning, and imagining. Time to get real. Time to anchor yourself on the earth. Time to expand your creativity out of your imagination and into something you can actually see or touch in the third dimension.

Jupiter

Connecting with Jupiter's energy this year requires a clear set of intentions. Without them, you may find yourself unable to count on him as your guardian angel, a role he quite frequently plays in your life. His buoyant optimism and enthusiasm is always heartening and inspiring and a place of welcome refuge. Well, in 2020, he is not only traversing Capricorn, aka Saturn's home and native land, but is hanging out there *with* Saturn, making him out-of-sorts and profoundly uncomfortable. He has no choice but to curb his enthusiasm, unless it's channeled in a direction that meets Saturn's demands. Hence the need for you to map out where you are going so that Jupiter can offer you the support you need. Without it, you may back away from achieving the goals you desire, believing that it's just too hard to overcome the challenges you encounter and thus deflating yourself at a time when you need to believe in yourself in a practical, realistic way.

Jupiter may not be filled with joy as he wanders through Capricorn, but that doesn't stop him from inviting you to expand your life in a fruitful, earthy, and successful way. Nor does it keep him from showing you that the only way to do that right now is through self-discipline, goal setting, and planning. He understands how deeply you believe in magic and synchronicity, and he's not saying those things are out of the question in 2020. However, you cannot rely on that alone to accomplish what your heart desires. You need the hopeful pragmatism inherent in Jupiter in Capricorn.

Saturn

As much as you often view Saturn as the unpleasant neighbor next door who is always complaining about what you do and how you do it, 2020 gives you the chance to move beyond that perception to a deeper appreciation of the gifts he represents. But first you need to stop assuming that his only role in your life is to act as a spoiler. Of course, you think him dull and demanding, unsympathetic and insensitive, which, from your perspective, he can be. However, Saturn knows that his job is always to reveal the true nuts and bolts of how to navigate life with purpose and accountability, something you often can't see or appreciate, for no other reason than you don't resonate with the idea that everything must be practical in order to be valuable. The key here is to remember that you can create your own definition of what is practical to you, which, ironically, is a very Saturnian process.

The truth is that Saturn is not trying to tell you what is practical in your life. He's just asking you to clarify it, so you have a foundation upon which to embody that definition. After all, *practical* and *practice* come from the same root word. So what is it that you would like to practice in your life? And how in 2020 can you do that in a way that builds a foundation for achieving your long-term hopes and wishes? That is what Saturn is challenging you to do. Not conform, not knuckle under, not acquiesce. Just commit yourself to creating a way to live your life with purpose, with direction. This brings you a deep satisfaction and a true sense of what you are able to accomplish, because it's out there and not just in your fantastical imagination. This is something you need, even though you are reluctant to acknowledge it. Time to set aside the belief that Saturn is a taskmaster and embrace him as a powerful and helpful mentor.

Uranus

After almost a year of coping with Uranus and all the upheaval he's caused in how you think and what you think, you are still struggling to figure out just what all this is about. He's challenged almost every cherished ideal and principle you thought was deeply entrenched and irreplaceable, thus exposing you to a truth about yourself: that you are just as stubborn about your point of view as anyone else. This shocks you and takes a sledgehammer to one of your most valued perceptions of yourself: that you are always open and compassionate and completely flexible. The key is to recognize that in order to value and protect yourself, you developed a hard shell around your thoughts and ideas as a way of maintaining a sense of who you are in the face of the insensitivity and the misconceptions you experience. It no longer serves you. In fact, it keeps you stuck in a space and place that no longer says much about the person you are growing into. And it keeps you attached to things and ideas that actually interfere with you truly knowing and being yourself.

All Uranus is asking you to do is rid yourself of that hard shell, take a good look at the thoughts and beliefs you cling to, question whether they assist you or undermine you, and set about creating a new template that reflects a healthier, vibrant, and more dynamic response to where you are right now rather than where you were. Part of this process includes letting go of anything ever said to you that was judgmental or unkind. This may be the most difficult aspect of working with Uranus, but it's necessary if you are to release yourself from the impact and the hold those words continue to have on you. No doubt it is surprising to see how easily you accepted what others had to say about you, and how deeply you took it to heart. Time to clean out everything in your mental attic and replace it with what you know about yourself, all of which is truly powerful, positive, and insightful. You just need to work with Uranus to shake up all the hardened defense mechanisms contained in your thoughts and beliefs. That way, you can reveal your true essence to the rest of the world and not suppress all the magic taking place inside you.

Neptune

No need to worry that all the pressure from Saturn and Pluto is going to dampen your capacity to dream and visualize. Neptune continues to infuse your life with all things magical and mystical, which is going to be a relief on the days when you feel you are encased in concrete and stuck to the ground, with no chance to float beyond the physical reality. Just be careful not to use Neptune's energy as a way to run away from or avoid reality. You are already feeling more than a bit tentative about yourself and about your connection to the planet. In fact, there may be days when you feel invisible even to yourself, and that is more than a bit disconcerting. How can you possibly get focused if you can't find yourself? That's not an easy question to answer when everything feels so fluid and foggy and ill-defined. But if you recognize that Neptune's intention is to dissolve anything that is not real and not substantial in your life so that you can clarify what you really are made of, then you have a focus to guide you. You need to make this focus physical, perhaps with dream boards, collages, painting, working with oracle cards, keeping a diary full of your hopes and wishes, yoga, dance, or whatever helps you express in the third dimension what you are feeling deep inside. This not only helps you process Neptune but also gives you a sense of where and how your life is going to expand.

Pluto

It really is a challenge to separate Pluto's impact on your world from Saturn's, at least for the first three months of 2020. These two planets are each seeking to be the one with the most influence over you, each pushing you in a seemingly different direction. Saturn doesn't want you to lose sight of the need for structure, while Pluto is constantly inviting you to tear everything down so it can be transformed. Sounds confrontational, until you see that the combination of the two offers you a rare chance to rebirth your reality with equal parts passion and pragmatism. There's no doubt that this process is not easily quantified or described. That intense push to transform your life and create a new beginning is likely to clash with the fear that if you don't rein in that very energy, you are headed for destruction, because, of course, Pluto is all or nothing while Saturn is cautious and measured. Pluto says surrender and let go, and Saturn says now wait just a minute. This has the potential to overload your circuits and make you feel like you are threading yourself through the eye of a needle. Your questions are twofold. Can I handle it? And is it worth it? Yes, to both. The crucial element in this process is your innate and prodigious talent for re-imagining what things look like and feel like. That way, the experience is no longer one of confinement and loss but one of transformation and joy. And you emerge as the butterfly from the cocoon, beautiful and with a new purpose and structure.

How Will This Year's Eclipses Affect You?

Eclipses signal intense periods that highlight major growth opportunities for us in the process of creating our lives. They are linked to the lunar phases—specifically the New and the Full Moon—and involve the relationship between the Sun, the Moon, and the Earth. A Solar Eclipse is a magnified New Moon, while a Lunar Eclipse is a magnified Full Moon. Eclipses unfold in cycles involving all twelve signs of the zodiac, and they occur in pairs, usually about two weeks apart.

This year there are six eclipses: two Solar Eclipses (one in Cancer and one in Sagittarius) and four Lunar Eclipses (one in Cancer, one in Sagittarius, one in Capricorn, and one in Gemini). This mixed bag of energies signals a shift from last year's focus on redefining nurturing versus babysitting, obligation versus accountability, family versus career, time for self versus taking care of business, and feelings versus rational thought. Three of this year's eclipses (the Lunar Eclipse on January 10 and the Solar

Eclipse on June 21, both in Cancer, as well as the Lunar Eclipse on July 5 in Capricorn) complete this cycle, while the new eclipse cycle calls on us to understand that there is no wisdom in living in an ivory tower, stuck in our belief that there is only one way to live life while cut off from that very life. Instead, we need to get down to the streets and actually experience our environment, talk to people, create a dialogue, and embrace diversity. Only then can we create a world that truly embodies freedom and opportunity. Three eclipses (the Lunar Eclipse on June 5 in Sagittarius, the Lunar Eclipse on November 30 in Gemini, and the Solar Eclipse on December 14 in Sagittarius) begin this process.

The first eclipse of 2020 takes place on January 10, and it's a Lunar Eclipse in Cancer, highlighting just how much you are working to find a way to nourish yourself by truly opening up your heart with complete faith in your capacity to protect yourself and to weather the internal emotional storms created by the insensitivity and lack of awareness of others. You now realize that your ability to merge with anyone who crosses your path leaves you disconnected from yourself and lost in determining what is yours and what belongs to them. With that shift, you are now ready to put into practice healthy boundaries that honor who you are and respect your right to choose how and when you share your sensitivity, your compassion, and your love, and with whom. It is no longer your job to psychically and spiritually support the entire planet. This releases a tide of new creative energy and an enthusiasm for the new life you are on the verge of initiating. The remainder of the year's eclipses unlock more steps and opportunities in this process.

Pisces | January

Overall Theme

There's no doubt that you begin the year feeling like you are heading for a brick wall at breakneck speed. The wall symbolizes any carefully constructed reality that needs to be torn down, while the speed is your desire to just do it and get it over with it. It's not your usual fluid way of dealing with life, but it's necessary, especially if you wish to actually transform your life instead of dreaming about it.

Relationships

Old patterns surface in how people treat you, and it leaves you wondering if you are actually making any progress in changing your approach to life—and relationships. Remember, this is still a work in progress. The key here is not to lament what is happening but to flex your newly developing ability to see yourself as valuable and not fall into your default position of deferring to what everyone else wants or needs.

Success and Money

Are you ready to tackle the challenge of seeing clearly how often you are content to accept the status quo in this area of your life? Doing the same old same old is simply not going to work. It's time to stop going with the flow and stand up for what you desire, at least within yourself. The truth is you *are* frustrated with your own complacency, but you can and are capable of taking charge and shifting that.

Pitfalls and Potential Problems

You, like everyone else, have some habits that seem to automatically take over when you're under the slightest amount of stress. Well, this month the stress is going to feel off the charts much of the time. Do not judge yourself for reverting to old behaviors. Observe them. Dig deep to find the roots of your reactions. It's difficult to change unless you know the why of your choices. Finding these answers liberates you and amplifies the trust you have in yourself.

Rewarding Days
4, 5, 27, 28

Challenging Days
10, 11, 12, 16, 17

Pisces | February

Overall Theme
It's likely that in spite of your innate optimism, you feel there's a cloud hanging over your head, one that promises to inundate you with unforeseen troubles and complications. This is not the current state of affairs in your life. Rather, it's the past visiting you in full force, along with a large dose of the energetic medicine that the rest of the planet is experiencing. Recognize this as an opportunity to psychically clean house and create new ways to protect yourself.

Relationships
Your deepest desire is to retreat from the hubbub of the human race. You just don't seem to have the energy, curiosity, or need to be with anyone but yourself. Celebrate this and your time alone. This is exactly how you continue building better relationships with others by valuing yourself first. Make sure you do something truly silly or fun or extravagant. It will light you up from the inside.

Success and Money
It's definitely a good time to link your hopes and wishes with a practical strategy for manifesting them. The key here is to play with each possibility, both intuitively and practically, so you can identify the one that currently has the greatest chance of success. Not that you need to abandon any of the others. It's just that their time has not come.

Pitfalls and Potential Problems
Put your guilt away. It really is appropriate for you to focus all your energy on your own life. It's part of a need to release any fears about the ongoing shifts in your life, as well as a needed time to recharge and reset yourself. You cannot make the significant changes that this year promises if you are carrying so many burdens.

Rewarding Days
10, 11, 23, 24

Challenging Days
6, 7, 26, 27

Pisces | March

Overall Theme

One minute you're up, refreshed, and hopeful, and the next you're stressed and bracing for the worst. This is the inherent Pisces state of being. You know, the two fishes swimming in opposite directions. Well, this month is exactly that. So you are in your natural habitat, but with a difference. The intensity pushing you from within is outside your comfort zone, and even though it's more of the same stuff that you've been contending with for more than a year, it feels like something is breaking. And you're right. A number of the negative patterns holding you back are indeed breaking.

Relationships

Much to your surprise, you find that everyone else feels as overwhelmed as you do, allowing you to share what is going on inside you. This raises your spirits, both because you are not alone and because you discover that you truly do have a support system full of people who cherish you and really want you to know how valuable you are to them.

Success and Money

A lot of progress is made in mapping out the next steps of your plan to transform your definition of success. No longer hampered by the belief that if you don't do it in the prescribed manner, you have no chance of accomplishing anything, you turn to your greatest assets—your intuition and your creativity—to guide you. The results astonish you and give you the necessary energy to push forward.

Pitfalls and Potential Problems

As the pressure builds within, take steps on a daily basis to take care of your physical and emotional bodies. This will give you the strength not only to meet the demands that pressure is putting on you to change and change *now* but to do so with grace and kindness. It's much better than succumbing to system overload and crankiness.

Rewarding Days

8, 9, 21, 22, 23

Challenging Days

4, 5, 17, 18

Pisces | April

Overall Theme

It's amazing how quickly lifelong patterns—ones that have restricted you, undermined you, and robbed you of your self-confidence—can be left in the dust, to be replaced by a direct pipeline to all the joy and optimism that lives in your core. Give yourself time to just feel both the gift and the potential in this shedding of what no longer works for you. It's not the time to take significant outward action.

Relationships

You are bursting at the seams with delight about life, about yourself, and about what is possible. And you really can't keep it to yourself. Nor should you. Be proud of yourself. This moment has been a long time coming. The one in which you show everyone exactly what you are made of, with all the flair and flamboyance that lives in your soul.

Success and Money

You are like a kid in a candy store. So many delicious and wonderful options are just waiting for you. All you have to do is choose. No more settling for what is doled out to you, for second-best, or for leftovers. You are ready now for the kind of success you decide is worthy of your time and attention. Bask in this reality as you ready yourself for the next steps.

Pitfalls and Potential Problems

You and time are not on the best of terms most days, weeks, months, and years, probably because so much of your consciousness lives outside it. Remember this as your enthusiasm rises exponentially and demands to be expressed. The truth is that freedom must first be experienced before it can be applied. You have just released a plethora of fears and restrictions, and you need to feel the space this created instead of rushing yourself.

Rewarding Days

5, 6, 23, 24

Challenging Days

2, 3, 28, 29

Pisces | May

Overall Theme

Life is a mixed bag as you feel the urge to push forward at the same time that you sense you need to retrace your steps. Seems paradoxical, yet there is so much you can accomplish by honoring both courses of action. Push forward confidently, after you review all your intentions and plans, to be sure you are on solid ground and haven't overlooked anything.

Relationships

Some unfinished business with those closest to you, including family, finds its way onto your agenda, even though the matters in question are not directly connected to you. This gives you the opportunity both to practice taking responsibility for only your actions and to observe how easily complications arise when there is a concerted effort to avoid the truth.

Success and Money

Before you take any more steps to bring your plans for a new future to fruition, you need to review your financial situation. This is necessary if you truly are planning for success. That way, you know exactly what every facet of your current reality looks like and you are not operating on a wing and a prayer. That won't work if you desire long-term, sustained success, the kind that creates financial security as much as it embodies your dreams.

Pitfalls and Potential Problems

"Review and respond" needs to be your mantra right now. Otherwise, you run the risk of tying yourself up in knots trying to figure out whether to move forward or back off. It's very tempting to simplify the mixed messages that this month offers. Life always operates on an ebb and flow. Recognize that and you navigate the situation with ease.

Rewarding Days

6, 7, 30, 31

Challenging Days

11, 12, 25, 26

Pisces | June

Overall Theme

Any concerns or worries you secretly tortured yourself with recede as the outward steps you took last month begin to bear fruit. This reinforces your trust in yourself, which is a welcome development after months of intermittent self-doubt and confusion. Now you know that taking a risk works when you choose to marry your imagination with a plan.

Relationships

You decide that it's time for a bit of fun and lightheartedness, especially since the emotional confrontations of last month's relationship issues ignited a drive in you to set aside difficulties long enough to reconnect with others by creating time and space for the simple pleasures of being together. After all, what better way to heal and give people the desire to sort things out than through laughter and play?

Success and Money

You take a step back to observe exactly where you are, not because you encounter any bumps in the road but because you now recognize the need to truly keep track of your forward progress. What's more, it is truly satisfying and inspiring to be able to create an ongoing picture of what you are accomplishing, and it gives you the necessary fuel to keep going.

Pitfalls and Potential Problems

Stop waiting for a disaster. It's not coming. Life is good, and you made it that way. Relax and enjoy. The only thing that can spoil all this elation is you failing to have trust in what you have created. It may be hard for you not to muddy the waters of your own life by searching for something, anything, to dim the light you are basking in. However, you can easily scuttle that tendency by simply ignoring it.

Rewarding Days

12, 13, 26, 27

Challenging Days

5, 6, 21, 22

Pisces | July

Overall Theme

One last push to realign your priorities and boundaries with your new-found capacity to listen to yourself first and foremost creates both a sense of relief and the kind of inner peace that's been hard to find this year. In fact, you no longer feel that you need to emotionally bench-press a thousand pounds just to get through the day. The emotional heavy lifting is behind you. Take a bow.

Relationships

You are inspired to finally open up about how profoundly life has pushed you to the edge during the last eighteen months, in part because you realize you have done more than survive. You are thriving, and you realize how important it is to celebrate your journey out loud. This brings unexpected benefits, not the least of which is a deepening of some very important relationships.

Success and Money

More than a couple opportunities pop up, and you are slightly taken aback. There's already so much going on that you aren't sure you can make space for anything else. Well, maybe you don't need to, unless you truly feel called to follow up on them. Perhaps they are just a sign that life is going to be abundant, and that rather than having to choose the lesser of two evils, you are going to be able to pick the best of several options.

Pitfalls and Potential Problems

You no longer feel that you are under a microscope, where everything you say and do is being monitored. This leads to a revelation: You were the one doing the scrutinizing. Why? Because you thought you might disappear otherwise. It's been quite a trial to maintain a sense of yourself while navigating a number of competing emotions: confused, unsure, and fearful yet passionate, focused, and ready to take action. Somehow you made lemonade.

Rewarding Days

9, 10, 23, 24

Challenging Days

4, 5, 19, 20

Pisces | August

Overall Theme

There's a bounce in your step, a fire in your belly, and a deep knowing guiding you. Whatever the world has in store for you, you are more than ready to meet the challenge. In fact, your motto is "Bring it on!" You now trust the foundation you worked so hard to revamp and rejuvenate, so much so that you now are able to make great use of one of your undervalued assets: faith.

Relationships

You go out of your way to nurture and take time for anyone in your life who is struggling to make sense of the shifting energetic tides. After all, your sensitivity is always on high alert, and it's difficult for you to ignore a cry for help, even if it's a silent one. The difference is that now you are able to be present without signing on to fix anything or take on the pain and discomfort of others.

Success and Money

Be careful about extravagant or impulse spending. It's likely to come in waves as you navigate some stressful situations created in your work environment. These situations are not directly connected to you or anything you did, but they have the potential to impact you, as someone tries to shift the attention away from themselves and drag you into the middle. Don't respond or engage, and not only will you emerge unscathed, but your stock will rise.

Pitfalls and Potential Problems

The only thing likely to create a couple of bumps in the road is your discomfort with impatience, yours or anyone else's. You don't always understand the difference between the drive to get something accomplished and the irritation of things not moving along quickly enough. This month, there's a lot of the former and not much of the latter. So take a deep breath and channel all that fervor that is fueling you.

Rewarding Days

10, 11, 23, 24

Challenging Days

15, 16, 28, 29

Pisces | September

Overall Theme

You suddenly feel a bit like a wet rag. Just know that you really pushed yourself, both internally and externally. Not only did you transform your whole outlook on your relationship with the physical world, but you also put it into practice without hesitation and with all engines firing. A timeout is appropriate. Slow it down.

Relationships

You really wish you liked people more right now. Well, what you are feeling isn't as much about others as it is about you. When you hit a low point, you are deeply aware that you simply don't have the resources to take care of anyone else. So you put up walls, or you try to. And then you get prickly. See this month as a golden opportunity to be honest and let people know what you are experiencing. The result? You get a lot of much-needed support.

Success and Money

You begin the month wondering if all your effort will be rewarded. It will. Just recognize that all the things you did in the last few months pushed you more than a little outside your comfort zone, and now you are having second thoughts—all of which disappear as the month goes on and you receive the okay to take the next steps in bringing your plan to fruition.

Pitfalls and Potential Problems

The reality is that you are not always in an ongoing conversation with your body, because your natural inclination is to be tuned into a whole bunch of other frequencies. This is at the root of any exhaustion you feel, especially this month. Take a break from anticipating, fantasizing, or planning life. Recharge yourself. Make it fun. Otherwise, it becomes just another task. And you don't need any more of those right now.

Rewarding Days

1, 2, 16, 17

Challenging Days

11, 12, 24, 25

Pisces | October

Overall Theme

Your preference is to stay focused on your long-term goals. Why? Because they energize you and show you a picture of yourself that is vital, vibrant, and full of promise. This is the best course of action right now, so it's okay to ignore anything that distracts you, undermines you, or raises the specter of guilt. Honor your intentions. Respect your intuition. Create what invigorates you. This is your path forward.

Relationships

Another deep dive into what makes you tick yields some further, surprising insights about how easily and how often you defer to what others need or want. This gives you a chance to continue redefining who you want to be in relationship to others, rather than how you can manage their expectations. This brings a breath of fresh air into your world and a growing pride in the changes you are making.

Success and Money

An unexpected financial reward, potentially a raise or a bonus, helps you understand how much the way you value yourself is undergoing a complete overhaul. Rather than wondering why this is happening, you embrace it as much deserved and definitely earned. This results in an internal review of your financial goals, the next step in grounding your life and your future.

Pitfalls and Potential Problems

Slow and steady progress is the goal in October. There's no need to panic or look for a way to get lost in uncertainty. Because your approach always begins with the intuitive and the imaginative rather than the rational and logical, you are always going to have periods when you wonder if your current trajectory is going to fall apart. It isn't. You are in the midst of creating something truly meaningful and spectacular.

Rewarding Days
13, 14, 25, 26

Challenging Days
15, 16, 29, 30

Pisces | November

Overall Theme

No doubt, this is a month of extremes—ones that you can use to your advantage, allowing you to shift your life in ways you hadn't even imagined. Your energy amps up exponentially and you can't seem to stop moving. At the same time, your intuition calls on you to pay attention. So do you put your foot on the gas pedal or the brake? Neither. This is not an either-or situation. Rather, it's both. You end the month with a sense of how to fuse your drive with your intuition.

Relationships

This is definitely a month when relationships are not a priority, at least not in terms of you processing or dealing with their overall role in your life. Instead, you just want to hang out and enjoy the company of those closest to you. This goes a lot further in building intimacy than does always being there to problem-solve or pick up the pieces. This not only nourishes you but creates joy and fun.

Success and Money

There are days when you feel you are pedaling as fast as you can and you just don't know if you can find another gear. Of course, you are excited and more than satisfied with what you are accomplishing. As long as you take time out every day to sit quietly and just be, you will find that next gear, no doubt surprising yourself in the process.

Pitfalls and Potential Problems

You really have been going full-tilt for some time, operating at a speed and on a frequency (the third-dimensional one) that took you to new heights in creating your life. You need a vacation. You can go far, far away or you can hang out at home. Just turn off the outside world. Your inner world needs a reboot, a time to fantasize and imagine, without any particular purpose. Do this and you reenter the earth's atmosphere with a renewed enthusiasm.

Rewarding Days

14, 15, 22, 24,

Challenging Days

5, 6, 29, 30

Pisces | December

Overall Theme

As the year comes to an end, you celebrate your emergence from the trials and tribulations of 2020 with a profound new appreciation for all that makes you who you are. No longer are you burdened by fear or judgment. You now know that you can take all those wisps of potential that whirl around in your mind and create something powerful and lasting, which is all that you really have ever desired.

Relationships

You really are in the mood to review where you've been and where you're going, and nowhere is this more important than in the area of relationships. You began the year wondering just who you were supposed to be in connection with others, and you end it knowing that the real question was how to be connected to yourself first. Answering that led to healthier, happier relationships.

Success and Money

You sense that your path is about to shift again, yet you know that it's the next step in taking what you created in 2020 and building upon it. This fills you with anticipation and excitement, partly because you now trust that you can use whatever happens as an opportunity and partly because you will always be energized by entering the unknown.

Pitfalls and Potential Problems

This is one month when you are not going to be sidetracked or overtaken by the negative, nor should you be. You are in awe of life, your life. You see the grace and the determination that you possess to make your dreams come true, and you are grateful for it all. So when that little voice says *but, but, but*—which it will—you acknowledge it. And smile.

Rewarding Days

7, 8, 25, 26

Challenging Days

9, 10, 29, 30, 31